Essentials of Personnel Assessment *and* Selection

Essentials of Personnel Assessment *and* Selection

Robert M. Guion
Scott Highhouse
Bowling Green State University

2006

LAWRENCE ERLBAUM ASSOCIATES, PUBLISHERS
Mahwah, New Jersey London

Lawrence Erlbaum Associates, Inc., Publishers
10 Industrial Avenue
Mahwah, New Jersey 07430
www.erlbaum.com

Cover design by Tomai Maridou

Cover illustration by Norisa Anderson, an established illustrator, cartoonist, and painter who resides on Vancouver's north shore in Canada. Email: norisa@landesign.ca

CIP information can be obtained by contacting the Library of Congress.

ISBN 0-8058-5282-4 (cloth : alk. paper)
ISBN 0-8058-5283-2 (pbk. : alk. paper)

Books published by Lawrence Erlbaum Associates are printed on acid-free paper, and their bindings are chosen for strength and durability.

Printed in the United States of America
10 9 8 7 6 5 4 3 2 1

It is a fine thing to have ability,
but the ability to discover ability in others
is the true test.

—Elbert Hubbard (1856–1915)

Contents

About the Authors ix

About This Book xi

I DECIDING WHAT TO ASSESS

1. Understanding Personnel Assessment 3

2. Analyzing Organizations and Jobs 20

3. Developing Predictive Hypotheses 51

4. Knowing What's Legal (and What's Not) 81

II KNOWING HOW TO ASSESS

5. Minimizing Error in Measurement 115

6. Predicting Future Performance 153

7. Using Multivariate Statistics 173

8. Making Judgments and Decisions 189

9. Analyzing Bias and Assuring Fairness 206

III CHOOSING THE RIGHT METHOD

10. Assessing Via Tests 235

11. Assessing Via Ratings 258

12. Assessing Via Inventories and Interviews 284

13. Combining Multiple Assessments 313

References 341

Author Index 363

Subject Index 369

About the Authors

Robert M. Guion is Distinguished University Professor Emeritus at Bowling Green State University, where he has been on the faculty since 1952. His published work includes *Personnel Testing* (McGraw-Hill, 1965), *Assessment, Measurement, and Prediction for Personnel Decisions* (Lawrence Erlbaum Associates, 1998), several chapters in edited books, and over 60 articles in professional journals. Honors include the Distinguished Scientific Contributions Award, Society for Industrial and Organizational Psychology; Award for Lifetime Contributions to Evaluation, Measurement, and Statistics, American Psychological Association (Div. 5); Stephen E. Bemis Memorial Award, International Personnel Management Association Assessment Council. Bob was named James McKeen Cattell Fellow for Distinguished Achievement in Psychological Science, American Psychological Society, and served as President of the Industrial Psychology Division of the American Psychological Association. He has served on numerous national committees for professional societies and for governmental agencies and has consulted widely with business and governmental organizations. He was involved in the development of the original Testing Order issued by the U.S. Department of Labor, a precursor of the Uniform Guidelines.

Scott Highhouse received his PhD in 1992 from the University of Missouri at Saint Louis. He is a Professor and member of the Industrial-Organizational (I-O) Area in the Department of Psychology at Bowling Green State University; which was recently ranked among the top three I-O programs in *U.S. News & World Report.* Scott is Associate Editor of *Organizational Behavior and Human Decision Processes*, and serves on the editorial boards of *Journal of Applied Psychology* and *Journal of Occupational and Organizational Psychology*. He is a member of the Society for Judgment and Decision Making, and was named a fellow of the American Psychological Association (APA) and the Society for Industrial and Organizational Psychologists (SIOP). Scott has published over 40 articles and several book chapters on decision making in employment contexts, and has consulted to private industry in the areas of employee assessment and selection.

About This Book

The first author wrote *Personnel Testing* (1965), which was intended and was used as a textbook in undergraduate and graduate courses in testing and selection. A second book was meant to reflect changes in assessment methods and in selection problems that occurred subsequent to that first book, and it was also intended to be a textbook. That book, *Assessment, Measurement, and Prediction for Personnel Decisions* (1998), had a much longer and more complex title; moreover, in an effort to be comprehensive, its content was also longer and more complex. It turned out to be more appropriate for professionals in the field and for those industrial and organizational psychology students preparing to become professionals than it was for undergraduate students or master's students preparing for broader human resources (HR) roles.

This book, *Essentials of Personnel Assessment and Selection*, distills from the 1998 book the essentials that managers and other well-educated people should know about the assessment processes so widely used in contemporary society—and so widely not understood. The comprehensive detail has been abridged or deleted, so instructors interested in using it for doctoral seminars would do well to supplement it with focused readings on the technical topics. The book is certainly appropriate for use as a text for advanced undergraduates and master's level students interested in becoming users of research-based assessment and selection information and techniques.

Like the earlier book, this volume emphasizes that good prediction requires well-formed hypotheses about personal characteristics that may be related to valued behavior at work. We continue to emphasize the need for developing a theory of the attribute one hypothesizes as a predictor, a thought process too often missing from work on selection procedures. New to this book is increased attention to some topics, such as team-member selection, situational judgment tests, nontraditional tests, individual assessment, and testing for diversity. Considerable attention was also given to updating the book to incorporate recent research findings.

In short, the goal was to produce an accessible guide to assessment that covers basic and advanced concepts in a straightforward, readable style. Evaluating job candidates is an emotional topic, fraught with unsubstantiated claims from test publishers and baseless accusations from social critics. The book provides a review of the most relevant statistical concepts and modern selection practices that will equip the reader with the tools needed to be competent consumers of assessment procedures and practices, and to be well-informed about the kinds of questions to be answered in evaluating them.

Finally, we would like to acknowledge the help of people who contributed their time and effort to make this book as good as we hope it is. Many people helped by critically reading parts of the earlier 1998 book, from which much of the content of this book was taken or adapted. These individuals include R. Lawrence Ashe, Walter Borman, Michael Doherty, Marvin Dunnette, Xiao Hong Gao, Milton Hakel, Richard Jeanneret, Frank Landy, Ann Marie Ryan, Frank Schmidt, Patricia Smith, and Vicki Vandaveer. Thanks again to all of you.

The authors and Anne Duffy, senior editor on this project, would like to thank the following reviewers who gave good advice and excellent suggestions to us:

Neil Christiansen, Central Michigan University
Fritz Drasgow, University of Illinois
Fred Oswald, Michigan State University
Charles Reeve, University of North Carolina, Charlotte

We are also grateful to Singapore Management University for providing the second author support to work on this book during his sabbatical, and to Jennifer Yugo for assisting in copyediting. Finally, we thank the second author's Organizational Staffing class members for providing feedback and discussion questions for this text.

—Robert M. Guion and Scott Highhouse
Bowling Green State University

I

Deciding What to Assess

1

Understanding Personnel Assessment

Assumptions of This Book
Validation and Its Limitations
Theory and Practice

- An extremely popular book right now, entitled *Moneyball* by Michael Lewis, describes how Major League Baseball's Oakland A's used massive amounts of statistical data to assemble a team of low priced high performers.
- A recent newspaper article announced that the National Football League's (NFL) Cleveland Browns organization hired the Baltimore Ravens' 38-year-old genius in player personnel to be its new general manager and senior vice president of football operations.

Professional sports places high value on the ability to identify talent and predict future player performance. Strangely, however, we have never heard of a popular book about a successful human resources (HR) department that used statistics to identify the characteristics of a good supervisor. We are also not aware of any *wunderkind* HR manager being named the chief executive officer (CEO) of a Fortune 50 corporation. Why is it that no one questions the importance of being able to identify talent in professional sports (not to mention Hollywood film making or major label music production), but personnel managers find themselves in a constant battle to prove their worth in industry? Sure, we hear a lot of verbiage about the importance of investment in human capital, but the HR department is still seen as the place to put "good old Joe." Indeed, the U.S. Department of Labor's still relevant report on the Glass-Ceiling Initiative (Martin, 1991) observed that women and minorities were often relegated to management positions in areas such as HR and public relations— positions not seen as central to the corporate mission.

Many believe that the answer to this state of affairs is to make staffing more "strategic," whatever that means. We believe, however, that personnel assessment in practice will not be taken seriously by management until the people who use it become serious advocates for it, acknowledge and master its complexities, and thoroughly and persistently communicate them to management. HR managers need to make a case to management for giving employee selection as much research and development (R&D) attention as is given to patent development. Staffing courses need to give the science of employee selection as much attention as they give to designing performance management systems or strategizing about human capital. Getting a "seat at the table" is about proving to management that you can find diamonds in the rough, using state-of-the-art techniques in performance prediction. It is not about talking the right business lingo or rejecting proven methods as old fashioned.

WISE DECISIONS

An organization functions through its members. New members are chosen in the belief that they will benefit the organization. They benefit the organization by accepting fairly specific organizational roles—sets of functions, duties, and responsibilities. When existing members of an organization seek a new member for a designated role, the dominant consideration is the suitability of a candidate for that role. Once in the organization, a person may keep the original role, be transferred or promoted, be trained for a somewhat changed role, or be terminated. All of these are personnel decisions. All of them are based, if the organizational leaders are not too whimsical and impulsive, on some sort of assessment of the person. Decision makers hope to make wise decisions, and competent assessments help.

Results of wise decisions can range from the mere absence of problems to genuinely excellent outcomes promoting organizational purposes. Good hiring decisions can result in substantial increases in performance levels and productivity. Consequences of unwise decisions can range from inconvenience to disaster. An examination of past U.S. presidential elections or NFL draft choices can provide ready examples of good and bad hiring decisions.

Wisdom in selection decisions depends greatly on knowing the characteristics that are truly important in an anticipated role and on not being distracted by irrelevant characteristics. Assessing relevant characteristics may be as easy as looking at a driver's license and noting whether or not it is current, but most are more abstract and harder to assess. If it is inferred from job analysis that qualifications include skill in getting along with others, that skill might be assessed in an interview, or from personal history information, but special efforts are needed to be sure that these assessments provide valid information related to future behavior on the job. Many qualifications are best assessed by tests or specially developed exercises.

This book emphasizes work organizations and how they may improve the chances that their personnel decisions will be wise ones. Wisdom in decision is elusive; there are opposing points of view about what is wise, desirable, and valued. We want to state our view explicitly.

Organizations exist when people join forces voluntarily to reach a common goal; they earn their existence by producing goods or services valued in at least a segment of the larger society. An organization, therefore, prospers according to its contribution to society (Eels & Walton, 1961), and individual members contribute by functioning well in their assigned roles. The interests of the consumers of the goods or services are compromised, no less than the personal interests of those in the organization, when a person who can function very well is denied a position given to one less qualified. Enough multiplication of such selection errors, and the organization fails—with resulting human and economic waste. Choices must be made if there are more applicants than openings. These choices could be random, or quasi-random, like "first come, first chosen." Choice might be based on social values, giving preference to veterans, women, or minorities. It might be based on nepotism, prejudice, or a similar-to-me bias. Or, it can be based on proven prediction of future performance.

We believe the principal basis for personnel decisions should be *merit*. Some people reject merit as elitist. Some consider profit-oriented concepts of merit inimical to the interests of a broader society. Some dismiss the idea of merit in the belief that situational factors (e.g., having a good boss) influence work performance more than the personal characteristics people bring to the job. However, if the merit principle is accepted, then methods for establishing relative merit are needed. We prefer psychometric methods that give standardized, even-handed assessments of all candidates, similar results from one time or situation to another, and demonstrable relevance to performance.

> The term *psychometric* results from the combination of two Greek words and, literally translated, means "measurement of the mind." The psychometric approach involves developing imperfect indicators of some underlying concept. They are imperfect because they are subject to measurement error.

It is wasteful to deny qualified people employment for invalid reasons, including whims known only as "company policy." Wasting human resources is as inexcusable as wasting physical resources. An organization has a responsibility to itself, to the society that supports it, and to the people who seek membership in it to be sure that it conserves and optimizes human talent.

THE ROLE OF RESEARCH IN STAFFING DECISIONS

The history of assessment for personnel selection is old. Ancient Chinese developed civil service examinations (Bowman, 1989; DuBois, 1970). Plato devised procedures for selecting the Guardians in his Republic. Another example is biblical. Gideon had too many candidates for his army. On God's advice, he used a two-stage personnel testing procedure. The first was a single-item preliminary screening test ("Do you want to go home?"); on the basis of the answers, he cut the number of candidates from 22,000 to 10,000. A behavioral exercise—to observe candidates drinking from a stream—was used for those remaining; three hundred were chosen. No one questioned the validities of these procedures because they were given by God. Unfortunately, many contemporary testers have behaved as if they, too, had God-given tests and did not need to worry about research evidence. Personnel researchers, however, recognize that tests and interpretations of test results are fallible and the validity of any given procedure for assessing candidate characteristics needs to be questioned. Such questioning has led to fairly standard procedures for evaluating (validating) selection procedures.

Fundamental Assumptions

Freyd (1923) acknowledged the following five assumptions fundamental to his outline of the research process. With some updating, they are also fundamental to this book:

1. People have abilities and other traits: mental abilities, psychomotor abilities, knowledge, specifically learned skills (including social skills), and habitual ways of dealing with things and events (including personality or temperament). We do not assume that traits are permanently fixed, either by heredity or early life experiences. We do assume, however, that some of them, especially abilities, are reasonably stable for most adults—stable enough that the level of ability observed in a candidate will stay pretty much the same for some time.

2. People differ in any given trait. Those with higher levels of abilities relevant to the performance of a job are expected to perform better, other things being equal, than those with lower levels.

3. Relative differences in ability remain pretty much the same even after training or experience. People with higher levels of a required ability before being hired will be the better performers on that job after training.

4. Different jobs require different traits. For example, one job may require specialized mathematical skills; another may require conscientious attention to procedural detail.

5. Required abilities can be measured. Cognitive abilities, for example, can be measured with many different kinds of tests.

Cognitive tests have been used successfully for employee selection and for many other purposes. The measurement of motivational requisites of successful performance has a less impressive record of success in employee selection. The record may be more impressive when the research effort expended on the definition and measurement of such traits approaches that expended on cognitive abilities.

Steps in Traditional Validation

Personnel research has traditionally focused on jobs that employ large numbers of people. For such jobs, traditional employment test validation follows steps.

Analyze Jobs and Organizational Needs. These procedures are sometimes casual and sometimes very systematic (see chap. 2). Both job and organizational need analysis inform judgments of whether the need is for improved selection or some other sort of organizational interventions, such as redesigning the job or training current employees. Clearly, no new selection procedure can solve a problem that springs primarily from inadequate equipment or inept management.

Job analysis asks what a worker does, how it is done, and the resources (personal and organizational) used in doing it. Jobs are analyzed to get enough understanding of the job to know what applicant characteristics are needed to perform it effectively.

Choose a Criterion. The criterion in personnel research is that which is to be predicted: a measure of performance, of a limited aspect of performance, or of some valued behavior associated with the assigned job role.[1] It might be a measure of trainability, production quality and quantity, or attendance or something else. Criterion choice is a matter of organizational values and organizational needs.

> The *predictor* is used to assess the job candidate's (future) suitability for the job. The *criterion* is used to assess the employee's (current) performance on the job. If we used a test of personality to predict number of sales made by our sales associates, then the predictor would be the test of personality and the criterion would be number of sales. *Validation* is the process of estimating the relation between the predictor and the criterion.

Form Predictive Hypotheses. It is likely that more than one kind of ability or trait must be measured if the criterion is to be pre-

[1]It is unfortunate that such an ambiguous word has become the standard term to designate the behavior or evaluation of behavior to be predicted. In court cases, for example, the term *criterion* is often used by lawyers and judges to refer to the basis for selecting people, such as a cutting score on a test. Such a difference in the denotative meaning of the word has caused much confusion between attorneys and their expert witnesses.

dicted in all of its complexity. Each predictor–criterion pair is a hypothesis open to research (see chap. 3). For example, an analysis of the job of potato chip sorter may have revealed that chip quality is an important work outcome to be predicted. One predictive hypothesis might be that individual differences in attention to detail should be related to better performance in monitoring chip quality. A predictive hypothesis may be rather casual and still prove to be a good one. More systematically developed, well-reasoned hypotheses will ordinarily be more likely to be supported by research.

Select Methods of Measurement. We tend, for good reasons, to have more research on tests and questionnaires than on other methods. Practical research follows success, and the predictive value of tests has been demonstrated more persuasively and more frequently than for competing approaches to assessment. Further, testing is easily standardized, enabling a fairer assessment than is possible when the method of assessment varies from one person to another (as with an unstructured job interview). Test use is not, however, free from problems. One serious problem is the tendency to only assess candidates on traits for which tests are available, rather than to assess characteristics (e.g., interpersonal skills) not easily assessed by available testing procedures.

Design the Research. Good research tries to assure that findings from the research sample can generalize to the population of interest, that is, job applicants. One aspect of research design is the choice of research participants. Inappropriate participants may spoil generalizability of results. Incumbents and applicants may differ in motivation to do well on a test, in means and variances on the measured predictors, or in demographics. Demographic diversity has become a watchword in organizational staffing. The research implications of tapping currently underused sources of job candidates in the search for diversity must be carefully monitored.

When the complexity of criterion performance calls for multiple predictors, some means of considering the predictors in combination is needed. Considering them in combination requires a choice of methods for forming a composite, and it is that composite that is to be evaluated. Sequential approaches to selection call for some rules for advancing from one step to the next. Any composite or sequence anticipated in operational use should be the composite or sequence used in research.

Collect Data. Predictors must be administered with both standardization and tact. The first of these is technical; the second is both technical and civil. Standardization of assessment procedure has long been accepted as a sine qua non of good practice; it has been virtually unquestioned throughout most of the history of personnel selection research. Everyone who is tested is given the same set of items, identically worded; any established time limits are rigidly followed whenever the test is given, and instructions are the same for everyone. With that said, it is important to appreciate the apprehension of people being assessed. Standardization does not mean treating people in a way that is not courteous and respectful.

Evaluate Results. Freyd (1923) referred to evaluating measurement; the idea subsequently became known as *validating* the predictor as measured. Whether called evaluation or validation, the traditional procedure has been to correlate scores or ratings on predictor variables with numerical values on criterion measures. If the correlation is high, then the predictor is said to be a good one (i.e., a "valid" one); and, if the correlation is low, then the predictor is said to be poor. (High and low are relative terms, evaluated more against experience than against specified coefficients.) In employment testing, empirical evaluation of predictions has traditionally been deemed essential.

The tradition of empirical validation needs to be qualified in light of views developed later in chapter 5. An even older psychometric tradition defines validity as how well the predictor (usually a test) "measures what it purports to measure" (Drever, 1952, p. 304). These views of validation are not the same. A test that purports to measure spelling ability may do so very well, but it is not likely to be very good at predicting how well mechanics repair faulty brakes. For this reason, we distinguish between the validity with which a trait or attribute is measured and the validity with which the measured trait predicts something else—between validity of measurement (psychometric validity) and validity as the job-relatedness of a predictor. Evidence for either concept of validity may be collected by any of several forms of empirical investigation.

Validation Designs

From the early days of employment testing, validation has followed one of two basic design methods: the *present employee* method, studying people already on the job, or the *follow-up* method, testing job applicants and getting criterion data later for those hired. The follow-up method is widely (but not universally) considered the better design because it tests actual applicants.

In an idealized follow-up design, the tests are given to all applicants but not scored until criterion data are available for those who are hired. (This is to assure that neither employment decisions nor subsequent criteria are affected by knowledge of the test scores.) Decisions are made as if the tests were not available at all, using existing methods—application forms, interviews, references, tests, hunches, or whatever—whether or not previously validated. After a time, criterion data are collected for those hired; the tests are then scored and the scores are compared to criterion data.

In the early days of employment testing, such ideal data collection procedures were rare; now they are virtually nonexistent. Nevertheless, the ideal provides a standard against which other designs can be discussed. Traditionally, the only other option was the present employee method where employees are taken off the job, tested, and the test scores are correlated with existing or concurrently obtained criterion measures. It is a faster method, and practical considerations often seem to favor it. These terms now seem archaic. Today's discussions are more likely to refer to "concurrent" and "predictive" research designs. These terms distinguish time spans for data collection, not the employment status of the research subjects. *Predictive designs* include a substantial time interval between the availability of predictor data and collection of subsequent criterion data; in *concurrent designs,* both are collected at about the same time. Thus, a predictive design may use present employees if the data to be evaluated can be collected from them at one time and criterion data collected some weeks or months later.

Does it matter whether the research design is concurrent or predictive? Opinions differ. Barrett, Phillips, and Alexander (1981) argued that the importance of the issue has been exaggerated. Acknowledging that the design differences are potentially important, they presented arguments to show that the differences in fact do not have much impact on the results of studies. If anything, concurrent studies have generally given somewhat larger correlations, at least for cognitive tests. Moreover, abilities are enhanced through job training and experience; people who do well on the job develop their abilities more than do those who do less well.

Concurrent and predictive designs are all variations on a single theme, the correlation between a predictor and a criterion. Validation research is not limited to that theme. This book considers other designs and considerations for assessing not only job-relatedness as an aspect of validity but also for assessing the meaning of scores on an assessment procedure. Because a predictor–criterion correlation is the traditional meaning of "validity coefficient," it serves as a way to introduce the problems and complexities of validation, but it is only an introduction.

Problems With Traditional Research

This recital of traditional personnel research is quite conventional, but it describes a paradigm that needs to be reexamined. It is subject to several potentially serious problems.

Numbers of Cases. Conventional research needs large numbers. "Large" once meant 30 or more; considerations of power in evaluating statistical significance have shown that "large enough" may require hundreds of research subjects. The power of statistical tests depends on the statistic. Generally, the more complicated the statistical analysis, the larger the sample needed. Major changes in the American workforce have occurred and seem likely to continue. Most people do not work in large corporations on jobs performed by hundreds of coworkers. Technological growth has produced a wider variety of jobs. Many employment decisions must now be made where only a few people are to be hired (perhaps only one) from a relatively small group of candidates. Further, more hiring is being done in professional, semi-professional, and managerial occupations, where one person must be chosen from perhaps as few as a half-dozen candidates. In short, the numbers for many decisions are too small for reliable correlation coefficients (i.e., less than 100). The traditional paradigm makes no provision for the small business, for choosing the replacement for a retiring manager, or for hiring a one-of-a-kind specialist.

Consideration of Prior Research. Traditional validation ignores prior research. Earlier, it was thought that validities were unique, specific to a situation at hand. Now it is known that validities often generalize well across different situations (see chap. 7).

Need for Judgment. The traditional approach to selection is purely statistical; it leaves no room for judgment. In one sense, that is good. The idea that human judgment yields better predictions than statistical equations do is a myth (or a superstition based on hope) that persists despite overwhelming evidence to the contrary. Nevertheless, statistical prediction is often impossible, infeasible, or insufficient; judgment is necessary (see chap. 8). Even with research, the circumstances for a candidate at hand may differ enough from the research circumstances that use of the research is questionable. The most obvious example lies in testing the skills of people with disabilities. One cannot intelligently (or legally in the United States) refuse to consider a blind applicant for a job in which visual acuity is not a genuine requirement just because the applicant does not match the research sample of people with sight. One can, of course, make some modification of the selection procedure (e.g., reading items orally), but the research does not apply to these nonstandard modifications (see chap. 4). The decision maker must therefore make a judgment based on the applicant's performance on a procedure of unknown validity, on interviewer judgments of unknown validity, prior work experience of unknown validity, or on a random basis known not to have any validity. To disqualify an applicant because the possible assessment procedures have not been validated is not very wise.

Global or Specific Assessments. A guiding theme of this book is that a predictive hypothesis can specify that people strong in a certain trait, or collection of traits, are likely to do well on the criterion. An alternative point of view is the *whole person* view—the idea that people are more than bundles of independent traits, that assessments should be holistic, looking globally at "the whole person." Dachler (1989) suggested that selection be considered a part of personnel development, considering patterns of behavior rather than scorable dimensions, focusing more on probability of future growth and adaptability than on fitness for a particular job. There is much to recommend his position.

Accepting one of these views may not wholly exclude the other. Two major differences between them are not insurmountable. First, traditional correlation uses measures of dimensions, not patterns. This does not, however, preclude correlating *X* and *Y* where *X* is the degree to which people fit a designated pattern of behaviors. Second, at least in the United States; the *Uniform Guidelines* (Equal Employment Opportunity Commission, Civil Service Commission, Department of Labor, & Department of Justice, 1978, Section 5I, p. 38298; see chap. 4) follows traditional methods. Although holistic evaluation of people and their future growth are nowhere mentioned in them, we suspect that a well-reasoned, well-developed selection procedure with evidence that it improves productivity, without violating the values of the larger society, will be permitted by the courts. Traditional research may seem to preclude more holistic approaches because not enough traditional researchers have thought about holistic approaches often enough or deeply enough to develop a solid paradigm for its use.

TESTING AND PUBLIC POLICY

The National Commission on Testing and Public Policy (1990) made eight policy recommendations for testing in schools and the workplace. We comment on four that are explicitly related to workplace assessment:

"Testing programs should be redirected from overreliance on multiple-choice tests toward alternative forms of assessment" (p. 26). Suggested alternatives include trainability tests, work sample tests, biodata, and assessment centers. It is worth remembering that multiple-choice tests currently have an edge over alternatives in demonstrated reliability and validity; the move to any alternative should be carefully evaluated.

"Test scores should be used only when they differentiate on the basis of characteristics relevant to the opportunities being allocated" (p. 27). This principle is well-established in employment testing, although far too many employers simply assume the relevance of tests on the basis of test names.

"Test scores are imperfect measures and should not be used alone to make important decisions about individuals ...; in the allocation of opportunities, individuals' past performance and relevant experience must be considered" (p. 30). Despite its apparent logic, this is a troublesome recommendation. True, test scores are imperfect measures and imperfect predictors. So are alternative assessments. To recommend that imperfect measures should not be used alone is

to recommend that sets—sometimes unique sets—of imperfect measures be considered jointly. The unstated assumption may be that the imperfections will cancel out, thereby improving predictions; that assumption is not supported by evidence. Public policy is usually formalized in laws; we would hate to see laws requiring that decisions be based combining valid but imperfect test scores with other information that has no evidence of validity.

"Research and development programs must be expanded to create and use assessments that promote the development of the talents of all our peoples" (p. 32). In a sense, the research being recommended seems to be going on already. However, the Commission's interest is in research on test use as a tool for developing society's human resources to the fullest. It is a useful recommendation.

THEORY AND PRACTICE

Good practice requires understanding of what one is doing. An existing, relevant theory can promote understanding, but its existence does not assure it. We call for more attention to theory to promote understanding of what is done in practice. Too much of what we know about personnel assessment and decision making, and therefore too much of this book, is limited to techniques. Better theories of work and work effectiveness can sharpen, prune, and expand those techniques and improve decisions.

An unfortunate but growing gap seems to separate academic science from organizational practice. Academics often seem interested only in building theories. Practitioners tend to decry the triviality and impracticality they perceive in academic theories, yet some of the theories they decry could inform many practical decisions in their organizations. There is, or should be, a symbiotic relation between theory and practice and between basic and applied research. To be practical, a theory has to be a good one, internally consistent, supported by solid data, and tested in practice to find out how well it works beyond the boundaries of an experimental situation.

A third member of this symbiotic partnership is society at large. Both science and practice must heed the social issues and problems they solve or exacerbate. Many scientific questions, especially in the behavioral sciences, stem from the concerns of that larger society. Practice within an organization is also practice within that larger society; for many practical decisions, both the relevant scientific foundations and their social effects must be considered.

Research should not be limited to just one chosen criterion; decision outcomes are likely to be plural. They need to be understood. Understanding requires human resources research and development programs at least on par with product and market research, and these programs work best if informed by competent theory. Outcomes and reasons for unexpected ones can be clarified through research, providing further practical guidance for decision making. All of this occurs within a community (including the larger society) that experiences the effects of outcomes and seeks to influence them. With a well-funded R & D program, unspecified and unintended outcomes, whether relevant to community concerns or to organizational needs, could be investigated much as medical research looks for side effects of medical interventions.

We must not, however, be so wrapped up in psychometric research, statistical analyses, and the contextual influences of the community that we forget that the purpose of all this is to optimize the process by which some people get rewards and opportunities and others do not. The central focus of this process—the one intended to reach the best possible outcomes—is a decision. Decisions are based on assessments; they also imply judgment, preferably informed judgment. Some information comes from research and theory; some comes from knowing the organization's needs; some comes from community influences. In fact, we do need more theory, and more of theory needs to be informed by practice.

DISCUSSION TOPICS

1. In the chapter, the authors argue for hiring based on merit. Is it ever appropriate to hire based on some other standard?
2. How do you think companies most commonly deviate from using psychometrically sound selection procedures? What are the consequences of this practice?
3. How does the selection approach of choosing the right person for the job differ from an approach aimed at choosing the job to fit the person? What are the implications of each approach?

2

Analyzing Organizations and Jobs

Organizational Need Analysis
Job Analysis
Methods of Job Analysis

Organizations face many challenges, only some of which require improved employee selection. Before deciding how to assess, what to assess, or even whether to assess, organizational needs must be identified. The scope of *organizational need analysis* is broader than can be addressed fully or appropriately in this book. It is important, however, to consider need analysis as providing the context in which selection and other interventions can be compared as possible solutions.

Organizational need analysis may lead directly to a hypothesis about appropriate selection procedures. Usually, however, hypothesis development requires analysis of individual jobs (or job families). Traditionally, *job analysis* has been considered necessary for building a selection system. Its use is strongly encouraged in equal employment opportunity (EEO) case law, it contributes to criterion development by identifying the most important aspects of performance, and it is a basis for choosing potential predictors.

ORGANIZATIONAL NEED ANALYSIS

Organizational need analysis is typically precipitated by a problem (e.g., poor productivity) or by changes in organizational goals. Effective need analyses generate hypotheses about future courses of action. In a given situation, some actions may be more effective than others. For example, a specific problem might be addressed by improved selection, improved training, job redesign, or changes in organizational structure or policy. Informed judgments of relative effectiveness (and relative costs) of the options determine the focus of further study and action.

Organizations function as systems, and the needs and actions that appear to focus on only one aspect of the organization will also have implications for others. If organizational need analysis suggests improved selection as potentially useful, then it also suggests criteria important enough to measure and predict. It may also identify personal characteristics needed. In these ways, organizational need analysis can identify a selection problem that cuts across organizational units.

Organizational Level Outcomes

Economic outcomes at an overall organizational level include profit or loss, stability or fluctuation of stock value, market share, and so on. Reasonable profit, stable or rising stock value, and growing market share please organizational leaders. Losses, fluctuations, and low market share are not pleasing; they are problems to be avoided or overcome. Overcoming them may call for new strategy, capital investment, high level personnel changes, changes in manufacturing processes or inventory controls, or human capital investments such as supervisory training or hiring more highly skilled employees.

People-oriented outcomes include performance (quality and quantity), workforce dependability (low turnover, absenteeism, or tardiness), workforce health and well-being (low stress and stress-related illness, few accidents), employee attitudes and motivation (job satisfaction, organizational commitment), or responsible versus counterproductive or antisocial behavior (no use of alcohol or drugs, theft, or sabotage). Some of these are organization-wide; others may be concentrated in specific units. An enormous number of variables may contribute to performance problems, including declining morale, worn equipment, inadequate training, poor quality of tools and work aids, poor supervision, or failure to select people based on assessment of genuinely important qualifications. Each suggests its own corrective action, and several may be needed. New selection procedures may be one of many necessary changes.

Some Approaches to Organizational Need Analysis

Organizational need analysis must attempt to gain expression of different views and, to the extent possible, reconcile them.

Conference Methods. Dialogue among people with different views is an essential condition for effective communication, which in turn is essential for clear identification and definition of problems and their solutions. One approach to need analysis, then, gets knowledgeable people together to talk about an issue or problem. Talking may sometimes become argumentative or excessively formal, so it can be useful to bring in an outside consultant who can facilitate the process and its focus.

The dialogue often begins with questions such as the following:[1]

1. What is the nature of the issue or problem at hand?
2. What is its history?

[1]Vicki V. Vandaveer suggested these illustrative questions.

3. What are the perceived outcomes or consequences of the problem? What observations have led to these perceptions? How consistent or how variable are people's perceptions?
4. What is occurring system-wide that is or might be related, or that might have an impact on the investigation of the issue or problem?

The facilitator probes beyond these basic questions, with the probes varying depending on the answers. Questions of structure, processes, key systems or subsystems, policies, and external forces might be explored. The approach is planned in advance only in a general way; it is not a standardized approach to be used consistently for all organizations, all issues, or all problems.

Organizational Assessment Surveys. On the other hand, survey methods are often proposed precisely because they are standardized. Questionnaires can be developed after interviews and conferences to be sure that major questions are asked. Any need analysis is useful when it helps people in organizations overcome force of habit in studying organizational problems. Raising questions about problems should be *systematic* and *ongoing*. To some organizational experts, systematic requires careful measurement, and ongoing means periodic. Regularly scheduled surveys can meet both requirements. Van de Ven and Ferry (1980) developed the Organizational Assessment Instruments (OAI) for survey research, one of many possible approaches to developing an organizational needs survey.

A General Approach to Need Analysis

Organizational need analysis is a managerial, not a research, function. Its immediate purpose is to generate, not to test, hypotheses. It must be done systematically, recognizing that the outcome of need analysis is a judgment (or a set of judgments) that can be framed in the language of hypotheses, and the quality of the judgment depends on the experience, knowledge, and wisdom of those who reach it. The best advice we can offer, whether the focus is on dialogue or on questionnaires, is to consider five general questions as carefully as possible:

1. What work outcomes are most in need of improvement? That is, what outcomes are most highly valued and not satisfactorily attained?
2. How widespread is the problem? Is it pervasive throughout an organization or organizational unit, or is it found in specific instances (i.e., specific people or specific units)?
3. At what level of analysis (individual or organizational) is the problem most accurately defined and approached? Consider, for example, a serious absenteeism problem. Should it be approached at the individual employee level or a broader organizational level?
4. What kinds of corrective actions are plausible? That is, what might reasonably be expected to help? Discussions with different people in the organization, and perhaps with outside consultants, can provide an initial list of plausible actions.
5. How effective have the various options been in prior use, in this organization or elsewhere? It is probably this question that gives some edge to attempts to improve employee selection decisions when the problem is one of improving performance levels. Most other activities lack the strong research base, with the substantial levels of predictive power and utility, that characterizes the testing literature.

Insiders—people who know the organization intimately—are necessary participants in seeking the answers; this is not something that a manager can delegate to an outside consultant and merely await the report—although an outsider can facilitate the discovery of answers and the reduction of internal barriers to their expression. Collectively, participants must have a wide range of knowledge, interest, and technical expertise. The best procedure for organizational need analysis may be to form a task force of bright people who know the organization from a variety of perspectives, augment them as necessary with hired specialists in various problem solutions or in discussion processes, and let them study, question, argue, and arrive at their best collective judgments.

JOB ANALYSIS

When organizational needs require improved personnel decisions for people on specific positions, jobs, or groups of jobs, job analysis (or position analysis) is necessary. The purpose is to understand them clearly enough to know what aspect of job behavior should be predicted and to identify variables or constructs that might be effective predictors—that is, to develop predictive hypotheses.

> *Job analysis* is a study of what a jobholder does on the job, what must be known in order to do it, what resources are used in doing it, and perhaps the conditions under which it is done.

What the jobholder does may be defined in several ways: as tasks, classes of duties or responsibilities, broad activities, or general patterns of behavior. What must be known includes job knowledge and job skills. Resources used may include those the person brings to the job (i.e., relevant experiences, general abilities, or other personal characteristics), tools and materials used (e.g., supplies or equipment), or the work products of other jobs or work units. Following McCormick (1979), with some additions and liberties of our own, Table 2.1 provides some standard definitions relevant to job analysis.

METHODS OF JOB ANALYSIS

Fundamentally, all job analysis consists of observing what can be seen and asking questions about what cannot. A job analyst watches, questions, understands, and summarizes the information

TABLE 2.1

Common Terms and Standard Definitions Related to Job Analysis

Term	*Definition*
Position	The duties and tasks carried out by one person. A position may exist even where no incumbent fills it; it may be an open position. There are at least as many positions in an organization as there are people.
Job	A group of positions with the same major duties or tasks; if the positions are not identical, the similarity is great enough to justify grouping them. A job is a set of tasks within a single organization or organizational unit.
Occupation	An occupation is a class of roughly similar jobs found in many organizations and even in different industries. Examples include attorney, computer programmer, mechanic, and gardener.
Job family	A group of jobs similar in specifiable ways, such as patterns of purposes, behaviors, or worker attributes. An example of a job family might be "clerical and technical," which could include receptionists, accounting clerks, secretaries, and data entry specialists.
Element	The smallest feasible part of an activity or broader category of behavior or work done. It might be an elemental motion, a part of a task, or a broader behavioral category; there is little consistency in meanings of this term.
Task	A step or component in the performance of a duty. A task has a clear beginning and ending; it can usually be described with a brief statement consisting of an action verb and a further phrase.
Duty	A relatively large part of the work done in a position or job. It consists of several tasks related in time, sequence, outcome, or objective. A clerical duty might be "sorting correspondence." One task in correspondence sorting might be "identify letters requiring immediate response."
Job description	A written report of the results of job analysis. A job description is usually narrative, sometimes given in a brief summarizing paragraph. It may be more detailed. Where job analysis was done by survey methods, the description may include listings of task statements found to define or characterize the job being studied, along with statistical data.

received to form a job description. Some jobs can be adequately analyzed just by watching workers work; others require extensive questioning by interview or survey. Job incumbents can be observed or questioned in several ways; a job analysis that provides the best job understanding usually uses several methods.

Observation and Interviews

Direct observation consists of watching and taking appropriate notes. It is the most obvious way to learn about a job, but it poses problems. The incumbent may work differently in the presence of an observer, perhaps going more by the book than is necessary, inflating the job by adding things not ordinarily done, or failing to do some things because of nervousness about being watched. It is time consuming and expensive. To observe a sample of several workers requires extensive observer time and skill. The biggest problem, however, is that much work is simply not observable. Consider the job of computer technician, in which case much of the content goes on in the head of the incumbent. Questions must be asked and answered to augment and interpret what can be directly observed.

Introspective reports of incumbents may be useful, especially in the development of *experience samples.* In this procedure, a job incumbent identifies with a brief note in a palm pilot or notebook what is being done at specific times during the day. The record allows the analyst not only to identify tasks and activities but sequences of them. Inferences from the experience samples should be verified in a follow-up interview of the incumbents who filled them out. Interviews are useful in other ways. An initial interview with an incumbent before observing work can clarify the nature and purpose of the observation, provide a broad view of the job being observed, and reassure the person being watched. Will the work be done all in one place, or will it be necessary to move around to see everything? Are certain crucial aspects of the work likely to be done so quickly that only an alert observer will see them? Such questions, answered during an initial interview, can guide the analysis. Verification interviews after observations can verify (or modify) other information, and the other information may stimulate incumbents to mention things otherwise overlooked.

The advantage of interviewing as an adjunct to observation seems obvious. What may be less obvious is that questioning, as in an interview, may need to be augmented with observations. Landy (1989) pointed out several problems with interviewing alone. One is that interview results may describe what should be done ideally or in theory rather than the way the job is actually done. Another is that experienced incumbents often have forgotten just how they do a job, as much of it has become automatic.

Functional Job Analysis (FJA). A job analyst must distinguish what people do on the job from what gets done as a result; FJA provides a grammar for doing so. Things people do are called *worker functions* (Fine & Cronshaw, 1999); they are action verbs in task statements in which the subject is always understood to be the worker, statements fleshed out in subsequent phrases more fully describing the task (Fig. 2.1). Instructions for using the FJA approach to develop an inventory of task statements are available in Fine and Cronshaw (1999). The system assumes that everything workers relate to in the course of their work can be subsumed under three headings: people, data, and things. These headings are even broader than they seem; interactions with *people* may include analogous interactions with animals; *data* includes a full spectrum of information, ideas, statistics, and so on; and *things* include virtually any tangible object touched or handled, such as complex machinery, books, or the top of the desk.

Critical Incidents. In the critical incident method, developed by Flanagan (1954), the job analyst meets with a group of incumbents (or others with expert knowledge of the job) and draws from them their recollections of things people have done that resulted in noteworthy consequences, good or bad. For each

Sentence Element	Task Statement
Subject: Who?	(Always the worker; unstated)
Action verb: Perform what action?	Schedules
Object of verb: To whom or what?	Appointments, meetings, events
Phrase: Upon what instruction? Source? Specificity:	Supervisor, caller, or memo; usually a vague "set it up," perhaps with deadline
Phrase: Using what tools, equipment, work aids:	Calendar, appointment pad, telephone, or conference room schedule book as needed
In order to ... : To produce or achieve what? (Expected outcome)	To assure presence of those expected to be present

Task Statement: Schedules appointments, meetings, or events according to instructions from supervisor or memo, or requests received from callers, using as needed appointment pads, calendars, telephone, or conference room schedule book in order to assure that all those expected to be present at the meeting or event will be able to do so.

FIG. 2.1. An example of a task statement developed by task sentence structure in functional job analysis.

incident, the description is limited to facts, not inferences, but it is detailed, reporting environmental contributing factors (e.g., equipment problems) or antecedents that may have contributed to the incident. Extraordinary events are more likely than ordinary ones to have memorable consequences and to be recalled, so this is not a good technique for getting complete job descriptions. It is, however, an excellent way to gain insights into crucial aspects of performance, and for developing employment interview questions.

> A typical critical incident interview might involve asking a supervisor to describe a recent action taken by an employee that was *unusually effective* in his or her job role. What were the circumstances leading up to the incident? What exactly did the employee do? Why was this so helpful in getting the job done?

Job Analysis Surveys. Observational and interview methods are useful when studying a single job where adequate information can be obtained from a few experts. When simultaneously studying sets of related jobs, especially in multiple locations, survey research may be the preferred method of collecting observations. Surveys are useful where many people have jobs with the same or similar titles but do different things. Even where jobs seem standard, such as police patrol officers, work performed may vary widely. A survey of job incumbents permits study of virtually all positions to determine whether there is enough uniformity among them to treat them as one job, or whether the positions should be grouped into different jobs with distinguishable patterns of duties.

Survey methods of job analysis are amenable to statistical analyses. They call for the development of items that can be combined into internally consistent job dimensions. Dimension scores can identify differences or similarities of positions within jobs, or be used to infer predictor constructs of greatest potential job relevance. Quantification helps even for analysis of a single job or position in a single location. Scores on major job dimensions clarify the degree to which one feature of a job is more important than another, and help in choosing criterion or predictor constructs.

Task Inventory Development

McCormick (1959) distinguished two types of inventories for surveys: job oriented and worker oriented. A *job-oriented inventory* is a set of brief task or activity statements (usually much briefer than the example in Fig. 2.1), each of which may describe what is done and what gets done as a result, for example, (a) "translates correspondence from French to English,"(b) "coordinates departing, en route, arriving, and holding aircraft by monitoring radar and communicating with aircraft and other air traffic control personnel," or (c) "writes special reports." Each example includes an action verb saying what is done and a further phrase describing what is accomplished.

In contrast, *worker-oriented inventories* describe work activities in terms that describe behavior, not accomplishments. McCormick's example, instead of describing a baker's job with the statement "bakes bread" (a job-oriented statement), described the activity with statements such as "manually pours ingredients into containers" and "observes condition of product in process" (McCormick, 1959, p. 411). These are worker oriented in that they describe behaviors that might be required in a variety of jobs (e.g., chemists, some quality-control inspectors, or candymakers).

The core of a job-oriented, or task, inventory is a set of task statements, or items, each with its action verb, direct object, and necessary delimiting phrases. Developing the set of statements is usually an iterative process in which the preliminary statements are edited, perhaps several times, during the various phases of inventory development. A first step in item writing is to consult available information such as training manuals, earlier job descriptions, organization charts, reference materials or manuals used in doing the work, or procedural guides and work aids. Such documents provide initial understanding of the job and may, perhaps, suggest some preliminary task statements. Information gleaned from documents can be augmented (or corrected) through on-the-job observations and interviews with knowledgeable people; such information can add to the pool of preliminary task statements.

Using Job Experts. Job experts, meeting in groups, can add, delete, or edit statements. Job experts may be incumbents, supervisors, engineers, quality-control staff, trainers, occupational safety officers, job evaluation staff, or others who have relevant knowledge about the targeted jobs. Job experts are sometimes known as *subject matter experts* (SMEs).

Writing Items. Inventory items must be descriptive but brief. They may be written by staff members or consultants, or in conference by groups of experts. They may be written at various levels of specificity. General statements are usually preferable to highly specific ones, but not always; what seems important is to keep the level at least somewhat similar across statements. Unfortunately, there seems to be no standard method for doing so. We offer a suggested, but untested, method:

1. Write preliminary items, each on a card, without concern for level of generality.
2. Have job experts sort them, independently, into sets with fairly consistent content.
3. Conduct a consensus meeting to reconcile differences in items placed in the different content sets.
4. Within each set, have each expert arrange the items in a hierarchy from most specific to most general, placing the most general at the top of the stack with more specific statements below to illustrate it.
5. Conduct a consensus meeting for a final arranging of statements and to judge the similarity of level among statements topping the sets.

If the experts think those statements are comparable in generality, then item development may be complete, but items judged too general or too specific probably need editing.

Item Categories. Grouping inventory items into categories promotes clarity. The *Job Requirements Inventory* developed by Lawshe (1987) has 14 categories, grouped further under 4 more general categories (see Table 2.2). The *Position Analysis Questionnaire* (PAQ) groups worker-oriented statements into information-processing categories. In multipurpose inventories, task items might be grouped under broader activities.

Response Scales. Ratings of importance or criticality are almost always requested. Ratings of complexity or task difficulty can help target levels of ability to be assessed. *Frequency* of task

TABLE 2.2

Outline of a Job Requirements Inventory

Performance Domain	*Number of Items*
Basic education proficiency requirements	
A. Understanding printed or written material	5
B. Performing calculations	9
Other proficiency requirements	
C. Understanding oral communication	4
D. Making oneself understood orally	4
E. Making oneself understood in writing	6
F. Understanding graphic information	3
Decision making and information processing requirements	
G. Exercising mechanical insight	7
H. Making estimates	5
I. Making choices and/or solving problems	5
Physical and sensory requirements	
J. Making visual or auditory discriminations	6
K. Using hands or fingers in work activity	4
L. Making gross body movements	4
M. Climbing or balancing	2
N. Exercising strength and/or endurance	12

Note. From Lawshe (1987). Reprinted with permission.

occurrence, or *time spent* on it, are commonly used scales. It is often important to ask whether or not the task can be performed as soon as one gets on the job or only after extended training or experience. Multiple scales are used because analysts want a variety of task information, but they may also increase reliability of ratings by forcing greater attention to them. A problem with multiple response scales, however, can be that the distinction seen by the investigator may not make much difference to respondents. Task inventories often call for ratings of both importance and frequency of performance; correlations between these scales often approach 1.0, suggesting that they mean the same thing to respondents. Nevertheless, both scales may be necessary (e.g., a lifeguard may hardly ever save a life, but it is the most important part of the job!).

The distinctive features of a job might define it and its critical components or its essential functions. A distinctive feature might be one that takes up the bulk of the respondent's work time, is crucial to some important work outcome (something would not result, or would not turn out well, if the task were not done effectively), or no one else does it. Such tasks may define the job; to differentiate among somewhat similar jobs, the following response scale combines all three. On a 4-point response scale, the responses may be:

0. I do not do the work described in this statement.
1. This statement describes something I may *occasionally* do, but it is neither an important nor a frequent part of my work.
2. This statement clearly *describes* my work; I do it, but it is not very time consuming, nor as important as other things I do, nor unique to my job.
3. This statement *defines* my job either because it is one of the most important things I do, or because it describes my work a great part of my time, or because no one else in my work unit is responsible for doing it.

It is best if local job experts choose wording they think communicates best for a given survey. Whatever the precise words, the scale is a composite of three scales and may therefore seem ambiguous. However, it has a unifying theme, job definition, and job experts seem not to be bothered by the ambiguity.

Pilot Studies. Inventories should be pretested for clarity and content. One kind of pretest asks a few people to read instructions and complete the inventory, "thinking aloud" throughout. As they verbalize their thoughts, ambiguities, unintended meanings, and other problems come to light. At some point, the draft inventory should be given to a sample of job incumbents. If possible, it should be completed in the presence of investigators so that problems with individual task statements or response scales can be observed and recorded. The task list for this preliminary study should include places for incumbents to identify tasks they perform that did not appear in the list.

Inventory Research and Data Analysis

Task Inventory Administration. If there are a great many potential respondents, or if they are widely scattered, a sampling plan is needed. In an industry-wide consortium, people in individual units are to be sampled, but a sampling plan is also needed for units to assure representation of various characteristics of the jobs being studied: organizations, organizational units, levels of responsibility, categories of job titles, or demographic groups. Experience levels should be proportionately sampled. Proportional sampling is the usual rule, but proportionality gives way to reliability if the proportional number of cases for some characteristic is too small for reliable analysis.

It is often desirable to gather data independently from incumbents and their supervisors. People who have held a job a long time, at least one permitting some autonomy, may come to do some things routinely without the supervisor's awareness; they may do some things so automatically that they are not aware of it themselves. Supervisors may expect some things to be done without checking to be sure they are or clearly communicating the expectation to the worker. An incumbent may inflate the nature of the job (Morgeson, Delaney-Klinger, Mayfield, Ferrara, & Campion, 2004); a supervisor may disparage it. If the incumbent and supervisor both complete the survey questionnaire independently, then the two versions of the job can be reconciled in meetings with job analysts. The resulting description can be more readily accepted as correct.

Grouping Task Statements. Task statements may be grouped to assist in distinguishing jobs within a group of jobs, to define criterion measures for evaluating performance, and to infer predictors of those criteria. Two ways are used to group task statements to facilitate meeting these objectives. They can be grouped rationally by job experts who, independently, identify broad categories and assign the statements to them. If statements are grouped as part of the inventory construction, grouping is by definition rational. The alternative is a statistical analysis of responses in a pilot study or in the actual job analysis. Cluster or factor analysis is often used, but these approaches have produced erroneous results (Cranny & Doherty, 1988). We suggest the following steps (or some variant of them):

1. When the list of task statements is available, and the responses from the survey are at hand, compute mean responses for each statement and select the most critical, important, or defining (or whatever response scale is used) tasks within each group; an arbitrarily chosen point on the scale will separate those selected from others.
2. For each group of task statements, have a panel of judges, meeting in concert, select a pair of statements describing the most clearly different tasks.
3. Have the panel sort the remaining statements (from Step 1) into one of three piles: like one, like the other, or like neither (presumably the "like neither" stack will be largest).
4. Repeat the process with the "like neither" pile until all of the most important or most critical task statements have been allocated.
5. Check for consistencies of responses across task statements within each group. Where inconsistencies are noted, either reassign the statement, or remove it from consideration.

Linkage of Required Worker Characteristics to Activities. It is important to distinguish between describing the job activities, and inferring the personal characteristics required for completing the activities. These personal characteristics have come to be known widely as KSAs, that is, the *Knowledges, Skills,* and *Abilities* required to do the work well. Sometimes the term is expanded to KSAPs or KSAOs, where the letter *O* or *P* stands for "other personal characteristics." We are not fond of these terms, in part because of problems distinguishing skills from abilities, or knowledge from skills, with reasonable satisfaction. Nevertheless, reference to KSAs or KSAPs has become so widespread, and is such a convenient shorthand, that we will use it rather than fight it. However, when we use it, a reader should see it as shorthand for the more inclusive term, *job requirements*.

Deriving the worker characteristics needed to perform the work activities is a critical component of job analysis. Indeed, it is this component that allows for the leap from describing the job to hypothesizing about what kinds of workers will do the job well. Sanchez and Levine (2001) noted that the translation of job activities into worker characteristics is what makes job analysis a *psychological* endeavor. Many job analysis inventories include items listing possible job requirements, and many ask respondents to link job requirements to tasks or, more often, activities. One way to request linkage judgments is illustrated in Fig. 2.2. In the inventory from which it is drawn, general duties were listed and KSAs were restricted to ability factors. Each cell represents a potential predictive hypothesis. Job experts entered a 0, 1, 2, or 3 in each of the cells, and mean judgments of experts were computed. Arbitrarily, a prestated mean value (perhaps 1.5, 1.7, 2.0) may be interpreted as suggesting a useful hypothesis, and that value might change from one predictor construct to another.

A linkage matrix like Fig. 2.2 can be used to generate predictive hypotheses in several ways. If an overall performance criterion is to be used, then a summary statistic for each ability column may be used; it might be a simple average or an average weighted by rat-

Linkage of KSA Categories to Major Job Duties

In the table below, the major job duties have been listed down the left hand side. The KSA categories agreed upon have been listed across the top. Each job duty is a row in the table; each KSA is a column. The place where a row and a column intersect is a cell. The definitions for the brief phrases here are given in the help sheets; please keep those definitions before you all the time you re going through this exercise.
Each cell calls for your judgment about the relevance of the ability listed in the column to performance of the duty listed in the row. You should record your judgment as a 0, 1, 2, or 3 according to this scale:

0 – not at all relevant to the performance of this duty
1 – relevant, but only slightly, to performance of this duty
2 – relevant to an important degree to performance of this duty
3 – of the highest relevance to the performance of this duty

Job Duty	KSA				
	Verbal Comp	Clerical Sp & Acc	Interview Skill	Number Facility	General Reasoning
1. Questions clients					
2. Evaluates documentation					
3. Explains, answers questions					
4. Refers clients to resources					
5. Codes information					
6. Develops budget worksheet					
7. Calculates needs, allowances					

FIG. 2.2. Linkage of KSA categories to major job duties.

ings of the importance of the various duties. It might be simply the number of cells in the column with cell means exceeding the prestated value. The same options exist if duties are grouped for independent performance evaluations. If job-relatedness is to be determined by criterion-related validation, errors in the linkages will be corrected by failure to find satisfactory correlations. If job-relatedness is to be determined by expert judgments, however, then the duty and KSA definitions must be tested in pilot studies to assure common interpretations, and the rules for inferring job-relatedness must be carefully considered in advance; any subsequent deviations must be justified, if indeed they can be, with very great care.

SOME WARNINGS ABOUT JOB ANALYSIS

1. *Different sources of information may yield different information, at least some of it wrong.* Different sources yield different information. Observing one incumbent rather than another may get biased information. An unusually effective worker may do different things with different resources. People with strong verbal skills can describe tasks and resources more clearly than others—and, perhaps, say more to embellish their jobs.

2. *Using all of the complex information a job analysis provides is not necessary for accurate prediction.* Overall performance in any job, or any aspect of job behavior can be optimally predicted by only a few predictors. After one or two variables, further variables rarely make more than trivial contributions to predictive accuracy.

3. *Job analysis tends to yield static descriptions of "the way we've always done it."* Job analysis typically describes the job as it is, not how it might be, ought to be, or will be in the future. Job analysis should, but rarely does, include planning for future contingencies and alternatives.

4. *Job analyses rarely recognize alternative ways to do the job or to qualify for it.* Most jobs can be done in more than one way. More attention should be given to "if–then" hypotheses: If an applicant can be expected to do the job one way, then one set of attributes will provide the best predictors;

but, if the applicant is likely to do it differently, then a different set of attributes may be better.

5. *Job analysis is typically descriptive, not prescriptive.* It might often be useful to describe *effective* ways to do a job. Differences in information from high performers and low performers can highlight the actions and personal resources that lead to effectiveness.

6. *No one method of job analysis is clearly superior to another.* For personnel research, the purpose of job analysis is to understand the job well enough to form sensible, rationally defensible hypotheses about the characteristics of people that predict criterion variables of interest. That purpose is not likely to be optimally met by any one method, nor is it likely to be met if one uses any method or set of methods uncritically.

Ready-to-Use Methods

Occupational Information Network (O*NET). The most extensive job analysis program was that of the U.S. Employment Service (USES) in developing the *Dictionary of Occupational Titles* (DOT; U.S. Department of Labor [USDL], 1977). The brief DOT descriptions were backed by extensive descriptions based on combined methods of observation and interviewing. The procedures were described in the *Handbook for Analyzing Jobs* (U.S. Department of Labor [USDL], 1972).

A new method of large-scale occupational analysis has been developed for the USDL. The O*NET database is accessible online at http://online.onetcenter.org/, and provides a set of ready-to-use instruments for describing jobs. O*NET uses general worker-specific descriptors that can be used to describe multiple jobs, as opposed to job-specific descriptors such as task statements. The database, however, also includes some occupation-specific information that can be used to develop local job analysis surveys. A number of potential applications of O*NET to job analysis and predictor selection have been presented (e.g., Jeanneret & Strong, 2003; Peterson, Borman, Hanson, & Kubisiak, 1999).

Personality-Based Job Analysis. In his presidential address to the Division on Measurement and Evaluation, American Psychological Association, Douglas Jackson said that job analysis techniques have largely overlooked personality predictors; a fact which he said accounted for their poor history. So challenged, a Bowling Green research group developed an inventory specifically intended to generate hypotheses about potential predictors among personality traits (Raymark, Schmit, & Guion, 1997). It is based on a list of 12 personality dimensions, shown, with definitions and contrasts, in Table 2.3. A sample page is shown in Fig. 2.3. Guion, Highhouse, Reeve, and Zickar (2005) developed a personality questionnaire, the *Self-Descriptive Index,* using work-related versions of items from the International Personality Item Pool (IPIP) database (Goldberg, 1999). Our experience with the instruments so far suggests that it can provide fruitful hypotheses about personality variables as predictors of success in several skilled trades.

Other efforts in this direction include a job analysis inventory geared to personality traits that has been used for occupations such as police, managers, and bus drivers (Inwald, 1992). There are also two inventories linked to specific instruments or theories. Costa, McCrae, and Kay (1995) described the NEO Job Profiler, designed for use with the Revised NEO Personality Inventory, and Gottfredson and Holland (1994) developed the Position Classification Inventory to match the Holland personality theory (for a summary, see Rounds, 1995).

Position Analysis Questionnaire (PAQ). A job-oriented inventory must be explicitly developed for each job or occupational group studied. This fact reduces the generality of job dimensions identified and renders comparisons across jobs and occupations

TABLE 2.3

Work-Relevant Personality Dimensions

Broad Trait	*Dimension*	*Brief Description*
I. Surgency		
	I-A: General Leadership	Tendency to take charge of situations, and motivate behavior of others.
	I-B: Interest in Negotiation	Ability to see and understand differing points of view, and achieve harmony.
	I-C: Achievement Striving	A desire to advance, and to excel relative to others or a personal standard.
II. Agreeableness		
	II-A: Friendly Disposition	Tendency to be likable warm and approachable.
	II-B: Sensitivity to Others	Tendency to be considerate, understanding, and have a concern for others.
	II-C: Collaborative Work Tendency	Desire to be part of a group and work well with clients, customers, and coworkers.

III. Conscientiousness		
	III-A: General Trustworthiness	A reputation for following through on promises, commitments, or agreements.
	III-B: Adherence to Work Ethic	A tendency to work hard and to be loyal.
	III-C: Attention to Details	A meticulous approach to one's own work or the work of others.
IV. Emotional Stability		
		A calm, relaxed approach to situations, events, or people. Adaptability to changes in the work environment.
V. Intellectance		
	V-A. Desire to Generate Ideas	A preference for original or unique ways of thinking about things.
	V-B. Tendency to Think Things Through	Considering the consequences or effects of alternative courses of action.

EFFECTIVE PERFORMANCE IN THIS POSITION REQUIRES THE PERSON TO:	Not Required	Helpful	Essential
Set 1			
1. lead group activities through exercise of power or authority.	☐	☐	☐
2. take control in group situations.	☐	☐	☐
3. initiate change within the person's work group or area to enhance productivity or performance.	☐	☐	☐
4. motivate people to accept change.	☐	☐	☐
5. motivate others to perform effectively.	☐	☐	☐
6. persuade co-workers or subordinates to take actions (that at first they may not want to take) to maintain work effectiveness.	☐	☐	☐
7. take charge in unusual or emergency situations.	☐	☐	☐
8. delegate to others the authority to get something done	☐	☐	☐
9. make decisions when needed.	☐	☐	☐
Set 2			
10. negotiate on behalf of the work unit for a fair share of organizational resources.	☐	☐	☐
11. work with dissatisfied customers or clients to achieve a mutually agreeable solution.	☐	☐	☐
12. help people in work groups settle interpersonal conflicts that interfere with group functioning.	☐	☐	☐
13. help settle work-related problems, complaints, or disputes among employees or organizational units.	☐	☐	☐
14. negotiate with people outside the organization to gain something of value to the organization.	☐	☐	☐
15. mediate and solve disputes at individual, group, or organizational levels.	☐	☐	☐
16. negotiate with people within the organization to achieve a consensus on a proposed action.	☐	☐	☐
17. mediate conflict situations without taking sides.	☐	☐	☐

(Go on to next page)

FIG. 2.3. A sample page from a personality-based inventory of general position requirements.

difficult. By definition, a worker-oriented approach is applicable across widely differing occupations. For this reason, many people prefer to use the latter approach to position, job, or occupational surveys. The most widely used is the Position Analysis Questionnaire (PAQ) by McCormick, Jeanneret, and Mecham.[2] Figure 2.4 shows a set of the individual items and some of the kinds of rating scales used. Several differences distinguish PAQ statements from most task inventory items in addition to being worker-oriented. Each statement has just one response scale, but scales may change from one statement to the next.

The recommended procedure for completing the PAQ involves the use of job analysts as data collectors. The job analysts may be people in the organizations (or outside consultants) whose major job is analyzing the jobs of others, or they may be other employees specifically chosen for this ad hoc assignment. They interview job incumbents, their supervisors, or both; after the interviews, the analysts themselves complete the PAQ forms. Alternatively, an analyst may meet with small groups of incumbents and supervisors who fill out the form in the presence of the analyst who can answer questions about the statements or the rating scales.

Direct Identification of Required Attributes. In most methods of job analysis, particularly the observe-and-question methods, required worker attributes are inferred from the analysis. A more direct method for identifying them is the Job Requirements Inventory (Lawshe, 1987b). A quite different, but equally direct, method is the Fleishman Job Analysis Survey (F-JAS). Fleishman and his associates were among the first to define and classify tasks according to their ability requirements. The heart of the procedure is a set of 52 abilities (Fleishman & Reilly, 1992a) for which definitions and rating scales are provided (Fig. 2.5). A useful feature of the system is its distinction between the defined ability and other abilities that might be confused with it. Each ability scale is a

[2]The Position Analysis Questionnaire is available from PAQ Services Inc.

RELATIONSHIPS WITH OTHER PERSONS

Code	Importance to This Job (I)
N	Does not apply
1	Very minor
2	Low
3	Average
4	High
5	Extreme

4 Relationships with Other Persons
This section deals with different aspects of interaction between people involved in various kinds of work.

4.1 Communications
Rate the following in terms of how *important* the activity is to the completion of the job. Some jobs may involve several or all of the items in this section.

4.1.1 Oral (communicating by speaking)

99	I	Advising (dealing with individuals in order to counsel and/or guide them with regard to problems that may be resolved by legal, financial, scientific, technical, clinical, spiritual, and/or other professional principles)
100	I	Negotiating (dealing with others in order to reach an agreement or solution, for example, labor bargaining, diplomatic relations, etc.)

4.3 Amount of Job-required Personal Contact

112 | S Job-required personal contact (indicate, using the code below, the extent of job-required contact with others, individually or in groups, for example, contact with customers, patients, students, the public, superiors, subordinates, fellow employees, prospective employees, official visitors, etc.; consider *only* personal contact which is definitely *part* of the job.

Code	*Extent of Required Personal Contact*
1	Very infrequent (almost no contact with others if required)
2	Infrequent (limited contact with others if required)
3	Occasional (moderate contact with others is required)
4	Frequent (considerable contact with others is required)
5	Very frequent (almost constant contact with others is required)

JOB CONTEXT

5 Physical Working Conditions

The section lists various working conditions. Rate the *average* amount of time the worker is exposed to each condition during a *typical* work period.

Code	Amount of Time (T)
N	Does not apply (or is very incidental)
1	Under 1/10 of the time
2	Between 1.10 and 1/3 of the time
3	Between 1/3 and 1/2 of the time
4	Over 2/3 of the time
5	Almost continuously

5.1.1 Outdoor Environment

135 | T Out-of-door environment (subject to changing weather conditions)

FIG. 2.4. Examples of items and rating scales in the position analysis questionnaire. From McCormick, E. J., & Jeanneret, P. R. (1988). Position analysis questionnaire (PAQ). In S. Gael (Ed.), *The job analysis handbook for business, industry, and government* (Vol. 1, pp. 825–842). New York: Wiley. Reprinted by permission of John Wiley & Sons, Inc.

INFORMATION INPUT

1.1 Sources of Job Information

Rate each of the following items in terms of the extent to which it is used by the worker as a source of information to performing the job.

Code	Extent of Use (U)
N	Does not apply
1	Nominal/very infrequent
2	Occasional
3	Moderate
4	Considerable
5	Very substantial

1.1.1 Visual Sources of Information

1 | U̲ Written materials (books, reports, office notes, articles, job instructions, signs, etc.)

2 | U̲ Quantitative materials (materials which deal with quantities or amounts, such as graphs, accounts, specifications, tables of numbers, etc.)

3 | U̲ Pictorial materials (pictures or picturelike materials used as sources of information, for example, drawings, blueprints, diagrams, maps, tracings, photographic films, X-ray films, TV pictures, etc.)

MENTAL PROCESSES

2.2 Information Processing Activities

In this section are various human operations involving the "processing" of information or data. Rate each of the following items in terms of how *important* the activity is to the completion of the job.

Code	Importance to This Job (I)
N	Does not apply
1	Very Minor
2	Low
3	Average
4	High
5	Extreme

39 | I̲ Combining information (combining, synthesizing, or integrating information or data from two or more sources to establish new facts, hypotheses, theories, or a more complete body of *related* information, for example, an economist using information from various sources to predict future economic conditions, a pilot flying aircraft, a judge trying a case, etc.)

40 | I̲ Analyzing information or data (for the purpose of identifying *underlying* principles or facts by *breaking down* information into component parts, for example, interpreting financial reports, diagnosing mechanical disorders or medical symptoms, etc.)

49 | S̲ Using mathematics (indicate, using the code below, the highest level of mathematics that the individual mush understand as required by the job)

Code	*Level of Mathematics*
N	Does not apply
1	Simple basic (counting, addition and subtraction of 2-digit numbers or less)
2	Basic (addition and subtraction of 3 digits or more, multiplication, division, etc.)
3	Intermediate (calculations and concepts involving fractions, decimals, percentages, etc.)
4	Advanced (algebraic, geometric, trigonometric, and statistical concepts, techniques, and procedures usually applied in standard practical situations)
5	Very advanced (advanced mathematical and statistical theory, concepts, and techniques, for example, calculus, topography, vector analysis, factor analysis, probability theory, etc.)

1. Oral Comprehension This is the ability to listen and understand spoken words and sentences.

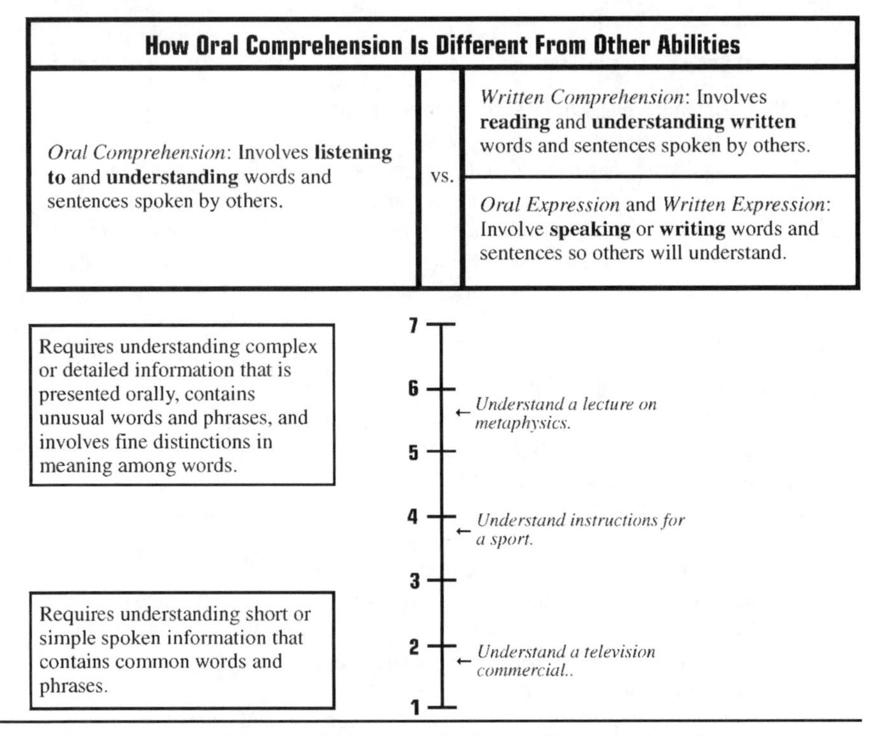

FIG. 2.5. Definition and rating scale for oral comprehension, one of the 52 abilities in the Fleishman job analysis survey.
From Fleishman, E. A., & Reilly, M. E. (1992). *Administrator's guide: F-JAS, Fleishman Job Analysis Survey*. Bethesda, MD: Management Research Institute. Reprinted with permission.

7-point rating scale with three tasks anchoring scale points; each is a task that virtually everyone can understand from ordinary experiences. For each ability, one task has one high, one low, and one intermediate scale value; the scale value identifies the mean ability scale value prior judges have assigned to the task. Job experts are expected to compare the tasks required by the job with the three anchor tasks and assign ability ratings; their mean ratings define the job's ability requirements. A companion volume by Fleishman and Reilly (1992b) provided information for the next step, establishing operational definitions for use in decisions. For each of the 52 abilities, ability definitions are given, followed by tasks and jobs in which the ability is used and, where available, examples of tests measuring the ability. From these, local operating definitions of worker requirements can be established. The recommended procedure calls for job experts as raters, usually job incumbents. In most cases, a job description or task list is presented to them in preparation for rating. The job as a whole might be rated, or broad job dimensions, or selected tasks.

Competency Modeling

The term *competency modeling* has become widespread in the popular HR literature. The notion behind the competency modeling movement is that traditional, or "old school," job analysis cannot meet the demands of the changing workplace. Although the meaning of the term *competency* remains unclear (Schippmann et al., 2000), the notion behind it is that one should identify the characteristics or attributes related to exceptional performance on the job. Sackett and Laczo (2003) observed that competency modeling's entire raison d'etre is the misguided assumption that job analysis focuses only on tasks done on the job, and not on the attributes required for success on the job. Indeed, there are many examples of worker-oriented methods presented in this chapter. Unfortunately, existing methods of competency modeling often fall short in terms of methodological rigor (see, e.g., Lievens, Sanchez, & De Corte, 2004).

General Caveats

Even the most careful job analysis is subjective. Job analysis is not science, even when it is used in scientific research or guided by scientific thought. It is an information-gathering tool to help managers or researchers decide what to do next. If well-developed and used systematically, it yields reliable information that leads to defensible predictive hypotheses with strong likelihood of being supported empirically. The insight needed to choose predictors that improve organizational functioning is more likely if one acquires correct information through well-considered job analysis. Not every job analysis must be comprehensive or even thorough, but they must be well-considered.

This chapter has barely scratched the surface of the topic of job analysis. Perhaps the most important caveat of all is to point out how much information is available that goes well beyond this chapter.

DISCUSSION TOPICS

1. What is the difference between an organizational need analysis and a job analysis?
2. Given the numerous methods available for job analysis, what are some considerations in deciding which method to use?
3. What is the role of the job expert, or SME, in the job analysis process? How would you go about selecting job experts?

3

Developing Predictive Hypotheses

Cognitive & Noncognitive Abilities
Personality
Criteria

A predictive hypothesis concerns the relation of one variable, a *criterion,* to at least one other, a *predictor*. A predictive hypothesis is not a universal truth; it may be expected to hold only within some boundaries. Specifying the operational hypothesis and its boundaries requires job and organizational knowledge and, beyond that, knowledge of psychology, psychological research, and psychometric tools.

CONCEPTUAL AND OPERATIONAL DEFINITIONS

Predictors and criteria can be defined at two levels: *conceptual* and *operational*. Hypothesis formation should ordinarily begin with simple theoretical statements about how predictor and criterion *constructs* relate. For example, one might expect, for an electronics assembly worker, "Quality of performance is a function of ability to make fine, precise manipulations of small objects." Performance quality is a criterion construct; the predictor construct is the ability to make fine, precise manipulations of small objects. This theoretical statement is not testable because no measurement operations are specified. If the predictor construct is conceptually defined as finger dexterity,[1] then its operational definition may be a score on a standardized test of finger dexterity.

> A *construct* is simply a general idea about something that is unobservable. Each predictor construct can be defined at a *conceptual* level (e.g., strong work ethic) and at an *operational* level (e.g., scores on a self-report measure of work ethic).

Some predictors are used even when the construct underlying them is unknown. Predictors defined only at the operational level can still be effective (one company reportedly found that high performing truck drivers had more tattoos than their lower performing colleagues). We do not disparage predictors that work (although, we may draw the line at counting tattoos). We believe, however, that finding out what they mean can promote understanding and, eventually, better measures.

Synergy of Theory and Practice

Professional practice is the hallmark of applied psychology, but continued application without understanding never progresses. Theory is understanding—or the attempt to understand. It is more than a hunch. Binning and Barrett (1989) pointed out that developing a predictive hypothesis requires both theory building and theory testing. With some modifications in terms and numbering, we follow their presentation in Fig. 3.1:

---

[1]The term *finger dexterity* is more precise than it might seem. French (1951, p. 208) defined it as "the rapid manipulation of objects with the fingers" and distinguished it from "manual dexterity" (which involves larger arm movements not part of finger dexterity) and "aiming" (which requires accurate eye–hand positioning).

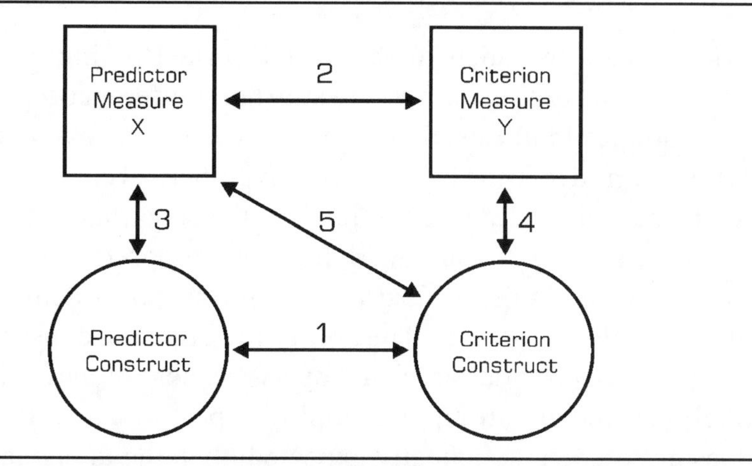

FIG. 3.1. Basic linkages in the development of a predictive hypothesis. From Binning, J. F., & Barrett, G. V. (1989). Validity of personnel decisions: A conceptual analysis of the inferential and evidential bases. *Journal of Applied Psychology, 74,* 478–494. Adapted with permission.

1. A predictor construct—an idea of a way people vary—is related to a criterion construct, a form of job behavior (e.g., absence, productivity, etc.) or a result of behavior. This is the basic theoretical statement at a conceptual level.
2. Predictor measure *X* is related to criterion measure *Y,* a relation expressible mathematically. This is a predictive hypothesis and, unlike the first option, is empirically testable.
3. Predictor measure *X* is a valid measure of, or reflection of, the predictor construct.
4. Criterion measure *Y* is a valid measure of, or reflection of, the job behavior construct. Tests of Inferences 3 and 4 are used in construct validation, evaluating simultaneously the idea of the construct and a designated measure as a valid measure of it.
5. The predictor measure *X* is related to the criterion construct in a manner consistent with its presumed relation to the criterion measure *Y*. The truth of this inference depends on the validities of Inferences 1 and 3.

Much can be added to this framework. Binning and Barrett (1989) in fact did so, but we will stop here; Inference 5 is the basic operational hypothesis.[2] It rests on the reasonableness of Inference 1, the inferred relation between two hypothetical constructs not directly measurable, and of Inference 3, the construct validity of the predictor as used. A framework like that proposed by Binning and Barrett (1989) is theoretical in calling for understanding, beginning with the constructs. The ability to define the constructs with some clarity provides an idea why assessment of a certain trait is likely to predict subsequent employee performance. If in fact it does not predict as logically expected, then the understanding of the criterion, the predictor, or both must be changed; progress ensues.

Specification of Population

To whom does the predictive hypothesis apply? Anyone? Only experienced applicants? New entrants into the labor pool? People with required credentials (e.g., degrees or licenses)? In short, who is an applicant? The question has both legal and technical implications. Definitions of applicant populations are elusive, but the basic idea is a population to which research results should generalize. Population boundaries may be defined by prior conditions, such as required credentials or passing a screening test.

Specification of Time Intervals

Usually (not always), criteria collected early—after a few months or perhaps a couple of years—are better predicted than those collected after longer intervals. Murphy (1989) suggested that validities and most valid predictors change with changes in career stage from a *transitional stage* of new learning to a *maintenance stage* of doing more or less routinely what had been learned. Cognitive

[2]It is Inference 9 in the full Binning and Barrett (1989) model.

variables, for example, may be better predictors of performance in transitional stages and motivational predictors better for maintenance stages. Helmreich, Sawin, and Carsrud (1986) found that achievement orientation did not predict performance well until after a "honeymoon" period on the job. The idea is that employees, like new spouses, are usually on their best behavior for the first few months. In time, however, employees (and spouses) revert back to their characteristic ways.

A study of pharmaceutical sales representatives found that agreeableness and openness (i.e., intellectance) predicted performance during the transitional period, but only conscientiousness predicted sales during the maintenance period (C. J. Thoresen, Bradley, Bliese, & J. D. Thoresen, 2004). For some jobs, the learning period may go on and on; Ghiselli (1956) identified an investment broker job in which performance improved linearly for 6 years. Cognitive ability may continue to predict performance for jobs with ever-changing tasks (Farrell & McDaniel, 2001). In generating hypotheses, one must decide whether they refer to predictions of performance during an early learning period, a later maintenance stage, or long-term career growth and development. The time interval can be approximate, but it should make sense.

Specifying Functional Relations

The term *functional relationship* implies that the level of one variable (usually *Y*) varies "as a function of" variation in another. The nature of the relation (i.e., the function) may ordinarily be expressed as a mathematical equation. Functions are discussed in more detail in chapter 6, but discussion of two issues should not wait.

First, predictive hypotheses usually assume (deliberately or by default) a linear function (one graphed as a straight line throughout the predictor range) as the relation between predictor and criterion. There are good reasons for the assumption, but there are also reasons for considering alternative functions. Consider the following example; we may hypothesize that more educated bank tellers will stay in the job longer than less educated ones. The reasoning might be that less educated tellers will make more mistakes and become more frustrated. It might be that more educated tellers had enough persistence to complete further schooling, and persistence may also keep them on the job.

Figure 3.2 shows three examples of simple functional relations plausible for various kinds of predictions. Panel *a* describes the common linear function in which any difference in *X* always has a corresponding difference in *Y*; that is, adding a point to a score implies the same added level of criterion performance whether the point is added to a low score, a moderate one, or a high one. In Panel *b*, this is not true in the higher predictor levels; adding a point to the lower predictor scores is associated with a bigger criterion difference than at the higher levels where the curve may be asymptotic to some criterion level. Panel *c* shows a similar loss of advantage at both lower and higher score levels; that is, differences in actual predictor levels in either a low scoring or a high scoring range have only trivial counterparts in criterion performance, whereas predictor differences in the middle range are associated with substantial criterion differences. These are by no means the only functional relations that may be plausible; others may also deserve consideration. Consider the previous bank teller example; it may be that educated tellers have better job opportunities elsewhere, or may quit because the job routine is boring. Whereas our first hypothesis was

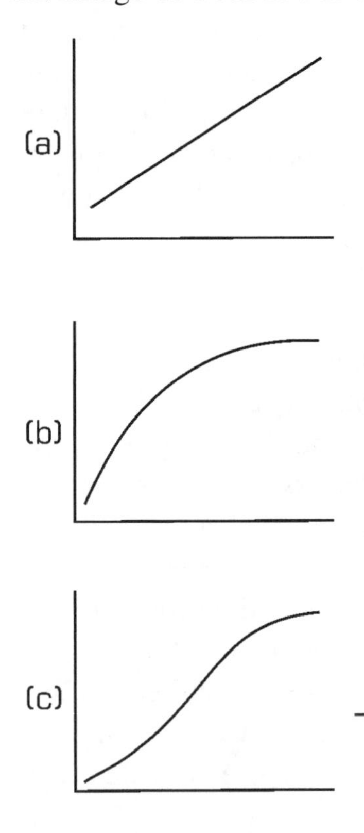

FIG. 3.2. Three examples of functional relationships.

based on a linear positive relation between education and tenure on the job, further consideration led to a revised, curvilinear hypothesized relation. Failure even to think of alternatives to the linear function means failure to test them. Although linear functions will ordinarily be specified, they should be specified intentionally, not by default.

A second issue was mentioned in chapter 2, the oversimplification inherent in assuming a single best way to do a job. A combination of traits may be relevant to performance, and it may be that trade-offs exist in the kinds of traits used by different people. For example, older typists may make fewer keystrokes per minute than their younger colleagues, yet they may type just as much through strategizing and looking ahead in the text more. This chapter is traditional in that it assumes continuous functions like those in Fig. 3.1 rather than the models implied by such trade-offs (and described in chap. 7).

CRITERIA

The word *criterion,* for a predictive hypothesis, is simply a "dependent variable, the variable to be predicted" (English & English, 1958, p. 130). There is little virtue in trying to predict a criterion nearly everyone (or no one) does well; it is not useful, and it will not work. Prediction of individual levels of criterion performance requires individual differences, that is, variance. If nearly everyone is at the low end of the scale, some other intervention is needed, such as better training or job redesign.

Criterion Constructs

Criteria are measures of behaviors or events that are important to the organization. Too often, they are simply accepted as givens, without much concern for their meaning. Clarity of the constructs they represent provides clarity for the meaning of predictions.

Inferring Constructs From Measures. Events worth counting, recording, and predicting may include accidents, quitting, completion of training, or receipt of letters of commendation (e.g., letters from the public praising something done by a police officer or by a truck driver). The meanings of such measures are often unclear.

Absence (or absenteeism) provides a useful example. What does it mean to count the number of days at (attendance) or away from work (absences) over a given period? Psychologists once interpreted absence only as withdrawal from an aversive situation. In this view, being late is a mild form of withdrawal, being absent is a stronger form, and quitting is the ultimate withdrawal from the job or organization.

Reasons for absence may not be readily apparent. Even classifying absences as necessary or avoidable is difficult. F. J. Smith (1977) computed average scores on six attitude scales for organizational units in Chicago and in New York. Scores were correlated with percentages of people attending work on a certain day. The study happened to be the day after a severe snowstorm in Chicago, but the weather was no problem that day in New York. Mean attitude scores did not correlate well with attendance in New York, but did in Chicago. Is attendance a matter of attitude? Only, it seems, if it requires more effort than mere habit.

This example shows that the meaning of attendance or absence is unclear. Why would an organization want to predict either? One reason is economic; absence is expensive. But before the cost, absence is psychological. Withdrawal or escape from work is psychologically interesting, but is it clearly indicated by absence? Probably not. Perhaps a trait construct such as *acceptance of responsibility* is one reason organizations worry about absenteeism, but absenteeism may not measure it very well.

> Most organizations are not concerned about truly uncontrollable reasons for absence as much as they are concerned about employees skipping work for no good reason. Thus, the *conceptual* definition may be voluntary absenteeism, but the *operational* definition may be number of days of work missed.

Starting with the measure (e.g., counting absences) and then trying to determine what it means is the wrong way to go. It makes more sense to decide first on the criterion concept; only when the concept is reasonably clear can a measure of it be tried and evaluated. With such a complex construct as responsible work behavior, a composite of several measures (maybe including attendance) may be more valid. Predicting one component, in short, may be less useful, and less well done, than predicting a *pattern* of behaviors tapping a common and clearly defined construct.

A Theory of Performance. Performance is a construct, measurable in many ways. J. P. Campbell, McCloy, Oppler, and Sager (1993) defined performance as cognitive, motor, psychomotor, or interpersonal behavior controllable by the individual, relevant to organizational goals, and scalable in terms of proficiency. Work outcomes (e.g., production), effectiveness (evaluation of outcomes), and productivity (an aggregate, not an individual, measure) are not part of their definition. Performance is work-related activity—behavior. Their definition differs from that given by the Society for Industrial and Organizational Psychology (SIOP): "the effectiveness and value of work behavior and its outcomes" (Society for Industrial and Organizational Psychology, 1987, p. 39). Regardless of definition, performance is not unidimensional; it may have many components. Ranking employees by level of proficiency in one component may not match their rank order on another.

Performance Components and Determinants. J. P. Campbell et al. (1993) postulated three determinants to account for proficiency in any performance component: *declarative knowledge,* or factual knowledge and understanding of things one must do; *procedural knowledge,* or skill in knowing how to do them; and *motivation,* or the direction, degree, and persistence of effort in doing them (see Kanfer & Ackerman, 1989, for background). At the workplace, both declarative and procedural knowledge may be combined as job knowledge; those with a wealth of knowledge that can be tapped by others are valued highly, but those for whom that knowledge is not accompanied by actual skill in applying it are often dismissed, somewhat contemptuously, as merely "talking a good job." The theory also suggests eight general factors of performance; with modification and abbreviation, they are shown in Table 3.1. Not all of them are relevant to every job (e.g., many jobs have no supervisory component); many may require a finer definition to be operationally useful for specific jobs (e.g., a job wherein the incumbent must communicate effectively to widely differing constituencies might require more specific communication components). They provide, however, a framework for construct definition.

Contextual Behavior. Valued behavior at work includes more than doing assigned job tasks. Regularly coming to work on time, staying with the organization rather than leaving, staying overtime on short notice when unexpected problems arise, helping others when needed, minimizing or solving conflicts within the work group, training or mentoring newcomers, justifying trust, or simply providing a good model for others all form part of the context in which work is done.

> *Contextual performance* refers to aspects of performance unrelated to specific tasks. These include activities directed at enhancing the interpersonal and psychological environment that facilitates task completion.

Borman and Motowidlo (1993), calling such things contextual activities, differentiated them from task or job performance in four ways: (a) Task activities contribute directly to the technical core of an organization's production of goods and services, contextual activities contribute to the organizational or social environment in which that technical core functions; (b) task activities differ across different jobs, contextual activities are common to many if not all jobs; (c) task activities are associated with skills or abilities, contextual activities are more associated with motivational or person-

TABLE 3.1

A Proposed Taxonomy of Higher Order Performance Components

1. *Job-specific task proficiency*
   How well the person does major substantive or technical tasks central to the job, i.e., job-specific behaviors differing from one to another. Joining two pieces of half-inch wood with dovetails and glue, and joining 2 4 studs and sills, are different core tasks for the cabinetmaker and the carpenter.
2. *Non-job-specific task proficiency*
   Tasks performed by virtually everyone in an organization, or at least virtually everyone in a job family. In the construction example, virtually everyone at a job site–cabinetmaker, carpenter, plumbers, electricians, and various helpers—must be able to make rough cuts, drill holes, hammer nails, and clean the work area.
3. *Written and oral communication task proficiency*
   Tasks requiring formal oral or written presentations to an audience, whether of one person or many. The critical, differentiating performance component is proficiency in writing or speaking to an audience. Examples vary from formally telling the boss of the results of a planning conference to the presentation of technical data to an audience of hundreds.
4. *Demonstrating effort*
   Consistency of effort, frequency of expending extra effort when required, and the tendency to keep working even under adverse conditions.
5. *Maintaining personal discipline*
   Avoidance of negatively valued behavior: alcohol and substance abuse at work, violating laws or rules, excessive absenteeism, etc.

(continued on next page)

TABLE 3.1 *(continued)*

6. *Facilitating peer and team performance*
   Supporting peers, helping them, or acting as a de facto trainer; being a good model for facilitating group functioning by keeping the group goal directed; and reinforcing participation by other group members.
7. *Supervision/leadership*
   Influencing subordinate performance through direct interpersonal interaction: setting goals for subordinates, teaching or training, modeling appropriate behavior, and rewarding (or punishing) in appropriate ways.
8. *Management/administration*
   Management activities distinctly differing from direct supervision.

Note. From "A Theory of Performance," in *Personnel Selection* (pp. 35–70), by J. P. Campbell, R. A. Oppler, & C. E. Sager, 1993, San Francisco: Jossey-Bass. Copyright 1998 by Jossey-Bass. Reprinted with permission.

ality variables; and (d) task activities are things people are hired to do, contextual activities are desirable but less likely to be demanded.

There are several questions to ask when choosing a contextual criterion: does it represent organizationally required behavior for everyone, or at least everyone within a specified group of jobs, or is it merely desirable? Also, are the desired behaviors more likely and more safely elicited from day-to-day managerial influence than from antecedent traits?

Trainability. How quickly tasks are learned may be an important construct, especially where people must frequently adapt to changing technology or assignments. Even on static jobs, the idea that anyone can become expert given enough time is a myth; those who need long learning time for complex tasks generally do not reach the level of proficiency after training reached by those who learn more quickly. It is organizationally useful to select or promote people who will learn their duties quickly or adapt quickly to job changes.

Status Quo, Change, and Criterion Choice

Organizations need to grow and adapt through change. Criteria should promote effective change, maintain useful stability in the face of change, and help develop an organization that continues to function effectively in a changing world. Whyte (1957) criticized American organizations who, through employment testing, choose conformers who resist change. Many of his criticisms were off target, but many criteria, if predicted well, tend dangerously to maintain the status quo. For example, the personality factor "conscientiousness" is widely advocated for selecting cooperative employees, but we have seen no discussion of how selection on this trait may create a workforce of followers. Avoiding criteria that merely reinforce the status quo requires intelligent recognition of the inevitability and usefulness of change.

PREDICTORS AND PREDICTIVE HYPOTHESES

What variables are likely to predict the criterion? How should they be measured? Forming a predictive hypothesis is a two-part logical argument: First, the criterion is related to certain traits and, second, that the chosen predictors are valid measures of those traits.

> The *predictive hypothesis* involves identifying what traits relate to the criterion, and reasoning that certain measures are valid measures of these traits.

Constructs are inferred from knowledge of the job or organization. People with different backgrounds may infer different constructs. Psychologists may choose constructs from factor analysis or general theories. Managers and job incumbents may rely on their experience, using what Borman (1987) called *folk theories*; if psychologists ignore ideas based on such experience, they risk ignoring some very good bets for predictors. Good hypotheses depend on prior knowledge and logic. One needs to know what has worked before, and what has failed to work, in similar situations. Some things are well-established. For example, job performance is predicted better by abilities than by other traits, and for most jobs cognitive abilities predict better than noncognitive abilities. Although many people find it hard to believe, the same factors that lead to success in school also seem to lead to success in one's career (Kuncel, Hezlett, & Ones, 2004).

Cognitive Factors

Cognitive abilities are abilities to perceive, process, evaluate, compare, create, understand, manipulate, or generally think about information and ideas. Common work-relevant cognitive activities include reading verbal or graphic materials, understanding the principles that make things work, planning events or procedures, solving problems, or perceiving signs of trouble in equipment or in human interactions or in contradictions in plans. Mental abilities are diverse and somewhat overlapping. More than 75 years of factor analytic research, however, has clarified and defined many components of mental abilities.

> *Factor analysis* identifies latent or underlying factors in the responses to measures. Verbal ability and quantitative ability are two of the (latent) factors underlying responses to items on tests such as the Graduate Record Exam (GRE).

Factor analysis examines intercorrelations among measures to identify or infer underlying (latent) traits accounting for the correlations. Several lists of mental abilities have been based on factor analyses, beginning with the Thurstone (1938) list of seven primary mental abilities: verbal comprehension, word fluency, spatial ability, perceptual speed, numerical facility, memory, and inductive reasoning. Subsequent research has made finer distinctions. Differences in the measures analyzed, in methods of analysis, and in the focus of researchers will result in slightly different factors and differences in their specificity. The possibilities for differences make it impressive that factor analytic results have been as much alike as they are. If every nuance is treated as a difference, then the lists of factors across studies can be very large. We will not try to list and define them all, but offer an illustrative (*not* definitive) list of frequently recurring cognitive factors in Table 3.2.

General Mental Ability

Even the lowest correlations between measures of mental ability are positive, suggesting a general mental ability. Traditionally, the general trait is called *intelligence*. Different authors, with different perspectives, emphasize different features of behavior called

TABLE 3.2

An Illustrative List of Cognitive Factors Identified Via Factor Analysis

Factor Label	*Description*
Verbal comprehension	The ability to understand words and their meanings, and to apply such understanding in verbal communications. Nearly any mental ability test will include a verbal comprehension score in some form.
Fluency	The ability to produce quickly a lot of ideas or associations. Different jobs may require different kinds of fluency, such as verbal fluency, ideational fluency, or number fluency.
Perceptual speed	The ability to identify figures make comparisons, or match visually perceived figures quickly and accurately. Perceptual speed is a generally useful predictor of clerical performance.
Spatial orientation and visualization	The ability to perceive spatial patterns, to orient oneself or an object relative to other objects in space. Engineers, mechanics, and others who must work from drawings need such abilities; drivers, pilots, or others who plan trips probably need it as well.
Number facility	The ability to do elementary arithmetic operations quickly and accurately. This is an obvious requirement for jobs requiring arithmetic computation.
General reasoning	The ability to understand relational principles among elements of a problem and to structure the problem in preparation for solving it.
Problem recognition	The ability to tell from early and perhaps subtle warnings that something is wrong or likely to go wrong; the problems may develop in equipment, people, social systems, or data. Sensitivity to potential or existing problems seems useful in jobs such as physician, air traffic controller, or machinery operation or monitoring.
Associative memory	The ability to recall bits of information previously associated with unrelated information; for example, to remember numerical information associated with names.
Span memory	The ability to recall in proper sequence a series of items (numbers, words, symbols) after a single presentation of the series, for example, looking up a telephone number and remembering it.

intelligent. One of the better definitions was given by Humphreys (1979): "Intelligence is the resultant of the processes of acquiring, storing in memory, retrieving, combining, comparing, and using in new contexts information and conceptual skills; it is an abstraction" (p. 115).

Spearman (1927) emphasized a general intellectual ability he abbreviated *g*, a symbol once again in frequent use. R. B. Cattell (1963) argued that the general factor had two components, *fluid intelligence* (*Gf*), involving basic reasoning, and *crystallized intelligence* (*Gc*), measured by tests such as vocabulary. Carroll (1993), in an encyclopedic reanalysis of mountains of factor analytic studies, proposed a three-stratum model. The first stratum consisted of the first order factors, somewhat like (but more narrowly and precisely defined) the list offered in Table 3.2. The second stratum included more general factors such as fluid and crystallized intelligence and others, and the third corresponded pretty well to Spearman's concept of *g*.

Job Specific Knowledge and Skill

"Know-how" is a folk construct. People who have it—who know and thoroughly understand a job's requirements—are better workers than those with less of it. To be useful, the term needs cleaner definition. Job knowledge may be general or limited to specific kinds of information or skill. The O*NET system of occupational information lists skills in three categories: *basic, cross-functional,* and *occupation-specific*. Basic skills are capacities developed over a relatively long period of time that promote or provide a foundation for learning other types of material. Cross-functional skills are those useful in a wide range of occupations. They include a variety of problem-solving, social, technological, systems, and resource management skills. Occupation-specific skills, of course, focus on tasks specifically required in occupations or jobs. The three categories are segments of a continuum from general to specific. The nearer a particular skill or knowledge is to the basic or general end of the continuum, the more likely it is to be expected of all qualified candidates; the nearer to the job specific end, the more likely it is to be the content of in-house training programs. For organizational entry, hypotheses usually emphasize more general skills and knowledge; for promotions, they may emphasize skills and knowledge specific to the work to be done.

Personality Constructs

Personality is a mixture of values, temperament, coping strategies, character, and motivation, among other things. Compared to cognitive traits, conceptual definitions of personality traits can be more easily developed for particular jobs or purposes, but finding operational definitions to fit them is more difficult. From the 1960s to the 1980s, research on personality predictors was sparse. Some people attributed the demise of such research to a critical survey of the published research on personality testing (Guion & Gottier, 1965). Two other influences were probably greater. First, the Civil Rights Act of 1964 explicitly permitted the use of "professionally developed ability tests," but it included no such enabling statement for personality inventories. Such inventories were targeted for severe social criticism, so many employers quietly stopped using them in fear of litigation. Second, the views of Mischel (1968), insisting that behavior is determined more by situations than by traits, were widely accepted. The idea of personality traits was widely abandoned by psychologists, but trait psychology, which never fully disappeared, reappeared in the 1980s.

A *personality trait* is a habitual way of thinking or doing in a variety of situations. It may be a general value, goal, or behavioral tendency to seek or avoid certain kinds of situations. It might be a need, even a metaphorical need, for a goal that is a state of being as well as an object or condition or experience. It may be a role that one habitually plays—the role of leader, clown, scholar, teacher, or a more nameless role having its genesis in other traits such as learned helplessness. It may be a constellation or combination of traits, a syndrome or type. The O*NET taxonomy does not refer to personality traits but "occupational values" and "work styles."

Most personality inventories measure several traits; if the list of traits named in them were placed end to end, it would stretch far! Consider the variety of constructs implied in this partial list of names of scales in existing measures of personality: alienation, anxiety, coping styles, emotional empathy, hopelessness, level of aspiration, perceptions of daily hassles and uplifts, response style, rigid type, risk-taking orientation, self-confidence, self-esteem, stress tolerance, team builder, Type A, and vigor. So many possible constructs must overlap; they require some means of reduction, commonly factor analysis.

The Five-Factor Model. Languages have thousands of words describing individual personalities. Many words have overlapping meanings; for example, *timid, shy, nervous,* and *irresolute* all describe people who tend to falter in social situations. Meaningful distinctions can be made among these terms, but the more general idea of social faltering can be inferred from the similarities. The example is an "arm-chair," or intuitive, factor analysis. Actual (statistical) factor analysis applied to such descriptive words has often resulted in five factors (e.g., McCrae, 1992). The five-factor solution, sometimes called the Big 5, has been found in languages other than English and in using different measurement techniques, including adjective checklists, phrases, and even a nonverbal approach. It has for some time dominated personality research; Goldberg (1993) described the domination as an "emerging consensus."

LABELING THE BIG 5

Names given the factors by various researchers have differed, as listed in Table 3.3. Some of these differences in preference can be attributed to bipolarity, with some names describing the positive and others describing the negative end of a bipolar scale. Generally, however, name differences seem to reflect the different nuances different researchers think most worthy of emphasis.

Our preference for Factor I is *Surgency*. It suggests the interpersonal aspect associated with extraversion, the common alternative, but it also includes the dominance and in-your-face visibility implied by wavelike "surging"; it is partly defined by adjectives such as aggressive, assertive, unrestrained, daring, and even flamboyant.

For Factor II, we prefer *Agreeableness*. It encompasses terms like likability or friendliness without putting much emphasis on conformity or compliance or implying emotional attachment to others.

For Factor III, we prefer *Conscientiousness;* it seems the most relevant to the work context. One set of key terms identified by Hofstee, de Raad, and Goldberg (1992, p. 158) includes *organized, neat, precise, exacting*; another includes terms like *conscientious, responsible*, and *dependable* clustering together.

For Factor IV, we prefer *Emotional Stability*. It is a familiar term, measured well by many inventories, positive rather than negative; it seems to generate no controversy, and it has frequently been a valid predictor.

Naming Factor V is not merely a matter of preference; substantive differences exist in the factors identified. "Openness to experience" is substantively different from "intellect," and neither reflects the central traits very well. We believe the most useful term is *Intellectance*; it is a liking for thinking about things, whether within the culture or in personal experience: problems to be solved, or things to be created.

Integrity and Conscientiousness. Factor III merits special attention. Employee theft of cash or merchandise is common enough that it has led to the use of tests to screen job applicants for honesty or integrity. These are not easy constructs to define.

TABLE 3.3

Interpretative Names Given to the Five Recurring Personality Factors

Factor I: social adaptability, extraversion, surgency, assertiveness, exvia, social activity, sociability & ambition, power, activity, positive emotionality, interpersonal involvement.

Factor II: conformity, psychoticism, agreeableness, likability, cortertia, paranoid disposition, friendly compliance, love, sociability, level of socialization.

Factor III: will to achieve, psychoticism, dependability, conscientiousness, task interest, superego strength, thinking introversion, prudence, work, impulsivity, constraint, self-control.

Factor IV: emotional control, neuroticism, emotionality, emotional, anxiety, emotional stability, affect, negative emotionality.

Factor V: inquiring intellect, culture, intelligence, intellect, intellectance, openness, independent.

Note. Adapted from "Personality structure: Emergence of the five-factor theory," by J. M. Digman, 1990, *Annual Review of Psychology, 41,* p. 423. Copyright 1990 by Annual Reviews Inc. Adapted with permission.

At first they seem to mean "theft-potential," but that is too narrow. A person of integrity is not simply a nonthief but one whose word can be trusted, whose work is reliably or dependably performed even without monitoring, and who can be counted on to do the right or good thing. A closer look at honesty testing and related validation research suggests the broader construct. Some test publishers have called their instruments predictors of "counterproductive behavior," but perhaps the more common, and more positive, construct would emphasize the *dependability* or *trustworthiness* aspects of conscientiousness (Goldberg, Grenier, Guion, Sechrest, & Wing, 1991).

Predictors under *conscientiousness* have been found to have the highest, albeit modest, mean correlations with job performance (Barrick, Mount, & Judge, 2001). Other factors have stable modest correlations within specific occupational groups. For example, agreeableness and emotional stability have been found to predict performance reliably in customer service jobs (Hurtz & Donovan, 2000). Thus, the five factors appear to have some utility for predicting performance, particularly when they are not correlated with other predictors in a selection battery.

Commentary. The five factors may be too broad for personnel assessment. Funder (1991) asserted that global traits (like the five) are best for explanations and theory development, but in prediction, narrower trait constructs are better. In choosing cognitive and psychomotor constructs, the trend favors more general ones, but for personality the trend seems to be toward greater specificity, favoring constructs more explicitly related to specific aspects of work. Examples include specific orientations such as *work orientation* (Gough, 1985) or *service orientation* (J. Hogan, R. Hogan, & C. M. Busch, 1984) or the breakdown of the Type A personality construct into two narrower constructs, achievement striving and impatience-irritability, each predicting different sorts of outcomes (Spence, Helmreich, & Pred, 1987). Even the *Hogan Personality Inventory* (R. Hogan & J. Hogan, 1992), heavily influenced by the five-factor model, includes seven scales, not five. It divides surgency into two components, ambition (the surgency emphasis) and sociability (the extraversion emphasis); intellectance is divided into one called intellectance and another emphasizing school success, liking academic pursuits and achievements. There is good reason to question the adequacy for applied purposes of the five broad factors.

Some critics say important personality constructs are not included in the Big 5. Apparent omissions include locus of control (Hough, 1992), self-evaluation (Judge, Erez, Bono, & Thoreson, 2003), activity level (Guilford, 1959), humility (Ashton, Lee, & Goldberg, 2004), and Type A personality (Tett, Jackson, & Rothstein, 1991). Some aspects of personality do not clearly fit the concept of a descriptive lexicon. Predictive hypotheses for decisions to be made among people well known in the organization may require a deeper probing of personality patterns than those where decisions are made among those new to or outside of the organization. McAdams (1992) referred to the five-factor model as a "psychology of the stranger," which does not entertain nuances among the factors or the "whole person" one comes to know when working closely together over extended time (p. 329). In short, maybe hypothesis development should consider a larger variety of constructs.

Research Design. Too often, personality test validation for selection decisions has relied on serendipity; research has not been planned or done very well. Guion and Gottier (1965) complained that most studies reviewed used concurrent rather than predictive designs. Personality traits are enduring, but they are surely malleable by experience. Self-confidence, for example, is likely to grow for those who do well on a job and to shrink for those who have been unsuccessful; variance in self-confidence is likely to increase with experience, and so is its correlation with success. Whatever justification exists for concurrent estimates of criterion-related validity of ability measures cannot be extended to personality measures.

> Identifying *job-relevant personality traits* involves specifying required behaviors of the job, and choosing traits that reflect consistencies in those behaviors.

The review offered other criticisms and concluded that "in *some* situations, for *some* purposes, *some* personality measures can offer helpful predictions. But there is nothing in this summary to indicate in advance which measure should be used in which situation or for which purpose" (Guion & Gottier, 1965, pp. 159–160). The overall conclusion was that the research had been so poorly done that generalized confidence in personality measures was unwarranted, and without clearer evidence of their validity in the situation at hand, they should not be used to make decisions concerning whether to hire or to reject people. The field of employment psychology is perhaps better prepared now, more than 40 years later, to study personality traits as predictors than it was at the time of that review. Meta-analyses have provided grounds for optimism.

The meta-analysis by Tett et al. (1991) classified studies as *confirmatory,* meaning a clearly stated hypothesis to be confirmed or rejected, or *exploratory,* meaning no such hypothesis. They also coded whether job analysis had been done. Generalized validity for confirmatory studies was better than for exploratory studies, and it was much better for confirmatory studies informed by job analysis. These, of course, are the studies based on a carefully developed predictive hypothesis.

Physical and Sensory Competencies

The Americans with Disabilities Act (ADA) and the Civil Rights Act of 1964 (as amended) have dampened what little enthusiasm existed for physical and sensory competencies for personnel decisions. For many kinds of work, however, they are potential predictors of performance and may be genuine prerequisites for some jobs and therefore defensible in litigation.

Physical Characteristics. Physical traits can be relevant to work outcomes; accommodation for physical differences may not be as simple as it might seem. Remodeling or computerizing a work area might be prohibitively expensive; providing work aids for some people might create hazards for others. Job analysis should show just how important apparent physical requirements really are and how the job might be done differently, and it should form a foundation for imaginative thinking about potential methods of accommodation. J. Hogan and A. M. Quigley (1986) reported that height and weight requirements had been approved in litigation only where there was no adverse impact or where job-relatedness was clearly demonstrated.

Physical Abilities. Many jobs, not merely laboring jobs, require physical skills. Package deliverers, fire fighters, power line repairers, tree trimmers, construction workers, and paramedics are among those for whom strength, endurance, and balance are relevant. Nevertheless, few psychologists have studied physical abilities and their relevance in employment practices; most of what we know has come from the work of Fleishman and his associates (Table 3.4). J. Hogan (1991a, 1991b) considered seven of these sufficient in personnel selection, arguing that static and dynamic distinctions rarely made sense in job descriptions. Condensing further, she identified three general fitness factors: (a) muscular strength, the ability to apply or resist force by contracting muscles; (b) cardiovascular endurance, or aerobic capacity, and (c) and coordination or quality of movement. A comparison of her taxonomy and Fleishman's is shown in Fig. 3.3. Different terms for similar abilities reflect slightly different emphases. She later combined strength and endurance factors; apparently, the physical requirements of jobs could be defined with but two factors: muscular strength and endurance and physical skill in movements. How general should definitions of physical abilities be? Again, it depends on the generality or narrowness of the criterion to be predicted.

Sensory Abilities. Vision and hearing ability are not unitary; "good vision" or "good hearing" means quite different visual or auditory skills for different jobs. Fleishman and Reilly (1992b) listed 12 different visual and auditory abilities, including with near and far acuity such specialized abilities as night vision, color vision, depth perception, and a corresponding variety of sounds related to hearing. Postwar vision research at Purdue University, and others, was reviewed in Guion (1965). No such extensive research has been done on hearing. It is likely that, in both cases, strong cognitive components are involved as well as the sensory ones. A certain pitch with low volume might be emitted from a piece of machinery; two people may have the acuity to hear it, but the better worker is the one who understands its implication.

TABLE 3.4

Fleishman's Taxonomy of Physical Abilities

Term	*Definition*
Static strength	Ability to exert continuous muscular force for short periods of time. Used in pushing or lifting heavy objects.
Explosive strength	Ability to exert muscular force in short bursts. Used in running, jumping, throwing things, or striking them (as in splitting logs with an axe).
Dynamic strength	Ability to use repeated or sustained muscular force over long periods of time; muscular endurance, resistance to muscular fatigue. Used in tasks requiring climbing or digging.
Trunk strength	Ability of stomach and lower back muscles to support parts of the body in repetitive tasks or over long periods of time. Used when working with tools while partially sitting or moving heavy objects while bent over.
Extent flexibility	Ability to bend, stretch, twist or reach out; a matter of degree, not of speed. Used when working in awkward, cramped settings or extending arms to reach something.
Dynamic flexibility	Ability to bend, and so on, quickly and repeatedly. Used in tasks like shoveling substances (snow, coal, etc.) to move them.
Gross body coordination	Ability to coordinate movements of arms, legs, and torso when the whole body is in motion, as in swimming.
Gross body equilibrium	Ability to keep or recover one's balance in unstable positions or conditions. Used in construction work, or in walking on ice.
Stamina	Ability to maintain challenging physical exertion over long time periods without getting winded; an aerobic ability. Used in fighting fires or in making extensive deliveries by bicycle or on foot.

Note. From *Handbook of Human Abilities: Definitions, Measurements, and Job Task Requirements* by E. A. Fleishman and M. E. Reilly, 1992, Palo Alto, CA: Consulting Psychologists Press. Copyright 1998 by Lawrence Erlbaum Associates.

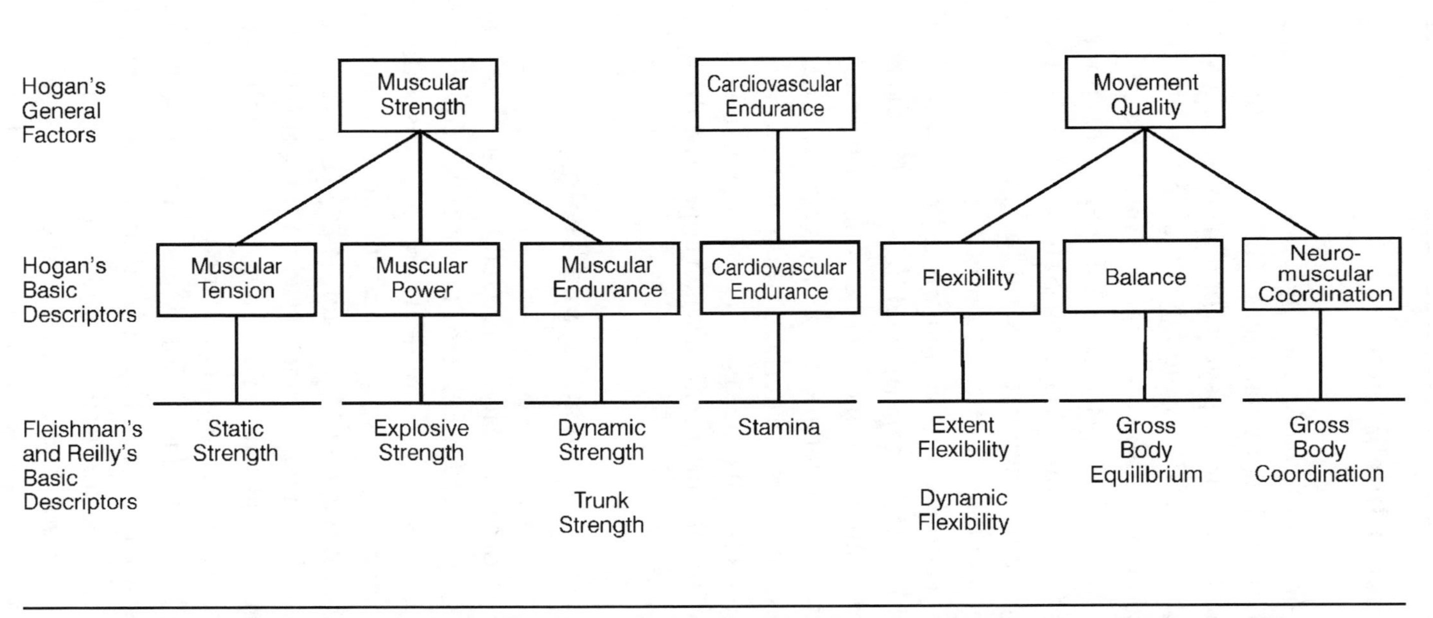

FIG. 3.3. A model of physical abilities, using the J. Hogan (1991a, 1991b) and Fleishman and Reilly (1992) descriptors.

Emotional Intelligence

The concept of *emotional intelligence* has received considerable attention in the popular press (Goleman, 1995), and is receiving serious attention as a psychological construct (Matthews, Zeidner, & Roberts, 2002). Although there appears to be no universally agreed on definition of emotional intelligence, it is generally described as the ability to accurately perceive, appraise, express, and regulate emotions (Mayer & Salovey, 1997). Certainly, such an ability would seem to be useful for a wide range of occupational arenas, including customer service, sales, politics, and many others. In a comprehensive and critical review of the literature, however, Matthews, Roberts, and Zeidner (2004) concluded that the construct currently lacks conceptual coherence, and attempts to measure emotional intelligence have fallen woefully short of standard psychometric criteria. At this point, we simply do not know if emotional intelligence is distinct from personality, or that it correlates with job performance when cognitive ability and personality are controlled.

Experience, Education, and Training

Some predictors are hypothesized without clearly articulated constructs; specified training or experience requirements are among them. Credential requirements are rarely useful; too often people with fine credentials do not have the competencies to match (Ash, Johnson, Levine, & McDaniel, 1989). They can be useful, if systematically evaluated and based on job analysis, (Howard, 1986; McDaniel, Schmidt, & Hunter, 1988b). Ash et al. (1989) suggested that education requirements, including a specific major, might be justified if the job requires extended knowledge comparable to that of recognized professions, the knowledge and ability requirements are hard to evaluate by other methods, the consequences of not requiring the degree and major are likely to be severe, and the degree program is the only way to acquire the knowledge demanded by the job. Even in these cases, however, it may be better to identify the competencies sought and to distinguish *preferred* from *demanded* qualifications.

Predictors for Team Selection

Individual candidates for assignment to a team must be assessed, and we stress here the assessment of individual candidates for team assignments. Technical competence is surely among them, but the skills, knowledge, and motivation needed to function well in a team go beyond the core technical skills. Stevens and Campion (1994) identified a generic list of teamwork knowledge, skill, and ability requirements. Their framework was based on two primary categories of KSAs that they termed *interpersonal* (i.e., conflict resolution, collaborative problem solving, and communication) and *self-management* (i.e., goal setting and performance management; planning and task coordination). Stevens and Campion (1999) used this framework to develop a selection test for teamwork settings, appropriately dubbed the "Teamwork Test." Although preliminary research on the Teamwork Test has been promising (McClough & Rogelberg, 2003; Stevens & Campion, 1999), its success may be based on its large general mental ability component. Personality approaches to team-member selection remain largely a matter of conjecture (cf. Kichuk & Wiesner, 1998).

An alternative approach to team–member selection is based on the idea of achieving optimal "fit" between the applicant's preferred teamwork style and that of the employing team. G. S. Anderson and Burch's (2003; Burch & N. Anderson, 2004) Team Selection Inventory extends the notion of person–job fit to the domain of teamwork. Thus, person–team fit is assessed by first assessing the work team's emphasis on safety, innovation, goals, and quality, and then assessing the relative importance the applicant places on these dimensions. The usefulness of this approach for predicting team–member performance remains to be seen.

DEVELOPING PREDICTIVE HYPOTHESES: A CAVEAT

Linking predictors to criteria is a local hypothesis, based on local job and need analyses. Better hypotheses await massive, cross-industry, cross-occupational research and meta-analyses. The ideal of an empirically developed matrix of such linkages has not been achieved. Without it, hypothesis development is necessarily local. Criterion constructs, other than overall performance, seem dictated by organizational needs. Choosing predictor constructs requires both local knowledge and scientific knowledge. Here is where one can get into trouble. Too much unrestrained scientific excitement leads to the use of esoteric constructs only because they are interesting—and overlooking constructs with good records. The best rule is for multivariate parsimony, the development of predictive hypotheses with relatively few predictors chosen from different categories. Cognitive constructs should always be included, but more often than is typical, the hypothesis should include personality and other noncognitive constructs. And always, the hypothesized predictors ought to make good sense to scientists and managers alike.

DISCUSSION TOPICS

1. Develop a predictive hypothesis, on both a conceptual and an operational level, using one of the five factors of personality.
2. How does contextual performance differ from traditional task performance? Would you like to be evaluated for your contextual performance in the classroom?
3. What kinds of factors would predict who would perform well as a team member in a group project? Consider group projects that have been assigned in your classes.

4

Knowing What's Legal (and What's Not)

Title VII
Uniform Guidelines
Affirmative Action
Negligent Hiring

In this age of litigation, personnel decisions based on whim, stereotypes, prejudices, or expediency are just plain foolish. This chapter emphasizes American laws promoting equal employment opportunity (EEO), particularly the Civil Rights Act of 1964, as amended. That legislation has dominated employment practices in the United States for over 40 years and is the foundation for other antidiscrimination laws. Its importance is widespread; it has influenced legislation in other countries, and American EEO laws apply anywhere in the world where U.S. citizens are employed by an American-controlled company. Businesses incorporated in other countries are subject to these laws for their operations in the United States.

THE CIVIL RIGHTS ACT OF 1964

The Civil Rights Act (1964) was to social policy in the United States what the continental divide is to the flow of rivers. It put the full power of the federal government to work on behalf of Black citizens having equal access to schools and public accommodations as well as employment opportunities. During congressional debate, in a misguided and unsuccessful effort to derail support for the proposed Act, a civil rights opponent offered an amendment to include gender as a proscribed basis for decision; another amendment added national origin. Both were accepted by the bipartisan management of the bill through Congress and became part of the Act. The Act's importance as a signal of a shifting concept of government cannot be overemphasized. Previously, the federal government had regulated things and standards (e.g., food and drugs, weights and measures). This Act regulated behavior.

> Although the Civil Rights Act was very broad, dealing with a variety of discrimination issues, *Title VII* of the Act was explicitly directed to employment issues.

Unlawful Employment Practices

Title VII of the Civil Rights Act specifies several unlawful employment practices:

1. Employers may not fail or refuse to hire, or discharge, anyone on the basis of race, color, religion, gender, or national origin.
2. They may not segregate or classify employees or applicants so as to deprive anyone of employment opportunities on the basis of race, color, religion, gender, or national origin.
3. Employment agencies may not fail or refuse to refer candidates on the basis of any of these characteristics. This holds

as well for labor unions with regard to membership or influencing employers to discriminate.

4. All provisions apply equally to employers, labor organizations, or joint labor–management committees controlling training programs.
5. Advertising employment or training opportunities may not indicate preferences for any group under any of these designated characteristics. Separate classified columns for "Help Wanted—Men" and "Help Wanted—Women" were discontinued, as were statements of preferences for characteristics that only men, or Whites, or speakers of English are likely to have.
6. It is unlawful to retaliate against people who have opposed unlawful employment practices under the Act.

Exemptions

The Act does not "apply to an employer with respect to the employment of aliens outside any State." Nor does it prevent religious organizations from hiring their own adherents to carry out religious work. Some preferential hiring is explicitly endorsed, such as preferential hiring of American Indians on or near reservations, or veterans' preference. Bona fide seniority systems were also protected. The Act does not prohibit or discourage discrimination on the basis of actual qualifications to do a job.

The Equal Employment Opportunity Commission

The Act established the Equal Employment Opportunity Commission (EEOC), empowered to investigate charges of prohibited employment practices; to dismiss charges deemed unfounded; to use conference, conciliation, and persuasion to eliminate practices where charges were found to be true; and to work with authorities in states or other jurisdictions where the practices are prohibited by local law. Where there is a finding of "reasonable cause" to believe the charge is true, the EEOC can file suit in the federal courts. Early in EEO history, working with employers through "gentle persuasion" lost out procedurally to the adversarial posturing of litigants.

UNIFORM GUIDELINES

The Uniform Guidelines on Employee Selection Procedures, identified hereafter simply as "the Guidelines" (Equal Employment Opportunity Commission, Civil Service Commission, Department of Labor, and Department of Justice, 1978), help guide employee selection aspects of the Act and Executive Orders. The course of the Guidelines development was not smooth (see Guion, 1998, for a history), but they, along with case law, now define "the legal context" for personnel decisions.

Adverse Impact and Disparate Treatment

Discrimination may be charged and litigated under two distinct legal theories. One is *adverse impact* (sometimes called disparate impact) in which an action is said to affect different groups differentially. Although the purpose of the law and its enforcement is to protect individual citizens from discrimination based on group identity, adverse impact refers to groups. Evidence that a group as a whole is less likely to be hired is preliminary (prima facie) evidence of discrimination against group members (but no more than that). A related view is called *disparate treatment,* or evidence that a candidate from a protected group is treated differently from other candidates in the employment process. In principle, all applicants should receive the same treatment—the same kinds of interviews, tests, application forms, and hiring standards.

The Guidelines note that adverse impact requires justification in terms of business necessity. That term does not imply something necessary for the survival of the business; rather, *business necessity* means that a selection procedure must be related to job behavior or performance—usually that it is a valid predictor of an important criterion—and therefore serves a useful business purpose not as well served by a known alternative with less adverse impact.

THE 80% (4/5) RULE

The 80% (four fifths) rule is used to determine the existence of adverse impact. Adverse impact exists if the selection ratio in one group (presumably the minority group) is less than 80% of the selection ratio in the other. Consider a situation in which a company has 80 White applicants and 20 Black applicants for a job. The 80% rule of thumb says that, if the company hires 25% of the White applicants (in this case, 20 of them), then it is reasonable to expect that 20% (i.e., 4/5s of 25%) of the Black applicants would be hired (in this case, 4 of them).

The 80% rule is simply an enforcement trigger used by federal agencies to move to an investigation. It lacks the force of law, and it must be interpreted in the light of other information. One employer might have an adverse impact ratio well under 80%, and therefore be suspected of potential discrimination, only because vigorous affirmative action has increased the number of nonqualified minority applicants. Another employer may have an adverse impact ratio above 80% because of the chilling effect of a reputation suggesting that application to that employer would be futile for members of certain demographic groups. Although a "chilling effect" argument requires substantial proof to succeed in court (e.g., *International Brotherhood of Teamsters v. United States,* 1977), its inclusion in the Guidelines emphasizes that the four fifths rule is subject to interpretation in specific contexts.

Options Under Adverse Impact. A selection procedure having adverse impact on any protected group may be modified, eliminated, or justified by validation. Modification is an option to be undertaken only with carefully designed research. Elimination is not an acceptable option for procedures with useful levels of validity. To abandon the use of a valid selection procedure because of fear of litigation is to return to essentially random selection—not a wise way to run a business. Of the three, validation in support of a business necessity defense is the only organizationally sound option. Organizational leaders should require it without waiting for federal agencies to do so. A selection procedure should be replaced if validation fails to show that it serves an important business purpose. Statistical validation is not the only way to show job-relatedness. Case law gives several examples where the business necessity defense was accepted on rational, "common sense" grounds.

Three options are presented in the Guidelines for using a valid selection procedure: Use cut scores to screen out only those deemed unqualified for the job, set up bands or other methods of grouping people into categories of predicted performance levels, and rank people for top-down selection. The different procedures may have differing degrees of adverse impact; the Guidelines assert that the probable level of adverse impact is least for cut scores and greatest for ranking. If a cut score is used and has adverse impact, then the choice of the cut score must be defended. If ranking has an adverse impact, then the principle of alternatives (as presented in the Guidelines) requires the employer to consider the use of a minimum cut score as an "alternative procedure" likely to have less impact. The Guidelines are silent on the fact that it may also have substantially less validity.

A further option is to substitute an alternative selection procedure with less adverse impact. Actually, alternatives should be considered from the outset. In planning the research, a predictive hypothesis should be formed with certain applicant traits hypothesized as predictor constructs (see chap. 3). Then one must choose one or more operational definitions of the hypothesized constructs to use in the study. In making that choice, prior literature should be considered, including literature describing evidence of validity and evidence of adverse impact—and evidence of other challenges to the validity of the methods.

Requirements for Validation

New research evidence, and the thinking stimulated largely by EEO regulations, has placed the Guidelines somewhat at odds with contemporary professional views. The Guidelines have treated criterion-related, content, and construct validity "as something of a holy trinity representing three different roads to psychometric salvation" (Guion, 1980, p. 386). Actually, the idea of three distinctly different kinds of validity has been inconsistent with professional views at least since the terms were introduced in the 1954 Technical Recommendations (American Psychological Association, American Educational Research Association, & National Council on Measurements Used in Education, 1954) and explicitly denied in the 1999 Standards. The more integrated view, that these terms refer to different *aspects,* or varieties of evidence of validity, is discussed more thoroughly in chapter 5.

Criterion-Related Validation. Obtaining a statistical relation between a predictor and criterion may not be technically feasible. The Guidelines explicitly recognize three conditions in the definition of technical feasibility: adequate samples, adequate score ranges on both predictor and criterion, and an acceptable criterion (i.e., unbiased, reliable, and relevant). If it is determined that criterion-related validation is feasible, the Guidelines specify that:

1. Job information must be reviewed, or the job must be analyzed, to determine criteria; a criterion must "represent critical or important job duties, work behaviors or work outcomes" (Equal Employment Opportunity Commission, Civil Service Commission, Department of Labor, & Department of Justice, 1978, p. 38300).

2. Samples used should be like the relevant labor market for the job in question.
3. Relations between predictors and criteria should be statistically expressed and should be statistically significant, typically at the 5% level of confidence.
4. If, in general, the results show that a selection procedure is a valid predictor of an important criterion, studies of fairness should be conducted (where technically feasible). The Guidelines are ambiguous about the definition of fairness to be used.

Content Validation. To establish content validity, the Guidelines require job analysis to identify work behaviors required for effective performance, their relative importance, and the work products expected to result. The analysis should focus on observable task behavior, although questions about what is observable are sometimes raised (e.g., is *planning* an observable behavior?). The requirement seems to restrict options to work samples (or, perhaps, to very narrowly defined job knowledge tests). The apparent narrowness is somewhat relieved by the inclusion of tests developed previously by others, in other circumstances, if the test content matches in some convincing way the content of the job as revealed by the job analysis.

> Relying on *content validity* evidence requires the use of a task-focused job analysis, rather than one that (only) focuses on the identification of KSAs.

Our interpretation of the guidelines suggests the following:

1. A content domain must be defined on the basis of a thorough job analysis, one that not only identifies tasks and resources used in doing them, but also determines their relative importance to the job overall. Implicit in this statement is the assumption that acceptable content validity arguments are job specific.

2. If the defined job content is but a portion of the job, then it must be critical to overall job performance.
3. The content of selection procedures defended on the basis of content validity must match the content defined by the job analysis.
4. Required prior training or experience may be justified as valid content if its content closely resembles the content of the job, as identified by job analysis.
5. Selection procedures defended only on the basis of content validity may be used only with a minimum cutting score.

Number 5 seems an odd requirement, and we do not endorse it. In a typing test based on content validity, for example, it is silly to say that one applicant who excels at the test cannot be preferred over one who scores at the bottom of the acceptable range. The requirement also fails to acknowledge that relations between test scores and criteria are almost always linear or at least monotonic—a point further discussed in chapter 6. Unless there is compelling evidence to the contrary, this means that persons with higher scores can nearly always be predicted to do better on relevant criteria than those with lower scores—even if the predictor is defended by content validity alone.

Construct Validation. The Guidelines also require job analysis as the first step in a defense invoking construct validity. It should identify behavior required for effective performance and constructs believed to underlie effective behavior. Such constructs should be clearly named, defined, and distinguished from other constructs, and selection procedures chosen should be supported with empirical evidence that they are related to the intended constructs.

Unfortunately, the Guidelines go on to say, "The relationship between the construct as measured by the selection procedure and the related work behavior(s) should be supported by empirical evidence from one or more criterion-related studies involving the job or jobs in question which satisfy the provisions [for criterion-related validation]" (EEOC et al., 1978, p. 38303). In short, despite some words supporting the use of construct validity arguments, this provision effectively rules out construct validity arguments. Under discussions of descriptive and psychometric validity in chapter 5, we give serious consideration to the nature of construct validity and of its role in establishing (or failing to establish) the job relatedness of a selection procedure.

Use of Valid Personnel Selection Procedures

"Transportability" of Validity Information. Acceptable evidence of validity may be based on validation research done elsewhere, but only with severe restrictions. The question is whether the outside research generalizes to the user's situation; some people refer to such generalizing as "transporting" the validity evidence. This provision predates the development of validity generalization research, and discussing it now seems rather quaint. However, it is still a part of the legal context, and there are often situations where one wishes to generalize from a specific study rather than from a body of related studies.

A generalized requirement, regardless of the nature of the validity evidence, is that the documentation and reporting be available in a form "similar to" the form required by the Guidelines. The following are other requirements for transporting criterion-related validity studies:

1. There must be evidence of the similarity of the job at hand and the job in the original study, identified by the same methods of job analysis.
2. The criterion in the original study is relevant to the local job.
3. The demographic characteristics of the applicant pool or research sample in the original study must be similar to those in the new situation.

Certainly the key characteristics of the job—those for which criterion data will be sought—should match in the two situations. It is less certain that broader similarity is truly necessary, and very nearly certain (from research done in the 1970s) that demographic similarity is not necessary; nevertheless, these requirements still define part of the legal context in which personnel decisions are made.

Testing for Higher Level Jobs. Employers frequently want to hire people who will advance in the organization. The Guidelines recognize this and further recognize that in many jobs advancement to higher levels is rare; in such jobs, hiring for the higher level may in effect be a pretext for discrimination. Employers are permitted to assess applicants for the higher levels only if the majority of those still employed after "a reasonable period of time" (rarely more than 5 years) progress to the higher level job, the higher level job will continue to require largely the same skills during that time, and the original job is not likely to provide the development of the requisite knowledge or skill.

Use of Scores. Four methods of score use are recognized: ranking (both top-down selection in which the highest scoring candidates are chosen first and the less systematic procedure where the candidate with the higher score is preferred over the one with a lower score), banding, pass/fail with a cut score, and combination with other tests. Little is said in the Guidelines about combining predictors, but there is a clear preference for cut scores, especially low ones. Ranking requires justification by data showing that variation in scores is related to variation in performance, that is, a criterion-related validation. Although words are used to suggest acceptability of content or construct validity arguments, the justification requirement nullifies them. Not all courts have accepted the Guidelines on this point, although many do. The idea of passing a test seems so ingrained in a society using cut scores for various kinds of licenses, diplomas, grades, and certificates that reference to passing or failing tests seems natural.

Where there are differences in mean scores of demographic subgroups (and there usually are), and where variances are about the same (and they might be), there is a necessary relation between the level of a cutting score and the degree of adverse impact. That is, a cut score can be set high enough that virtually no one in the lower scoring group can pass it. The way to reduce adverse impact, therefore, is to lower the cutting score. How low? The Guidelines themselves do not say, but some enforcement agencies in some situations have argued that the cutoff should permit hiring people at approximately the same score of the lowest scoring employee who is retained and on that basis presumed satisfactory. This position ignores the statistical realities of linear or other monotonic relations between test scores and performance. It ignores congressional intent in supporting, in Title VII, employers' rights to set qualifications. It ignores the fact that selection procedures are typically adopted for the sake of improving levels of proficiency in the workforce, not simply for maintaining what may be an unacceptable status quo.

In a different vein, it ignores the realities of selection procedures. In civil service jurisdictions, the typical pattern is to establish an eligibility list giving the names of all candidates who have exceeded a low cut score; selection is then done by ranking (top-down) those on that list until the list is "exhausted." An exhausted list typically still has names on it of people who have passed the test, but the passage of time and difficulties in finding people still interested in the job induce the authorities to initiate a new examination and start over with a new eligibility list. Even though a passing score is established, actual practice makes the de facto passing score somewhat higher.

In the private sector, the difference between a minimum cut score, if one is even considered, and the de facto score is even more pronounced. Hiring rates differ with the times. In a period of recession, for example, a company may do little hiring, and it will choose from the best of the many applicants presenting themselves for consideration; the lowest score among those hired may be quite high. When unemployment is very low, when virtually "any warm body" will do rather than leave a job totally unfilled, the de facto cutting score is reduced drastically. Such variability seems to be unacceptable to the authors of the Guidelines; they seem to assume that, unless ranking is justified, a fixed cut point will be established. Nothing is said about selection above that point. If more people score above the cut score than can be hired, then how should new employees be chosen? At random? The Guidelines do not say.

Reporting and Record Keeping Requirements

The Guidelines specify stringent record keeping requirements. Although not matters of psychological or psychometric principle, these are important to management. They are so important to litigation that any employer affected by the Guidelines should study them in great detail and with informed legal counsel. Moreover, various agencies have issued (and revised) record keeping requirements independently of the Guidelines.

CASE LAW FROM SELECTED EEO COURT DECISIONS

A *statute,* such as the Civil Rights Act, is a set of words adopted after legislative debate, compromise, and amendment. Application of these words to a specific instance is not always clear. Each party in a dispute may honestly believe the words to be on its side. The courts have the responsibility of applying the words and their legislative history to the specific case. In the U.S. federal courts, the dispute is first heard by the judge or jury in a District Court; the judge or jury is the "trier of fact" who determines the facts of the case and interprets them in the light of the relevant statutes and prior court decisions. Attorneys' arguments, testimony from witnesses, and study of the law and interpretation developed in prior cases all contribute to the judge's decision.

When a jury is involved, the judge instructs it as to the law. In the end, one party prevails; the losing party may appeal the decision to a Circuit Court of Appeals (the appellate level), which has jurisdiction over District Courts in its geographical area. At the appellate level, lawyers present their cases to a panel of judges; these judges do not hear witnesses or determine facts but hear and study arguments to determine whether an error of procedure or of legal interpretation has occurred.

The decision of the lower court may be confirmed, reversed, or remanded for reconsideration or retrial. Decisions at the appellate level become binding precedents for the district courts of that circuit; that is, those decisions guide District Court judges in future cases involving the same or similar legal issues. A district judge does not always follow precedent, but strong and compelling reasons, based on the facts of the case and their differences from the facts in the precedent case, are needed to justify deviation. The highest level of appeal is to the U.S. Supreme Court. Decisions at this highest level are binding precedents for all other federal courts, with the same possibility that the triers of fact in a new case may find important differences justifying a different legal path.

At all three levels, decisions rendered become part of *case law,* which is the body of judicial interpretations of the statute. The relative weight of decisions in case law is greater at the higher judicial levels, so we concentrate on a few decisions rendered by the Supreme Court and some recent ones from lower courts. We do not give details of cases but will give implications for personnel practices. See books by Gutman (2000) or Lindemann and Grossman (1996) for more on case law.

Griggs v. Duke Power Co. (1971)

When the Civil Rights Act of 1964 was enacted, 14 of 95 employees at the Duke Power Company in North Carolina were African

American. The plant had five departments, including a labor department. The company had required a high school diploma in all departments except labor, which was the only department with Black employees. On July 2, 1965, the effective date of the Act, the company extended the high school requirement to the labor department and required acceptable scores on two aptitude tests installed at that time.

The lower courts ruled that the requirements were permissible as long as the company did not *intend* to discriminate on the basis of race. The unanimous Supreme Court decision reversed the lower courts, and included many far-reaching provisions (*Griggs v. Duke Power Co.,* 1971):

1. *Intent vs. effect*: The court stated unequivocally that good intentions cannot excuse the use of procedures that create obstacles, unrelated to performance, for minorities. It is the effect of a practice, not the intent behind it, that is important.
2. *Business necessity*: The Court said that the Act prohibits the use of practices that appear to be fair but have discriminatory effects. "The touchstone," it said, "is business necessity." Although the Court seemed to equate business necessity with job-relatedness, other cases were needed to clarify the still-controversial concept.
3. *Job-relatedness*: Whether job-relatedness is sufficient to show business necessity was not clear from this one decision; that it is a requirement for professionally justifying use of a selection procedure was not in doubt. When the decision was announced, many psychologists equated job-relatedness with validity, but later decisions have shown distinctions.
4. *Deference to Guidelines*: Only the 1966 EEOC Guidelines were available when the case was heard. The Court asserted that Guidelines issued by the EEOC were "entitled to great deference." That did not give the Guidelines the force of law, but Guidelines provisions are to be carefully considered in Title VII cases.

5. *Use of tests of job qualifications*: The court affirmed that the purpose of the law was to require that selection decisions be based on qualifications rather than on race or color. The EEOC's endorsement of tests that are job related was entirely consistent with congressional intent.

Dothard v. Rawlinson (1977)

The Alabama legislature had established minimum weight and minimum height requirements (120 lb, 5′ 2″) for employment as prison guards in state correctional facilities. A woman was rejected for a guard trainee position because of failure to meet these requirements; she sued. These requirements would exclude about one third of American women but only a bit over 1% of American men. Accepting these statistics as evidence of adverse impact (i.e., the *burden of production* had been met), the Court in *Dothard v. Rawlinson* (1977) said the *burden of persuasion* shifted to the defendant to show job-relatedness, a position consistent with the history of testing Guidelines. Virtually all federal EEO regulations had taken the position that adverse impact triggered a demand for a showing of validity; the shift in the burden of proof that was implicit in *Griggs* and was made explicit in *Dothard*. Table 4.1 shows the burdens on the plaintiff and defendant in Title VII claims.

> The court distinguishes two kinds of evidence under burden of proof: The *burden of production* involves putting forth enough evidence to provide a *prima facie* case. The *burden of persuasion* refers to "going forward" with the evidence. The burden of persuasion carries the risk of "nonpersuasion" meaning that, failure to meet a preponderance of evidence standard, the issue is decided against the party that bears this burden.

Regents, University of California v. Bakke (1978)

This case (*Regents, University of California v. Bakke,* 1978) was heard under Title VI, the educational section of the Civil Rights

TABLE 4.1

Burden of Proof in Title VII Discrimination Claims

Burden	*On Whom?*	*Disparate Impact*	*Disparate Treatment*
Production	Plaintiff	Provides direct, statistical evidence that members of a protected class are being adversely affected by a specific employment practice	Demonstrates that he or she: • belongs to protected class • applied for the job and was qualified • was rejected and job remained open
Persuasion	Defendant	Demonstrate that practice in question is job-related and consistent with business necessity.	Provides nondiscriminatory reasons for the decision.

Act, but it had implications for debates of future amendments of Title VII. California had two independent admissions programs, a regular program for most applicants and a special one for minorities who claimed disadvantaged status. Bakke, a White applicant to the Medical College of the University of California at Davis, was rejected in each of 2 years when minorities with substantially lower scores were admitted; he sued successfully in California courts. The U.S. Supreme Court affirmed that the admissions system was unacceptable and that Bakke should be admitted, but it reversed the judgment that race cannot be legally considered. Its view was that racial diversity among medical students might be a legitimate consideration among others, but that the two-track system used at Davis violated constitutional protections.

Connecticut v. Teal (1982)

Connecticut v. Teal (1982) ruled against using the "bottom line" as a safe harbor in a case involving a multiple component promotion system. First, candidates for promotion were required to pass a written test. Those who did were placed on an eligibility list from which selections were based on prior work performance, recommendations of supervisors, and seniority. Test results caused adverse impact, but on the bottom line more Black than White candidates were promoted. The Court's view was that Title VII sought to assure every *individual* equality in employment opportunity, not to provide overall equality for racial groups. Any component of the overall process that precludes further consideration is subject to adverse impact analysis and the subsequent requirement for evidence of job-relatedness. This decision was extremely important in organizations using a "multiple hurdles" approach to personnel decisions.

Watson v. Fort Worth Bank & Trust (1988)

Since the 1966 EEOC Guidelines, attempts have been made to regulate subjective assessments (e.g., unstructured employment interviews) as well as formal tests. *Watson v. Fort Worth Bank* (1988) examined the applicability of the adverse impact trigger to a case in which promotions were based primarily on supervisors' subjective recommendations. The Court was aware of its dilemma. Requiring adverse impact analysis for every unstructured consideration could lead to the adoption of surreptitious quotas to avoid litigation. Not requiring it could mask strongly discriminatory effects of apparently benign procedures. Even objective data such as test scores or diplomas could be combined with subjective interviews, the composite therefore being subjective, and the entire thrust of *Griggs* and its adverse impact trigger could disappear as a mechanism for enforcing Title VII.

Given these poles, what should courts do about subjective practices? On this question, the Supreme Court was divided. The decision of the plurality said that two standards of proof are required to show discrimination prima facie. First, a plaintiff must identify the *specific practice* being challenged—not easily done when the practice is a private, subjective judgment. Second, with the practice identified, the plaintiff must also present statistical data strong enough to convince the presiding judge that the practice has the effect of *causing loss* of equality of opportunity for members of a protected group. The decision argued that a "burden of persuasion" does not transfer to a defendant; as in other matters of evidence, the defendant has the opportunity to criticize or refute either the data or the causal inference.

The Court also said that the cost of alternative procedures is a factor to be considered; cost had not heretofore seemed to be a matter of much concern to the Court and certainly not to enforcement agencies. Similarly, for the first time, the Court also said that expensive validation studies were not needed, even for tests, when common sense and good judgment affirmed the job-relatedness of the practice. Indeed, in matters of judging job relevance, lower courts were urged to defer in many matters to the greater expertise of employers in questions of business practice.

Wards Cove Packing Co. v. Atonio (1989)

In *Wards Cove Packing Co. v. Atonio* (1989), a five-justice majority affirmed most of the plurality decision in *Watson v. Fort Worth Bank* (1988). It affirmed the extension of adverse impact analysis to subjective procedures, the need to specify the practice being challenged, and maintaining the burden of persuasion on the *plaintiff*. Prior to *Watson,* the burden of persuasion shifted to the defendant, after the plaintiff had met the burden of production. It added a further requirement that evidence of adverse impact compare the demographic data on a specific job to the available supply of people for that job; that is, adverse impact statistics must be based on relevant labor markets. The Court also reduced the "business necessity" language to "business justification," saying that a practice need not be essential to survival of the business or in some other sense indispensable.

THE 1991 AMENDMENT TO THE CIVIL RIGHTS ACT

Differences in opinions about fairness in employment were neither resolved nor clarified by 25 years of EEO enforcement and litigation. If anything, they froze as polar opposites, held not as reasoned policy but as deeply held emotional commitments. For some, Supreme Court decisions like those in *Watson* and *Wards Cove* seemed overdue statements of sanity in the EEO arena. To many others, they seemed to signal a weakening of basic EEO principles, including the Court's standards in *Griggs*.

A Civil Rights Act of 1991 was passed and signed into law. It amended Title VII, among other things. Worries about quotas seemed to be put to rest by prohibiting "race-norming." (Race-norming is a way to get the numbers right by using percentiles or standard scores in different score distributions for different subgroups and using top-down selection based on the percentiles.) Shortly before the congressional debates, controversy erupted over the practice in state Employment Services referrals using the U.S. Department of Labor's General Aptitude Test Battery (see Hartigan & Wigdor, 1989). Race norming does not seriously affect mean job performance, but making it illegal quieted the charges of a quota bill. Of the Supreme Court decisions opposed in the 1990 bill, only the *Watson* view that the burden of persuasion remained with the plaintiff was changed by the 1991 Act. Definitions of business necessity and of job-relatedness were to have been codified by the 1991 Act. Nevertheless, they remain as ambiguous (some say "flexible") as before, and commonsense definitions may yet prevail. Another provision addresses intentional discrimination, providing even for jury trials and for compensatory and punitive damages. Good sense, if not morality, requires organizations to make sure that intentional discrimination on irrelevant grounds, or even the appearance of it, does not occur.

AFFIRMATIVE ACTION

Employers must not only avoid unlawful discrimination, but must take affirmative action to reduce the effects of prior discrimination. Early examples of affirmative actions included recruiting efforts, special training programs, direct mentoring, or extended probationary periods. Some affirmative action programs are voluntary, but many are imposed by court orders or consent decrees. Affirmative action is not a requirement under Title VII, although it is in the Guidelines. It has been a requirement for government contractors under the various Executive Orders, including the still-effective 11246, since 1961. It has been controversial since the development of the Philadelphia Plan in 1969, and the controversy is usually emotional.

The Philadelphia Plan

The affirmative action requirement in EO 11246 posed a special problem for the building trades; contractors do not generally have their own crews of skilled employees. They often hire those sent by unions. Office of Federal Contract Compliance (OFCC) investigations found few minorities in trade unions in the five-county Philadelphia area, despite a substantial minority population. The Secretary of Labor issued an order calling for increased proportions of minorities in each of six trades in each year of a 4-year period. Any building contractor submitting a bid for a federal contract was required to submit with it an affirmative action program to show goals within these standard ranges and a plan for reaching them.

Contractors faced a dilemma when the Comptroller General of the United States issued an opinion that commitment to the plan was illegal and that disbursement of federal funds for a contract with such a program would be withheld as unlawful. An association of contractors sought help from the courts. The appellate court supported the plan, and so did the Supreme Court, in effect, by declining to hear the case. Thus began the equating of affirmative action, once largely matters of recruiting and training, with numerical goals and time tables.

Reverse Discrimination

Affirmative action was initiated not to provide favoritism for groups of people, but to compensate partially for the effects of past discrimination. When courts find that an employer has a history of discrimination, affirmative action programs or even outright quotas may be mandated as remedies. When an employer independently sees evidence of adverse impact on a particular job or set of jobs, that employer may voluntarily establish affirmative action plans, goals, and time tables. Doing so, however, runs the risk of a reverse discrimination charge, and the plan must explicitly correct prior discrimination (see *Weber v. Kaiser Aluminum & Chemical Corporation,* 1977).

> *Affirmative action* is not the same as nondiscrimination, and the courts have not looked favorably on *voluntary* affirmative action—in the absence of prior discrimination.

Employers still feel that they walk a fine line in the conflict between obedience to the Executive Order and compliance with Title VII. The EEOC, at least, will not hold an employer liable (for reverse discrimination) for voluntary affirmative action programs if facts show an actual or potential adverse impact from practices in existence or planned, the plan corrects for prior discrimination as shown by discrepancy between the relevant proportion of the employer's workforce and the relevant labor market, and the available labor pool among protected demographic groups is "artificially" limited.

Developing Affirmative Action Plans

To establish a local affirmative action program, the employer should first identify jobs with evidence of either adverse impact or disparate treatment. If there are such jobs, then the responsible practices should be identified and corrective plans developed. The plans need not be (and to be effective probably should not be) restricted to hiring intentions. They may include special recruiting, educational or training programs, and plans for identifying and advancing those whose abilities are underutilized in their current positions. They must be limited, both in time and scope; they should not go beyond correction of prior adverse impact or disparate treatment either from a desire to "do good" or from fear of litigation.

Diversity as a Business Necessity

A recent Supreme Court decision in *Gratz v. Bollinger* (2003) concerned the University of Michigan's use of bonus points for minority applicants. Like *Bakke,* this case was heard under Title VI, but the implications for employment decision making are obvious. In the mid-1990s, the University of Michigan's College of Literature, Science, and the Arts had instituted undergraduate selection guidelines under which every applicant from an underrepresented racial or ethnic minority group was automatically awarded 20 points of the 100 needed for admission. The university relied on the judgment in the *Bakke* case, suggesting that consideration of race as a factor in admissions might serve a compelling government interest in some cases. The university argued that the educational benefit resulting from a racially and ethnically diverse student body served such an interest. Large corporations, such as 3M and General Motors filed briefs with the Court, stressing the need to employ racially and ethnically diverse workforces. The Court's decision in the case was mixed, and seemed to ignore many of the well-established principles of testing and assessment for employment (Tenopyr, 2004).

The Court accepted the notion that diversity is a compelling state interest, justifying its consideration in undergraduate admissions. At the same time, it struck down the university's selection system that grants bonus points to minorities, arguing that such a procedure is tantamount to quota selection. In delivering the opinion of the Court, Justice Rehnquist argued that consideration of race as a factor must be done at the individual level, not at the group level. In other words, each applicant must be considered as a whole, and preference is to be given on a case-by-case basis. Justice Rehnquist used the example of an applicant with artistic ability so great as to equal the talent of Picasso, yet this student receives only 5 points under the university's selection guidelines. Every minority student, however, would automatically receive 20 points under the same system. The Court's argument seems to suggest that, instead of receiving 20 points, minority applicants might be scored on the basis of *how much* diversity they would bring to the student body. The idea of individual differences in diversity seems a strange concept indeed.

In a dissenting opinion, Justice Souter gave credit to the university for its transparent selection system. According to Souter, "I would be tempted to give Michigan an extra point of its own for its frankness. Equal protection cannot become an exercise in which the winners are the ones who hide the ball." Like Justice Souter, we worry that the *Bollinger* decision may encourage organizations to "hide the ball" in their attempts to increase diversity. Doing so would imply using a selection system that does not have clearly defined standards regarding each qualification, and its relative importance in the hiring decision.

AGE DISCRIMINATION

The Age Discrimination in Employment Act of 1967 (ADEA; Age Discrimination in Employment Act, 1967) prohibits discrimination against anyone age 40 years or older. It encourages employment decisions about older people on the basis of ability, not age. It applies to hiring, early retirement programs, promotion, benefits packages, and so on. It is enforced through the EEOC.

Most ADEA litigation involves terminations, that is, firing, reductions in force, or involuntary retirement. A few companies have openly had age limits for jobs involving public safety (e.g., bus drivers), defended as bona fide occupational qualifications (BFOQs). Faley, Kleiman, and Lengnick-Hall (1984) showed that courts (at least initially) were more receptive to such arguments in ADEA cases than in cases of racial or gender discrimination, apparently on the grounds that employers should not have to experiment with the safety of third persons (e.g., passengers) to develop empirical proofs.

One hurdle to employees filing an ADEA claim has been the presumed need to show intentional discrimination. A recent supreme court decision in *Smith v. City of Jackson* (2005), however, ruled that evidence of disparate impact on older workers could be used in establishing a prima facie case. The ruling in *Smith,* along with the general aging of the workforce, indicates that more ADEA claims are likely to be filed in future years. Defense of an ADEA claim involves showing that factors other than age were determining considerations. For promotions, transfer, or terminations, these factors are usually performance ratings.

DISCRIMINATION AGAINST DISABLED PERSONS

The Americans With Disabilities Act of 1990 (ADA; Bureau of National Affairs, 1990) prohibits discrimination against qualified people who have disabilities. A *disabled person* is defined as one with a physical or mental impairment that substantially limits one or more major life activities, or who has a record of such impairment, or who is regarded as having such an impairment. "Major life activities" include caring for oneself, walking, speaking, seeing, hearing, and working. An impairment might be a physiological or mental condition, cosmetic disfigurement, anatomical loss, mental illness, retardation, or learning disability. The ADA does not protect people whose employment on a given job would threaten the safety or property of others.

The law requires employers to focus on what a candidate can do, not on disabilities. For a job to be filled, the employer must be able to distinguish essential functions of the job from those that, even if important, may not have to be performed by every incumbent. A clerical job, for example, may require operation of certain machines, reaching certain file drawers or shelves, and delivering occasional materials to people in other offices. If any one of these is deemed an essential function of the job, then a qualified candidate must be able to do it. The ADA prohibits only discrimination against *qualified* candidates with disabilities. It does not require preferential hiring of qualified but disabled candidates; it explicitly encourages hiring the candidates *most* qualified to perform essential functions, irrespective of disabilities.

Reasonable Accommodation

Employers must offer reasonable accommodation to overcome barriers a disability may pose for an otherwise qualified candidate. An unusually short person may be considered disabled. The disability may be a barrier to the filing function if file drawers or shelves are too high, but providing a stool may be enough accommodation to enable a short person to carry out that essential function. Thinking of accommodation as a major architectural change is often unwarranted; Jeanneret (1994) reported that about two thirds of all accommodation requests cost less than $500. Congress, EEOC, and the courts have stressed reasonableness; accommodation is not required if it would impose an undue hardship on the organization.

General Employment Procedures

Candidates may not be asked on application forms or in interviews about disabling conditions, although questions about their abilities to perform essential functions are permissible. Those with known disabilities may be asked to describe or demonstrate how they might (with or without accommodation) perform those functions, but they may not be questioned about the disability itself. Reasonable accommodation applies to application forms and interviews as well as to the job and job environment; accommodation might include providing application forms with large type, completing them orally while someone else fills in the blanks, providing an accessible interview location for people with mobility problems, providing an interpreter to sign for deaf candidates, or readers for blind ones, and so on.

Medical examinations or background checks are frequent parts of the employment process. Under the ADA, these procedures are permitted only after making a conditional job offer (i.e., conditioned on satisfactory results of these post-offer procedures). Putting off the medical examination until a tentative decision is made poses problems for some kinds of testing. Psychomotor tests might be used in medical diagnosis, and personality inventories might be used to diagnose other disabilities, but both are more often used as predictors of performance. When the evidence says that such tests have been evaluated for predicting performance on essential job functions, they need not be treated as part of the medical examination.

NEGLIGENT HIRING, DEFAMATION, AND WRONGFUL DISCHARGE

EEO law has dominated the legal context for nearly half a century, but other kinds of laws also need attention. Among these are laws of *torts,* that is, wrongful acts resulting in injury. The employer can be sued for damages if an employee does something that results in injury to a coworker, a customer, or some other third party. The suit might be based on the doctrine that an employee carrying out assigned duties is an agent of the employer. More often, in states where they apply, the doctrines of negligent hiring and retention are being used. These hold that an employer can be found negligent in hiring or keeping an employee if an injury was caused by an employee acting "under the auspices of employment," the employee is shown to have been unfit for the job, the employer knew or should have known about the unfitness, the injury was a foreseeable consequence, and the hiring or retention of the employee was the *proximate cause*[1] of the injury.

Grounds for Action Under Negligent Hiring

Grounds for action under negligent hiring require that there be an injury. In most litigation, the injury is physical (results of assaults or of accidents, rapes, or other physical violence). A consequence of criminal behavior (e.g., theft) may be the injury. Emotional or psychological injuries might be litigated. The "auspices of employment" is rarely at issue. It is not restricted to carrying out actual job duties as the employer's agent; the activities or event causing injury may include more than assigned task performance, although liability seems restricted to activities carried out while the employee is on the job or in some sense representing the employer (e.g., wearing the employer's uniform). Employees on their own time, or commuting from work to home, are not acting under the auspices of employment.

Showing that an employee is "unfit" is not necessarily showing incompetence on the job. Much litigation in this area involves violence, so a person with a history of violent reactions to interpersonal frustrations may be deemed "unfit" for employment in jobs where potentially frustrating contact with others is likely. Being "unfit" includes (from case law) not only mental or personality disorders but also more ordinary deficiencies. An employee's competence in driving may be considered in determining fitness in a job in which driving ability is hardly a defining characteristic (e.g., a social worker) but in which the employee must drive from one site to another. It is unclear whether checking for a valid driver's license is enough to avoid liability for an employee at fault in an injury-producing accident between sites, but a finding of un-

[1]Proximate cause means that the injury must be a reasonably expected or probable consequence of things done or not done by the employer. If an employee with a long history of lying causes injury by threatening a potential customer, then failure to learn of that history is not a proximal cause of the injury; there is no necessary or prudent connection between being a liar and threatening people (Ryan & Lasek, 1991).

fitness seems likely if the employee had a history of multiple at-fault traffic accidents.

The most common basis for dispute in negligent hiring and retention cases is whether the employer should have foreseen the possibility of unfitness. An employer should take steps to identify potential problems. In the previous example, perhaps checking for the license would be a sufficient precaution, but greater care would be shown by checking accident or driving records or insurance papers or perhaps giving a special driving test. It is necessary to exercise prudence and identify possible consequences if a person who is unfit in any specific way is put on the job.

Appropriate Methods of Assessment

Most writers on negligent hiring emphasize reference checks and background investigations—advice easier to give than to follow. Another legal doctrine, known as defamation, has made reference checks all but worthless. About the only information prudent employers give when asked about former employees is confirmation or disconfirmation of dates of employment and last job held, and some refuse even that. There is safety in the refusal. To be actionable under a charge of defamation, information given by the previous employer must be shown to be false, but the burden of proof falls on the employer, who must show that the statement made is true. Saying that an employee was discharged because of the supervisor's *opinion* that the employee was not trustworthy can be true if the opinion is a matter of record; it is therefore not defamatory. The same information given in a context of innuendo permits the inference that the employee did in fact violate trust, without factual support for the inference, and it may be defamatory under the principle known as "slander *per quod*." Statements that do not hold up under legal scrutiny, whether false, partially true, or unsupported by evidence, may also serve as the basis for suit for wrongful discharge. All in all, the risks are usually deemed too severe to take on behalf of inquiry from outside the organization.

Background investigations run similar risks and may also violate a candidate's rights of privacy. Many kinds of public information can be tapped, but always with some risk that the information is erroneous. Questions of validity of references and background investigations are not new. Moreover, some resulting information cannot be used for employment decisions. Courts have repeatedly ruled against the use of arrest records, for example, to deny employment to those in demographic groups experiencing unusual arrest frequency—although convictions may be used. There is always a question of cost. Thorough background investigations are likely to be fruitless for young applicants and very expensive for older ones with more background to investigate.

A FINAL COMMENT

Not all aspects of the legal context for employment decisions have been described. Omissions include, for example, record-keeping requirements, rules governing immigrants, requirements for federal employment of part-time people, the polygraph protection act, state laws, or laws of other countries. Moreover, what is described here is subject to changes in statutes, regulations, or court decisions.

We have tried to emphasize that personnel decisions must be made according to existing laws. The law is dynamic, ever-changing, and varies by state or local jurisdiction. Changes follow or accompany (or are accompanied by) changes in the ideas and attitudes of society in general, whether emerging spontaneously or in response to leadership. Even imperfect law is an expression of, and an instrument of, social policy. Perhaps, then, the objective of this chapter is better described as trying to emphasize that personnel decisions must be made not only according to organizational policies and interests, but according to social policy and interest insofar as it can be understood.

DISCUSSION TOPICS

1. What is meant by business necessity? What did the 1991 Civil Rights Act contribute to clarifying this issue?
2. What are the advantages and disadvantages of having the burden of persuasion on the defendant? On the plaintiff?
3. Some organizations rely heavily on promotion from within. Would it be appropriate for these organizations to test for KSAs needed for a higher level job to fill a position that may not need these skills?
4. Should the ADEA protect people under age 40 from age discrimination?

II

Knowing How to Assess

5

Minimizing Error in Measurement

Measurement Theory
Reliability
Validity

Assessment is a broader term than measurement. Measurement is a special case of assessment. It is based on a more defined scale along which scores can be ordered with relatively fine gradations (e.g., measurement of mechanical ability). Measurement seeks precision. In contrast, many other assessment procedures are ad hoc or used for specific practical purposes where precision is not useful or perhaps not possible. This chapter focuses on minimizing error in measurement. In other words, it focuses on enhancing measurement precision.

BACKGROUND

Quetelet, a Belgian astronomer and mathematician, noted that if the center of a distribution of human observations was correct, or represented perfection, then nature erred equally often in either direction. He later found that distributions of social and moral data also followed this "normal law of error." That law was important to Galton's studies of the inheritance of genius, and he used a crude index relating offspring and parent ability to test the proposition that ability is inherited. His index eventually led Pearson to develop the product moment coefficient of correlation. It treats the standard deviation of a more or less normal distribution (the normal law) as a useful unit of measurement. It continues to be the unit in most psychological measurement.[1]

J. M. Cattell (1890) and others of his era developed several perceptual and sensory tests and tests of memory, which Hull (1928) considered academic aptitude tests. Employment tests were developed by Munsterberg at Harvard, clinical tests by Kraepelin in Germany, and intelligence tests by Binet, Simon, and Henri in France. Most mental ability tests of the early 20th century used Binet's question-and-answer approach. The same period saw projective personality tests and standardized school achievement testing. By midcentury, a specialized group of test experts, concerned about the proliferation of tests used with or without clear measurement properties, developed a set of "Technical Recommendations" for the development and evaluation of tests and test use (American Psychological Association, American Educational Research Association, & National Council on Measurements Used in Education, 1954).

Different kinds of psychological measurement have all emphasized individual differences. Some have emphasized theories of psychological processes, but few have offered theories of the attributes measured. Usually the technique came first, followed later

[1]Boring (1961) pointed out, first, that one cannot assume that a mathematical function such as the "normal law" applies to a particular variable until it has been demonstrated empirically, which Galton and most of his followers failed to do. He then went on to say, "The *a priori* assumption that the normal law applies to biological and psychological variables, and therefore provides a device for changing ordinal scales into equal intervals has continued well into the present century. The scaling of mental tests in terms of standard deviations ... in some ways preserves this ancient fallacy" (p. 123).

by questions of what the measures mean. Reliability was the dominant topic in measurement during much of the second quarter of the 20th century; later, validity became the dominant concern. In employment practice, validity is often equated with effectiveness of prediction, but in psychometric theory it refers more generally to score meaning.

RELIABILITY: CONCEPTS OF MEASUREMENT ERROR

People differ. So do measures, for many reasons: flaws in measurement, the vagaries of chance, or traits measured—including traits not intended to be measured. Flaws, chance, and unintended traits are *measurement errors*. Concepts of reliability and validity both involve error, although in different ways.

Measurement Error and Error Variance

Errors happen in measurement. Two people using the same yardstick to measure the same table may get different results. A chemist using the most sophisticated equipment available may weigh a crucible several times, with results apparently differing only trivially, and settle for the average as the "true" weight. Mental measurements are still more subject to error. Intelligence is an abstract, complex concept, nearly defying definition, yet it is routinely measured with tests. There are always measurement errors, but scores usually do reflect fairly well the level of the trait being measured. It is sensible to assume, despite error, that one who scores high on an arithmetic test really is pretty good at arithmetic. The basic assumption of psychological testing is that any measure contains an element of error and an element of correctness, or "truth."

What accounts for differences in test scores? A measuring instrument, whether a yardstick or a test, is a constant stimulus; variance in measures stems from people's responses to it. Table 5.1 shows why people get different scores on the same test. The first

TABLE 5.1

Reasons for Individual Differences in Test Performance

Reason	*Examples*
I. Reasons that are more or less permanent and that apply in a variety of testing situations.	A. Some traits (e.g., reading ability) influence performance on many different kinds of tests. B. Some people are more test-wise than others. C. Some people grasp the meaning of instructions more quickly and more completely than others.
II. Reasons that are more or less permanent but that apply mainly to the specific test being taken.	A. Some of these reasons apply to the whole test or to any equivalent forms of it. a. Some people have more of the ability or knowledge or skill being measured by the test. b. Some people find certain kinds of items easy while others may be more confused by them. B. Some reasons apply only to particular items on a test. If the test happens to contain a few of the specific items to which the person does not know the answer, that person will have a lower score than someone else who is luckier in the specific questions asked.
III. Reasons that are relatively temporary but would apply to almost any testing situation.	A. A person's health status may influence the score. B. A person may not do as well when he or she is particularly tired. C. The testing situation is challenging to some people; others may feel less motivation to do well. D. Individuals react differently to emotional stress. E. There may be some relatively temporary fluctuations in testwiseness. F. A person varies from time to time in readiness to be tested. G. People respond differently to physical conditions (light, heat, etc.).

IV. Reasons that are relatively temporary and apply mainly to a specific test.	A. Some reasons apply to the test as a whole (or to equivalent forms of it). a. People differ in their understanding of a specific set of instructions. b. Some people may "stumble" sooner into certain insights useful in tackling a particular test. c. Differences in the opportunities for practicing skills required in test performance. d. A person may be "up to" a test or "ripe" for it more at one time than at another. B. Some reasons apply only to particular test items. a. Momentary forgetfulness may make a person miss an item that might otherwise be answered correctly. b. The same thing can be said of momentary changes in level of attention or carefulness.
V. For measures involving interactions between examiner and examinee, for measures using open-ended responses to be evaluated on a complex basis, for measures involving ratings (e.g., performance evaluations, evaluations of work samples)—for all of these, scores may be influenced by characteristics of someone other than the examinee.	A. Conditions of testing may vary in conditions intended to be standard or controlled. B. Interactions between examiner and examinee characteristics (e.g., race, gender, age, or personality). C. Bias or carelessness in rating or other evaluations of performance.
VI. Some reasons just cannot be pinned down. After everything else has been taken into account.	

category of reasons in Table 5.1 suggests that scores will differ because of those general, long-term characteristics of applicants that will influence scores on virtually any test, including such characteristics as general understanding of language, terms, and expressions, of instructions, and of the skills used in test taking. The second category suggests that scores will differ because of individual differences in the characteristics measured by the test. It also suggests that some applicants with limited vocabularies may be lucky enough or unlucky enough to find specific words in the test that they do or do not happen to know. With a different set of words, these applicants would have scored much differently.

The third category lists temporary characteristics of the applicants that could influence scores on any test; a person who is very nervous or distracted might do much better on a test under different circumstances. The fourth category includes reasons that are temporary and specific to the test or some part of it, such as temporarily getting stumped by a word usually known or recognized. The fifth category describes reasons for differences among scores that reflect conditions of administration of the test, such as interaction with the examiner or idiosyncrasies of scorers. Some have nothing to do with the examinee, and others may be applicant reactions to the conditions. Category VI reflects pure chance.

Notice that Category II-A is the one of primary interest in measurement; other categories reflect unwanted variance in scores. Classical psychometric theory begins by assuming that any measure X (obtained score) is the algebraic sum of a true measure (true score) t and a measurement error (error score) e, or

$$X = t + e \tag{1}$$

Further assumptions are that true scores and error scores are not correlated, error scores in one measure are not correlated with error scores in another, and error scores in one are not correlated with true scores on something else. Together, these assumptions say that error scores are truly random. In fact, however, some errors are not purely random. A true score, if really true, contains no error, but the theory defines it as the mean of an infinite number of a person's obtained scores on parallel measures of the same trait (Thurstone, 1931), that is, measures with the same means, standard deviations, and distributions of item statistics. But, if every obtained score in that infinite set contains the same error, then the mean is the score one would intuitively consider "true," plus or minus that repeated, constant error. The theoretical error score, in short, does not include errors the person makes constantly over repeated testing; it includes only unpredictable, random error. If errors were only random, then the mean of repeated measures would approximate an intuitively "true" score. The constant error across repeated measures for each person influences the mean of repeated measures precisely as it influences each individual measure.

> One example of *systematic error* that differs from person to person might be a tendency to prefer some types of item formats. Some people enjoy these formats, whereas others find them confusing.

Distinguishing systematic, repeatable errors from errors that vary randomly across repeated measures allows rephrasing the basic equation as

$$X = s + e \qquad (2)$$

Instead of t (true score), Equation 2 considers an individual's actual score X to consist of a systematic score s (a composite of an intuitive true score and any systematically repeated error), and e, the random error. Equation 2 describes the score of just one person; the s score includes that person's own private constant error. These personal errors differ for different people, so a set of them has some variance.

A different sort of error is constant for everyone in the set. It influences all measures in the set equally and therefore has no variance. Classical reliability theory is concerned with data sets and variances, so the equation is expanded from describing a person's score (X) to one describing variance across people's scores:

$$\sigma_x^2 = \sigma_s^2 + \sigma_e^2 \tag{3}$$

where σ_x^2 is the total variance (i.e., differences from person to person) in a sample of scores, σ_s^2 is the variance or differences due to systematic causes, and σ_e^2 is variance due to random error.

Reliability

Technically, reliability is consistency in sets of measures or items. Equation 3 shows where the consistency comes from: from the trait being measured and individual systematic (nonrandom) errors, with little variance due to any kind of random errors. As a basic concept, then, *reliability* is the extent to which a set of measurements is free from random-error variance. In equation form, the conceptual definition of a reliability coefficient is:

$$r_{xx} = 1 - \frac{\sigma_e^2}{\sigma_x^2} \tag{4}$$

where r_{xx} is the theoretical reliability coefficient, σ_e^2 is the variance of the random sources of error, and σ_x^2 is the total variance. The smaller the error variance relative to total variance in obtained scores, the more reliable the measures in the distribution. Keep in mind that this is a conceptual discussion; many different reliability coefficients can be computed from the same data, but each is simply an estimate of the theoretical reliability coefficient. In discussions of reliability, "measurement error" refers to random sources of error. We could also define reliability as the proportion of total variance attributable to systematic sources, but it is important to recognize that it is not defined as the proportion of total variance due to "true" variance. Such a definition would imply a specific trait, a specification irrelevant to an understanding of consistency (Tryon, 1957).

Reliability as a Necessary Condition For Validity

Reliability is often termed the sine qua non of mental measurement; if a test is not reliable, then it cannot have any other merit. Imagine if every time you stepped on the bathroom scale it produced a different reading of your weight. Such a scale would be worthless (surely your weight would not change as a result of stepping on and off the scale!). However, evidence of reliability is not in itself sufficient evidence that a measure is a good one. There is still the very important question of whether systematic sources of variance are relevant to the purpose of measurement. If systematic sources of variance on the vocabulary test were due to test-wiseness, and not ability in vocabulary, then those systematic sources are not relevant to the purpose of measurement. This is a matter of validity. Validity is the major consideration in test evaluation. Reliability is important because it imposes a ceiling for validity. The theoretical relation of reliability to validity is shown by the formula:

$$r_{x\infty y\infty} = \frac{r_{xy}}{\sqrt{r_{xx}\, r_{yy}}} \tag{5}$$

where $r_{x\infty y\infty}$ is the *theoretical* correlation that would exist if predictor x and criterion y were perfectly reliable, r_{xy} is the validity coefficient actually obtained, and r_{xx} and r_{yy} are the respective reliability coefficients. This is known as correcting the validity coefficient for *attenuation,* that is, for unreliability.

It may be important for theoretical purposes to ask what the correlation would be if the two variables were measured with perfect reliability. That question is rarely important in personnel research.

When we have an imperfect employment test, we use it anyway, use something else, or improve its reliability; in any case, we use a less than perfectly reliable test. There is little value in dreaming about the validities that might have been if only we had a perfectly reliable test.

In some situations, however, it is useful to know the level of validity with a perfectly reliable criterion, that is, to know how much of the *reliable* criterion variance is associated with predictor variance. We can find out by correcting for criterion unreliability only:

$$r_{xy\infty} = \frac{r_{xy}}{\sqrt{r_{yy}}} \qquad (6)$$

where y is the criterion, y^{∞} is the perfectly reliable criterion, and x is the test. This is the correction for attenuation in the criterion. Assume a validity coefficient of .40, better than many, but not noteworthy. Assume also a criterion reliability coefficient of .25, a terribly low reliability. Substituting in Equation 6, $r_{xy\infty} = .40/\sqrt{.25} = .40/.5 = .80$, the estimated correlation with a perfectly reliable criterion. The coefficient of determination for this hypothetical correlation is .64; the test accounts for 64% of the total *explainable* variance. Clearly, this offers reasonably effective prediction, given the limits of criterion unreliability. A validity coefficient expressed as the relation of the predictor to the explainable criterion variance is a more standardized statement than the uncorrected coefficient, is less subject to the vagaries of random criterion variance, and generally makes more sense.

ACCURACY, RELIABILITY, AND VALIDITY

Accuracy should not be confused with reliability. A thermometer or test may provide exceedingly inaccurate measures that are quite reliable even so. Nor should accuracy be confused with validity. Consider the thermometer example.

To determine its accuracy, a set of temperature readings could be paired with criterion readings obtained for the same situations using instruments in the Bureau of Standards. If the correlation between our faulty thermometer readings and the standard readings were high, then we could conclude that the thermometer gives "valid" measures of temperature—but not necessarily accurate ones. The thermometer with the 20-degree constant error could be perfectly valid, as shown in Fig. 5.1: The connected dots show perfect correlation despite the constant error. The unconnected ×s show both perfect correlation and perfect accuracy. Lest this be considered a peculiar circumstance of the consistency of the error, Fig. 5.2 illustrates a possible perfect correlation where the amount of error in a test thermometer is greater at high temperatures than at low ones.

Accuracy, in relation to a standard, must be a function of both *strength* of relation (correlation) and *kind* of relation to the standard. To be accurate, a measure must be highly correlated with a standard measure of the same thing, and the relation must be a specific form of a linear one. This is all very well for physical measures; we can refer sensibly to the accuracy of predictions or of measures defined by standards in some Bureau of Standards. There is, however, no such bureau for cognitive or temperament traits. The concept of accuracy, therefore, is meaningless for psychological constructs.

RELIABILITY ESTIMATION

Reliability is traditionally estimated by computing a correlation between two sets of measures presumably measuring the same thing in the same sample of people in the same way. The two sets of scores might be scores on two different but equivalent forms of the same test, scores on the same test given at different times, or scores on two halves of a test. For each person, the two systematic scores are expected to be the same; systematic variance therefore causes, im-

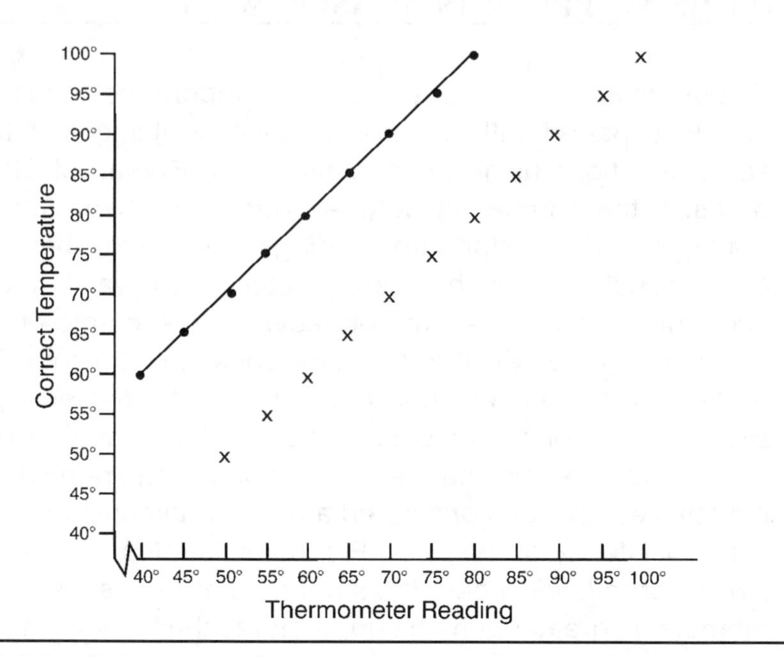

FIG. 5.1. Perfect correlation where inaccuracy is due to constant error.

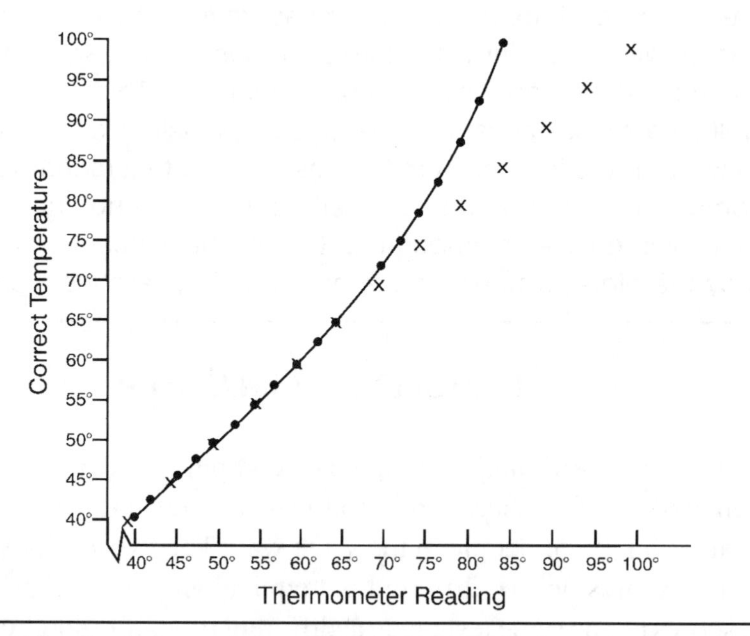

FIG. 5.2. Perfect correlation where inaccuracy is due to both constant error and scale differences.

proves, or at least maintains correlation. Error scores are not the same, being random, so error variance comes from conditions or personal characteristics that differed in the two sets of scores. Random error variance inhibits or lowers correlation coefficients. If the effect of a source of variance is consistent in the two sets of scores, then it is treated as a source of systematic variance. If it differs, it is treated as a source of error variance. Different estimates of reliability differ in the sources of variance treated as *systematic* (correlation-causing) or as *error* (correlation-reducing). Each method for estimating reliability is a specific set of procedures for defining what is meant by reliability—an operational definition of reliability. Different operational definitions emphasize different sources of error variance. Giving a test a second time in exactly the same form and manner as before, the so-called test–retest method, considers stability the source of consistency. This method treats errors due to particular items on the test, for example, as variance contributing to individuals' true scores (i.e., as a systematic source). Another method correlates scores obtained from equivalent forms of the same measuring device. This method treats peculiar items as a source of error variance. Either of these methods may be varied by allowing different amounts of time to elapse between measurements. If the two measures are obtained at pretty much the same time, a short-term effect on test performance (e.g., alertness or tiredness of test takers) is treated as a systematic source, but it is treated as error when the time interval between is large. Dividing a test into two equivalent halves is another method. With this technique, even very temporary characteristics, ordinarily considered sources of error in other procedures, may enhance correlation. Five kinds of operational definitions of reliability that treat variance sources differently are compared in Table 5.2, using the categories from Table 5.1.

Coefficients of Stability

Stability means scores are consistent over time. A *coefficient of stability* defines random error as individual differences in score change

TABLE 5.2

Allocation of Variance in Different Estimates of Reliability

	Treatment of Sources of Variance[a]							
Estimate Method	*I*	*IIA*	*IIB*	*III*	*IVA*	*IVB*	*V*	*VI*
Immediate test–retest	S	S	S	S	S	E	E	E
Delayed test–retest	S	S	S	E	E	E	E	E
Immediate equivalent forms	S	S	E	S	S	E	E	E
Delayed equivalent forms	S	S	E	E	E	E	E	E
Split half	S	S	E	S	S	S	E	E

[a]S = systematic variance; E = error variance.

(inconsistency) over an appreciable time period. *Test–retest* (using the same test) is useful if item sampling is not a problem. Test–retest correlation may be spuriously high if previous responses are remembered. Testing with an *equivalent form* (defined in the next section) after the time interval increases variance attributed to error, eliminating memory as an irrelevant source of systematic variance.

Coefficients of stability are useful for psychomotor or sensory tests if intervals are long enough to counteract practice or fatigue effects. Longer time intervals are needed for cognitive tests. The appropriate time interval depends on how long people remember particular content and how often the content is practiced. A lot of skill practice or information use produces overlearning; those with initial high scores would surely repeat them, but over time those with low scores would improve; differences in benefits of practice are treated as error variance.

Coefficients of Equivalence

Two test forms with different items are equivalent if they have matching content (each has the same number of each kind of item), and their means and standard deviations do not differ significantly.

Equivalent forms are developed by specifying logical and statistical properties (item type and content; item difficulties, validities, or intercorrelations; or test means and standard deviations) to which each of them will conform. Such item matching should yield correlated forms with essentially the same "true score" distributions. A *coefficient of equivalence* defines reliability as the extent to which a set of measures is free from errors due to sampling a test content domain. Actually, because genuine equivalence is hard to achieve, reliability estimates computed as correlations between equivalent forms are rather conservative (i.e., low). The conservatism is not so great with tests of well-defined content like vocabulary or arithmetic, but it may seriously distort reliability estimates for less well-defined areas such as temperament and motivation or for measurement by ratings.

Coefficients of Internal Consistency

Coefficients of internal consistency treat variance due to variations in item content as a major source of error variance, and they show how much the variance is systematically based on a common concept measured by the test as a whole. In other words, they indicate how much the items in the test are getting at the same thing. Coefficients of internal consistency are widely used because of their convenience; they need only one administration with just one test form (if there is no time limit).

Kuder–Richardson Estimates. Techniques involving analysis of item variance are estimates of internal consistency. The most common of these methods was presented by Kuder and Richardson (1937) in a series of formulas; these formulas require the assumption of homogeneity (Cureton, 1958). The Kuder–Richardson formulas may be considered averages of all the split-half coefficients that would be obtained using all possible ways of dividing the test. The preferred formula (Richardson &

Kuder, 1939) known as Kuder–Richardson Formula 20 (K–R 20) from the numbering of equations in the original derivation, is

$$r_{xx} = \left(\frac{n}{n-1}\right) \cdot \left(1 - \frac{\sum pq}{S_x^2}\right) \tag{7}$$

where n is the number of items in the test, p is the proportion of correct responses to a given item, $q = (1 - p)$, and S_x^2 is the total test variance. Note that error variance is given as the sum of item variances, pq. This is a harsh assumption and may indicate why this formula gives a lower bound estimate of reliability (Guttman, 1945).

It is now more common to find references to Cronbach's *coefficient alpha* (Cronbach, 1951), a more general version of the K–R 20 equation,

$$\alpha_n = \left(\frac{n}{n-1}\right) \cdot \left(1 - \frac{\sum S_i^2}{S_x^2}\right) \tag{8}$$

where α_n is $r_{xx'}$ the reliability coefficient called alpha for a test of n components (items or sets of items), S_i^2 is the variance of item responses or other component scores, and S_x^2 is the total score variance. If item responses are dichotomous, then $\Sigma S_i^2 = \Sigma_{pq}$, and the equation for alpha is the same as K–R 20. Alpha can be used for items with response scales, ratings, or scores on small sets of dependent items such as a set of items based on a single passage or illustration.

Useful as it is, the alpha coefficient should not be used merely for convenience, and it should be interpreted only as internal consistency, not confused with equivalence or stability. It is appropriate for most norm-referenced tests of abilities because these are typically constructed to provide homogeneous sets of items. It is not appropriate for domain-referenced tests constructed to represent a not-necessarily-homogeneous content domain.

Interrater Agreement

Two different observers seeing the same behavior or product may evaluate it differently—a source of error variance. With tests and rating scales scored by observer judgments, such a source of error can be large. The score depends not only on the behavior of the person observed or rated, but also on scorer or rater responses and characteristics. *Interrater reliability*, like other operational definitions, is often expressed as correlation. If there are several raters or scorers, a correlation matrix can be computed and an average determined, or intraclass correlation can be used. With dichotomous ratings, it may be expressed as the percentage of agreement between pairs of raters.

Comparisons Among Reliability Estimates

Estimates by various methods turn out to be similar. If variance in a set of measures is generally systematic, with little of it attributable to random error, then different operational definitions of reliability should agree fairly well. For this general statement to be so, the systematic variance has to be attributable to long-term, general characteristics of examinees, including the characteristics one is trying to measure. However, different methods make different assumptions, procedural and mathematical, and define error differently; researchers, test developers, and test users should use estimates that make sense for the circumstances they face. When a test is used to predict performance over a long period of time, stability is more important than internal consistency. If retesting is common enough to justify equivalent forms, then coefficients of equivalence are needed. If production should be consistent month in and month out, then an alpha coefficient over a period of several months is appropriate. The absolute values of stability, equivalence, and alpha coefficients may not differ very much, but small differences in reliability can make great differences in the appropriateness of decisions about individual people (Wainer & Thissen, 1996).

Standard Error of Measurement

So far, reliability has been defined and discussed in terms of distributions or sets of measurements. However, the basic datum is always a single measure, and the *reliability of an individual score* may be important—increasingly so as ADA and selection for single positions preclude use of large data sets. The standard error of measurement, expressed in test score units, serves that purpose. Rearranging the definitional equation for reliability, we get

$$s_e^2 = s_x^2 (1 - r_{xx}) \quad (9)$$

or

$$s_e = s_x \sqrt{1 - r_{xx}} \quad (10)$$

where s_e is the *standard error of measurement.*

Standard errors of measurement have three uses in personnel decisions: to determine whether scores for two people differ significantly, to determine whether a person's score differs significantly from a hypothetical true score, or to determine whether scores discriminate differently in different groups, for example, different demographic groups or groups defined by different score ranges. The latter use should be more common than it is.

> If individuals were to repeatedly take a test, with no change in their standing on the attribute being measured, then scores would vary around their true score on the attribute. The *typical* distance between their true score and their observed score defines the *standard error of measurement.*

In mass employment, it is important to know if test scores distinguish people reliably in those regions of the distributions where hard decisions are made. They should; one evaluation of a test can ask whether the range with the minimal standard error of measurement is the crucial range for decisions. Standard errors may be computed independently for different regions, given enough cases.

INTERPRETATION OF RELIABILITY COEFFICIENTS

Some people simplify reliability interpretation by stating a minimally satisfactory coefficient. It is not that simple. Interpretation must consider other information, including the intended use of the measures. For basic research, high reliability may not be critical. Decisions about individuals, however, require highly reliable measures. A reasonably sought level of "highly reliable" may depend on the history of a particular kind of measurement; "high" for interviews is lower than for standardized tests. Several other factors need to be considered in interpreting coefficients, including sample and item characteristics (see Guion, 1998).

One particularly important factor influencing reliability is the number of items in the test. With some exceptions (e.g., Li, Rosenthal, & Rubin, 1996; Wainer & Thissen, 1996) reliability is generally influenced by the length of a test or period of observation. Determining how long a test must be for adequate reliability is expressed in this formula:

$$n = \frac{r_{nn}(1 - r_{xx})}{r_{xx}(1 - r_{nn})} \tag{11}$$

where n is the number of times the existing test must be multiplied for a desired level of reliability, r_{nn} is that level, and r_{xx} is the reliability coefficient before lengthening the test. Use of the equation assumes that increments are equivalent to the existing procedure. It may be applied only to coefficients of equivalence or of internal consistency.

Reliability improvement improves validity. Properly increasing test length by a specific value of n, estimated validity will be shown by

$$r_{x_n y} = \frac{r_{xy}}{\sqrt{\frac{1}{n} + \left(1 - \frac{1}{n}\right) r_{xx}}} \tag{12}$$

where $r_{x_n y}$ is the validity expected for the lengthened test x, and n is the factor by which the test is to be lengthened (R. L. Thorndike, 1949). Using selected values in this equation will show that, where a test is reasonably reliable to begin with, not much added validity will be gained through lengthening the test. Where, however, a low validity coefficient is due to low test reliability, lengthening the test can be useful.

VALIDITY: AN EVOLVING CONCEPT

The classical notion of validity used criteria only to judge the excellence of tests as trait measures. A test, it was generally said, "purports" to measure something, and validity is the degree it measures "what it is intended or purports to measure" (Drever, 1952, p. 304). This view differs from a later view of validity as the effectiveness of test use in predicting a criterion measuring something else and valued in its own right. The early concept of validity evaluated test scores as measures of a trait of interest; the later one evaluates test scores as predictors of something else. Investigations of both ideas have been called validation, results of either are called validity, and data collected for one of these evaluations may (but may not) be useful for the other. The distinction has not been commonly recognized.

People tend to use a verbal shorthand, referring to "test validity" as if validity were a property of the method of measurement. It is not; it is a property of the *inferences* drawn from test *scores*; the inferences (interpretations) may be descriptive or relational.

> It is the *inferences* we make from test scores that are either valid or not valid—not the tests themselves. If we believe that a test should predict job performance, then we would validate that inference or belief by correlating scores on the test with job performance measures. If we believe that a test should measure perceptual accuracy, then we could correlate its scores with a different, preferably better, measure of the same sort of perceptual accuracy.

Three Troublesome Adjectives

Early attempts to clarify the validity concept (American Psychological Association, American Educational Research Association, & National Council on Measurements Used in Education, 1954, 1966) described criterion-related, content, and construct validity as aspects of validity; however, no general definition of validity was offered. Criterion-related validity was shown by the relation of test scores to an external criterion. Content validity was a matter of the fidelity of sampling a content domain in the construction of the test. Construct validity was more complex, requiring a showing of reasons both for inferring a particular construct from the test scores and for not inferring alternative constructs. The three came to be treated as if they were three different *kinds* of validity, not *aspects,* an error of interpretation forcefully criticized by Dunnette and Borman (1979) and by the first author as psychometric trinitarianism (Guion, 1980). At least since Cronbach (1971), validity concepts have emphasized the meaning of scores: how a score can be interpreted, or what can be inferred about a person with that score. Inferences are constructs, and the "unitarian" view that has emerged treats the notion of validity, with no modifying adjective, as an expanded view of what was called construct validity (Messick, 1989, 1995a).

Descriptive and Relational Inferences

Descriptive inferences interpret scores in terms of the characteristics revealed by the measurement procedure itself. For example, a high score on a cognitive ability test suggests that the test taker is high in intelligence. *Relational inferences* interpret scores in terms of different but correlated characteristics. For example, a high score on a cognitive ability test suggests that the test taker will perform well on a job that is mentally challenging. These are not wholly independent. The validity of descriptive inferences depends on several sources of information, relational data among them; it is closely associated with the idea of construct validity. Relational inferences are not well understood without understanding the descriptive properties of the related variables. Nevertheless, the distinction emphasizes different demands on validation: the difference between evaluating the success with which a construct is measured and evaluating its use. Both are important, but so is the distinction. For personnel decisions, the distinction is between interpreting scores as traits and interpreting them as signs of something else.

A relational inference is made when one infers from a score a corresponding level of performance on a criterion; it is usually evaluated by correlations. There is almost always more than that to be inferred from a well-understood test score. Validity is more than a correlation coefficient. To be sure, a test can be designed to do no more than predict a criterion—having no meaning at all if the criterion changes. A change in the job or technology or context can destroy the validity of such a limited relational inference, and no one will know why.

Usually, several constructs can be offered as plausible descriptive interpretations. One may be intended by the developer or user; others may be unwanted contaminants. If scores can sensibly be interpreted in terms of the intended construct or meaning, but not in terms of the intrusive others, then the intended descriptive inferences are surely valid, apart from any relational inferences that may also be valid.

Psychometric Validity

Validation for descriptive inferences seeks confirmation of the meaning of test scores intended by the test developer (or some subsequent meaning intended by a test user) and disconfirmation of plausible alternative meanings. Because such validation is procedurally different from traditional employment test validation, we distinguish evaluating (validating) descriptive inferences from validating relational ones. For personnel assessment, with apology for yet another adjective, we call the result of the former *psychometric validity*. The result of the latter we call *job-relatedness*, at least in personnel decision contexts.

> Evidence for descriptive inferences is *psychometric validity,* and evidence for relational inferences is *job-relatedness*.

This chapter emphasizes psychometric validity. It is intended to examine classical psychometric theory and look beyond the comfortable limits that corral validity within a coefficient. Validity is itself an inference—a conclusion reached from an abundance of information and data.

The simple, fundamental question of psychometric validity is, "How well has the intended characteristic been measured?" More precisely, the question asks, "With what confidence can the scores resulting from the measurement be interpreted as representing varying degrees or levels of the specified characteristic?" There is never a simple answer. Answers are judgments, not numbers, and they are to be supported by data and logical argument. They depend on the relative weight of evidence—the weight of accumulated evidence supporting an interpretation relative to the weight of accumulated evidence opposing it. One looks not at single bits of information but at the preponderance of the evidence.

VARIETIES OF PSYCHOMETRIC VALIDITY EVIDENCE

Evidence Based on Test Development

Sometimes a model is so elegant and convincing (e.g., the measurement of information), or so routine and natural (e.g., measuring linear distance with a yardstick), that the measures are accepted without much question. However, most measurement in psychology lacks such models, and evaluation is needed. We suggest these questions to guide evaluation of the procedure's development:

Did the Developer of the Procedure Have a Clear Idea of the Attribute to Be Measured? This is a question of intentions; the developer of the procedure must have had something in mind to be measured. It may have been a thoroughly established construct—or little more than a vague idea of a continuum along which people or objects could be ordered. It may have been a theoretical construct such as latent anxiety, or something empirically tangible such as the smoothness of a machined surface, or something observable such as coordination of motor responses to visual stimuli. These are all abstractions, attributes of people or objects of concern. It is a small but positive sign of validity if development followed a clear conception of the attribute to be measured. It is a large, negative piece of evidence if the developer has not bothered or is unable to describe the attribute measured, how it matches or differs from other attributes under other names, or whether it is an attribute of people, of groups of people, or of objects people do something with or to.

Are the Mechanics of Measurement Consistent With the Concept? Most psychological measurement is based on the responses people make to standard stimuli presented according to standard procedural rules. If the developer had a clear idea of what was to be measured, then it should have governed a plan for procedures, and further questions like these need answers:

- Is the presentation medium appropriate? Does printing a test on paper or showing it on a computer fit the definition of the attribute to be measured?

- Are there rules of standardization or control, such as time limits? If so, were they dictated by the nature of the trait being measured, or were they chosen for convenience?
- Are response requirements appropriate? It is not appropriate to use a recognition-based multiple-choice item type for a construct defined in terms of free recall; it is not appropriate to use verbal questions and answers for constructs defined as physical skills.

Satisfactory answers to such questions provide only slight evidence of validity, but unsatisfactory answers—or no answers at all—are reasons for questioning assertions of validity.

Is the Stimulus Content Appropriate? The content of a measurement procedure should certainly fit the nature of the attribute to be measured. This is more than so-called content validity. Of course, if the attribute to be measured implies a specific content domain, such as knowledge of the content of a training program, then content-oriented test development—with its insistence on domain definition and rules for domain sampling—constitutes useful and strong evidence of validity. But the principle applies also to more abstract constructs such as those developed by factor analyses. For tests of factorial constructs, item types defining the factor in prior research should be used, or evidence should show that the item type chosen taps the factor satisfactorily.

Was the Test Carefully and Skillfully Developed? After determining that the developer had a clear idea in mind at the outset, and that it stayed in mind long enough to plan the measurement operations and content, you should look for evidence that the plan was carried out well. The evidence depends on the plan. If equipment is required, then the evidence might include a record of the alternatives considered and the reasons for choices. More broadly, when judgments were required (and they nearly always are), they and the reasons for them should be a matter of record. Useful evidence also comes from answers to questions like these:

- Were pilot studies done to try out ideas, especially if they are unusual, about item types, instructions, time limits, ambient conditions, or other standardizing aspects of the test?
- Was item selection based on item analysis? Were appropriate item statistics computed and used?
- Did the data come from an appropriate sample? Was the sample large enough to yield reliable statistics?
- Does the final mix of selected items fit the original plan, or is there some imbalance? Was the item pool big enough to permit stringent criteria for item retention?

Evidence Based on Reliability

Is the Internal Statistical Evidence Satisfactory? Classical item analysis looks for two item characteristics: *difficulty level,* usually expressed in the reverse as the percentage giving the correct item response, and *discrimination index,* typically expressed as the correlation of item responses to total scores. Item statistics can be examined for spread and average difficulty or discrimination indices to see if they are appropriate for the anticipated measurement purposes. A test that is too easy or too hard for the people who take it will not permit valid inferences. Item statistics should be evaluated, of course, in the light of the circumstances that produced them. Their usefulness may depend on such things as sample size, appropriateness of the sample to the intended population, and probable distributions of the attribute in the sample. No universally correct statement of the most desirable item characteristics can be made. Ordinarily, one might consider a variety of item difficulties a sign of a "good" test. For some kinds of personnel decisions, however, a narrow band of difficulties might enhance discriminability in a critical region and be considered better evidence of validity than a broad band.

Responses should be somewhat related to total score on all items; otherwise, no clearly definable variable is measured. Usually, a rather high level of internal consistency is wanted. A high coefficient alpha does not provide positive evidence that the item set as a whole is measuring what it is supposed to measure, but it does offer assurance of systematic content. If other information (e.g., meritorious care in defining the construct and in developing items to match the definition) makes it reasonable to assume that most items have indeed measured the intended concept, then a satisfactory alpha is reasonable evidence that the scores reflect it without much contamination. Constructs vary widely in specificity; some are very narrowly defined, such as any one of the 120 constructs in the Guilford structure of intellect model (Guilford, 1959), or very broadly defined, such as a construct of creativity that may include many narrower constructs. Tightly defined constructs require high internal consistency coefficients.

Are Scores Stable Over Time and Consistent With Alternative Measures? Stability over some not-too-brief time period seems essential, especially if internal consistency is relatively less important. If equivalent forms of the test have been developed, then they should in fact meet at least minimal requirements of equivalence (common means and variances) as well as correlate well. If scoring is done by observers rating performance or its outcome, then certainly interrater agreement is an essential ingredient of reliability. Because reliability limits validity, evidence of high reliability suggests good descriptive validity, but consistency may be due to consistent error.

Evidence From Patterns of Correlates

Correlating scores on a measurement procedure to be evaluated with other measures may yield evidence of validity. Such research provides information of two kinds, both equally important to conclusions about validity. One is *confirmatory evidence,* which confirms (or fails to confirm) an intended inference from test scores. It is evidence that relations logically expected from the theory of the attribute are in fact found. The other is *disconfirmatory evidence,* which rules out alternative inferences or interpretations of scores—evidence that relations not expected by the nature of the construct are in fact not found. Confirmatory evidence that does in fact confirm the intended interpretation is a necessary but insufficient condition for accepting scores as valid measures of an intended trait. Evidence is also needed that plausible alternative interpretations can be rejected (i.e., disconfirmed).

Multitrait–multimethod matrices are commonly used to study correlates with other variables. Two or more traits are identified (one measured by the assessment method at hand), and they are each measured by two or more methods. Confirmatory evidence of validity exists if correlations among measures of the same trait across methods are higher than correlations among traits within common methods (D. T. Campbell & Fiske, 1959).

One form of statistical evidence that has pleased some people remarkably well is a nice *validity coefficient* (i.e., the correlation between a predictor and some criterion). Many people place far too much faith in a single validity coefficient. A nice validity coefficient might stem from a common contamination in both the instrument being validated and the criterion. Suppose that performance ratings of school principals are contaminated by a general stereotype that a good principal is physically tall, imposing in stature, looks like scholar, and speaks in a low, soft voice. If the measure to be validated is an interview rating of administrative potential, and if these ratings are influenced by that same stereotype, then there will be a nice validity coefficient. It does not follow that the interview ratings are good indicators of administrative ability.

Another problem with a single validity coefficient is that it seeks only evidence confirming (or failing to confirm) a particular inference. It says nothing to confirm or to disconfirm alternative inferences. Validity coefficients are, of course, valuable bits of evidence in making judgments about validity, but do not confuse validity coefficients with validity, and do not base judgments about validity on validity coefficients alone.

Does Empirical Evidence Confirm Logically Expected Relations With Other Variables? Specifying an attribute to be measured, and maybe explicating a theory of the attribute, is the first step in planning a measurement procedure. The theory of the attribute will suggest that good measures of it will correlate with some things but not with others, and at least some of these hypotheses can be tested. Evidence supporting them also confirms the validity of the scores as measures of the intended attribute. Traditional criterion-related validation procedures follow this logic. One might hypothesize from one's theoretical view of mechanical aptitude that those with high scores on a test of it will do better in an auto mechanics' school than will those with low scores. To test the hypothesis, scores are correlated with grades in the school. A significant, positive correlation is evidence of validity for both relational and descriptive inferences. Testing other hypotheses, perhaps showing correlations with the number of correct troubleshooting diagnoses in a standardized set of aberrant pieces of equipment, or the speed with which a bicycle is taken apart and reassembled, gives further evidence of psychometric validity. Every such hypothesis supported adds further confirming evidence of the validity of interpreting scores as measures of mechanical aptitude as it has been defined. Failure to support hypotheses casts doubt on the validity of the inference or on the match of the theory of the attribute with the operations—of the conceptual and the operational definitions of the attribute.

Does Empirical Evidence Disconfirm Alternative Meanings of Test Scores? In practical terms, this means ruling out contaminations. Work sample scores should not be biased by the particular equipment an examinee happens to use. Performance ratings should not be biased by differential stereotypes among raters. Work attitude scores should not be biased by a social desirability response set. A test of spelling ability should not be biased by a printed format that requires excellent visual acuity. Many such problems can be guarded against during test development, but some need empirical study. Failure to disconfirm the more plausible contaminants may suggest validity problems.

Are the Consequences of Test Use Consistent With the Meaning of the Construct Being Measured? A *theory of an attribute* should identify outcomes or consequences of test use relevant to the construct. For example, if the attribute to be measured involves flexibility in thinking about problems, the theory of the attribute may include flexibility in solving problems of malfunctioning equipment. If a test of the attribute is used to select mechanics, then one consequence of its use is that high scorers are likely to think of and try alternative explanations for mechanical problems—hence, to solve more of them. If they actually do solve more problems than do low scorers, then it is evidence of valid measurement of the construct as well as evidence supporting the predictive hypothesis.

BEYOND CLASSICAL TEST THEORY

Classical psychometric theory has served well and is sufficient for many practical uses. Extensions of classical theory, and alternatives to it, have been developed. They are useful, but they may sometimes require more resources (e.g., subject pools, opportunities for repeated measurement, etc.) than most personnel researchers will have. Even so, they offer concepts worth considering. These discussions are brief and elementary, but some awareness of these methods is needed by anyone even slightly involved in personnel assessment.

Factor Analysis

Factor analysis investigates the dimensionality of a set of scores by identifying sources of systematic variance ("factors") common to two or more tests in a set. The systematic source of variance intended for one test may be a systematic source of error in another; ability to understand the material may be the trait intended to be measured by a reading test, but it may be a contaminating source of systematic error in an arithmetic test. In principle, factor analysis identifies dimensions by finding clusters of highly correlated variables, which are minimally correlated with other clusters of variables. All of these methods, from the simplest to the most complex, use a common set of variables, all measured in the same sample, providing a matrix of correlations or covariances.

A small correlation matrix, good only for illustrative purposes, is shown in Table 5.3. The variables are four different tests. Each cell in the matrix shows the correlation coefficient computed for a pair of them, such as the correlation of .62 between Tests A and B. Let Test A be a hypothetical test of general mental ability, B a vocabulary test, C a test of reading speed, and D a perceptual speed test. What factors account for scores on them? It is easier to understand what happens in factor analysis if we work backward from an answer to the question. Possible answers are given in Fig. 5.3, showing underlying, latent factors and their contributions to score variance on each test. In this example, Test A should correlate well with Test B because most of the total variance in each is due to individual differences in language ability. The correlation between Tests A and C may be even higher; more of the total variances from these tests stem from common dimensions—in this case, two of them. Test D correlates only slightly with A and C (only small

TABLE 5.3

Correlation Matrix Showing Hypothetical Relations Among Four Tests

	A	*B*	*C*	*D*
A	—	.65	.63	.15
B		—	.52	.00
C			—	.17
D				—

Test	*Factors Actually Measured*	*% of Total Variance*
A: Mental Ability	Language Ability	55
	Perceptual Speed	40
	Error	5
B: Vocabulary	Language Ability	70
	General Reasoning	28
	Error	2
C: Reading Speed	Language Ability	35
	Perceptual Speed	50
	Word Fluency	10
	Error	5
D: Perceptual Speed	Perceptual Speed	6
	Finger Dexterity	70
	Visual Acuity	10
	Error	14

FIG. 5.3. Dimensions contributing to total text variance in each of four hypothetical tests.

common sources of variance) and not at all with B (because they measure nothing in common). Error, of course, refers to the unreliable component of scores attributed to random sources which, by definition, should be uncorrelated across the four tests.

This backward approach is, of course, unreal. In practice, we know only the correlations between the tests and we draw inferences about the factorial structure of the tests from the correlations. A matrix like Table 5.3 would not allow us to determine the full structure of these tests. Of course, in this matrix, fancy statistical analysis would be unnecessary anyway. One can simply look at the correlations and know that Tests A, B, and C are all measuring the same thing to some degree, and Test D does not measure it. Knowing something about these tests, we can simply look at the matrix and draw some inference about the nature of that "same thing." Obviously, Tests A, B, and C all require test takers to understand verbally expressed ideas. Therefore, it is plausible to infer that the ability to satisfy this requirement is one underlying cause of the correlations observed; it can be tagged "language ability," and it is a "factor."

Three of these tests, according to Fig. 5.3, require at least some perceptual speed; an actual factor analysis (if it could be done on a 4-variable matrix) would identify perceptual speed as a factor. The matrix is too small, however, to identify some of the dimensions in Fig. 5.3. The data for a factor analysis must include at least two variables for each anticipated factor. General reasoning ability, word fluency, finger dexterity, and visual acuity are also sources of variance in the matrix, but each influence scores on only one test, and they could not be identified by a factor analysis of this matrix. Although specified as systematic sources of variance in creating the example, factor analysis of such an inadequate matrix would treat them only as sources of error variance—as if the variance they produce were random—because they are not systematic sources across two or more variables. At a minimum, four more tests would have to be included in the set for these factors to be identified.

GENERALIZABILITY THEORY

Generalizability theory examines the limits or boundaries within which score meanings generalize. Scores may be influenced by particular circumstances and be useful only if the assessment generalizes to other circumstances (e.g., other times, other behavior samples, other test forms, other raters or interviewers). An assessment is a valuable aid to decisions only if inferences drawn from it are like those drawn under other conditions. Generalizability theory, as developed by Cronbach, Gleser, Nanda, and Rajaratnam (1972) described principles for testing the limits of the generalizability of inferences from trait measurements. Here we present only their basic logic.

Assessments are done in given sets of circumstances—by a certain person, on a particular day or time of day, in a certain room or other location, with specific ambient temperature or noise or distractions, and so on. If score interpretations were limited to any single combination of these specific circumstances, then they would have little interest to anyone; such circumstances are usually expected to be matters of indifference, variables that have at most a trivial influence on the outcome. We want to generalize the assessment inference to the one we would have made from assessment of the person on another occasion, in another setting, or with another administrator or ambience.

Traditional reliability estimation inquires into limited kinds of generalizability. Internal consistency coefficients refer to generalizing across the various items or observations. Stability coefficients tell whether inferences generalize across testing occasions. A generalizability study can answer both kinds of questions by collecting data in an analysis of variance design.

> A *generalizability study* simultaneously estimates variance attributable to sources such as persons, items, and occasions.

If all items are used for all persons on all experimental occasions, the design is "fully crossed," expressed as $p \times i \times o$, and shown by Venn diagrams as part *a* of Fig. 5.4. Part *b* depicts a design in which two (presumably equivalent) sets of items are used on two occasions, as if using equivalent forms in a test–retest reliability study. Items would be "nested within" occasions, expressed as a $p \times i{:}o$ design. These are only two of the many different designs one might choose for studies of two sources of variance other than the traits of the people assessed. Clearly, either design provides more information than does a single reliability coefficient.

ITEM RESPONSE THEORY

Statistics used in classical test theory—item statistics, distribution descriptive statistics, and the various correlations of reliability and validity estimation—depend on the distribution of the measured construct in the sample providing the data. If the sample

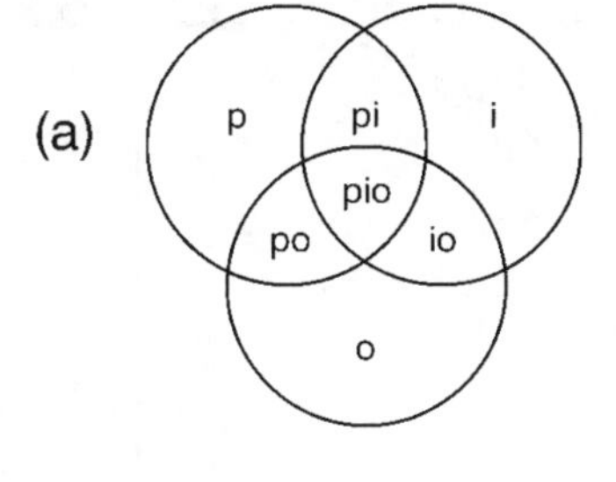

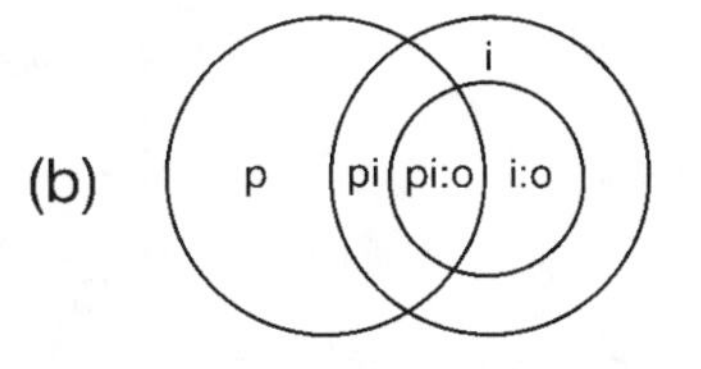

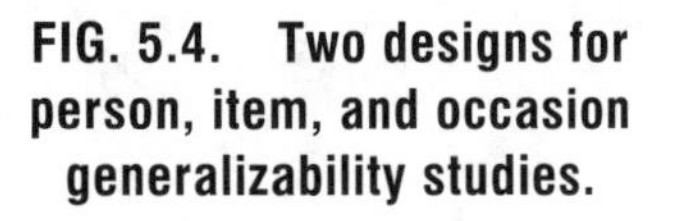

FIG. 5.4. Two designs for person, item, and occasion generalizability studies.

is truly representative of the population from which it is drawn, then these sample statistics can be taken as reasonable estimates of population values. However, if sample distributions differ markedly from population distributions, then they may be poor descriptors of population values. This problem led to the development of *item response theory* and procedures for developing relatively *sample-free* estimates of population values.

> With classical test theory, individuals' score on a test reflects their standing relative to the rest of the sample of test takers. With *item response theory*, their score reflects their standing on the latent factor measured by the test.

Item response theory (IRT) is based on the commonsense idea that people with a lot of a specific ability are more likely to give the right answer to an item requiring that ability than are people with less ability. A systematic relation can be assumed between levels of the trait and the likelihood of a specified item response. The relation can be modeled as a mathematical function, or equations, defining an *item characteristic curve*. Figure 5.5 shows item characteristic curves for three items. The abscissa is a theoretical scale of the latent ability, designated *theta*, θ; the ordinate is the proba-

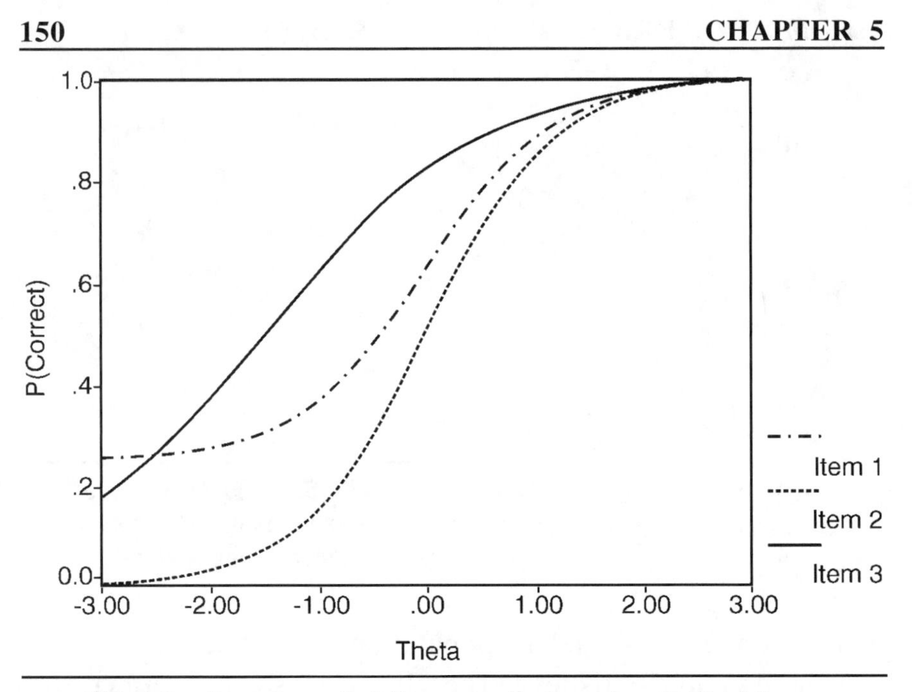

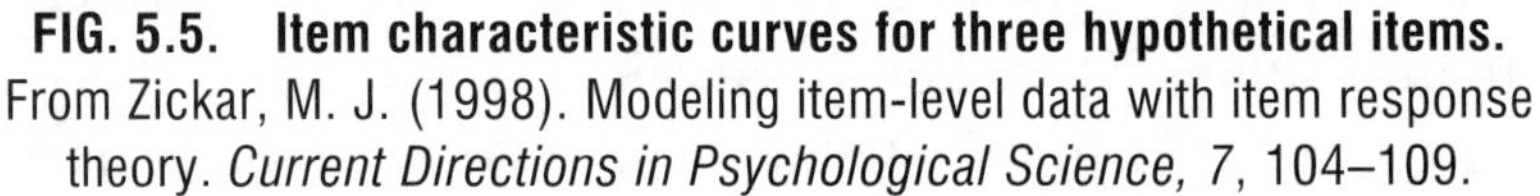
FIG. 5.5. Item characteristic curves for three hypothetical items. From Zickar, M. J. (1998). Modeling item-level data with item response theory. *Current Directions in Psychological Science, 7*, 104–109.

bility of a correct response. An item characteristic curve may have many forms, but the most common is a positive, monotonic curve. It assumes that the probability of a correct response continually increases (or continually decreases) with ability level, but not at a constant rate. People in a low ability range have little likelihood of giving a correct or keyed response; regardless of specific levels of low ability; the slope of the curve in the low range is very slight. In a middle range of ability, the change in probability increases sharply with increasing increments in ability—up to a certain point—after which there are further but progressively smaller changes; that is, the slope of the curve is increasingly steep up to a point.

Computerized Adaptive Testing With IRT

Think of an examinee on one side of a table and a test administrator, with a very large deck of cards, on the other. Each card has on it a test item and, visible only to the administrator, a difficulty level. The administrator chooses an item of low difficulty first. If the examinee answers it correctly, then the administrator chooses a second, harder item. If the first answer is wrong, then the second item chosen is easier. A few more items are similarly chosen to identify the likely region of θ. A few more items are chosen most appropriate for information in that region. The result can be a very precise estimate of θ for that person with only a few, carefully chosen items. The scenario is unlikely. The idea of someone sitting with a large deck of cards picking out items is, frankly, boring. The scenario is not at all unlikely, however, if the examiner is a computer and the cards are entries in its data bank. A computer program can do it almost instantly. The result is called *computer adaptive testing*. This is discussed further in chapter 10.

Analysis of Bias and Adverse Impact

IRT is useful for EEO concerns because item parameter estimation is independent of the ability distribution in the sample studied. If the trait measured is not itself correlated with gender, race, or idiosyncracies of a particular culture, then subgroups based on gender, race, or culture should yield the same invariant ICC parameters within linear transformations. IRT analysis is in fact sometimes used to identify items that function differently in the different subgroups. Differential item functioning is discussed in chapter 9.

DISCUSSION TOPICS

1. How would you explain reliability and validity to a high school student? Why is reliability a necessary condition for validity?
2. Why is it inappropriate to speak of a test as being valid or not valid?

3. Identify a theory of a predictor–criterion linkage. Consider what confirmatory and disconfirmatory evidence you could use to test your theory.

6

Predicting Future Performance

Criterion-Related Validation
Regression & Correlation
Significance Testing

Employment testing is future oriented, always at least implying prediction. Predictions, like measures, should be evaluated by comparing, in an accumulated record, the match of explicitly predicted and actual performance—that is, the likelihood that an assessment-based prediction is true. Traditionally, the relation is determined and evaluated statistically through criterion-related validation.[1]

Criterion-related validation seeks answers to two basic questions. First, what *kind* of relation exists between a predictor and the criterion predicted? This question is answered by a regression line, straight or curved, or an equation. Second, what is the *degree*

[1]Occasionally, someone will abbreviate the term *criterion-related validity* and speak or even write about "criterion validity." This should be avoided; logically, criterion validity refers to the validity of a criterion, a psychometric evaluation of the criterion measure, not to the statistical concept of the degree of relation between a criterion and another variable (or collection of variables) that predicts it.

of relation? Is there any relation at all? How strong is it? Is it significant? How accurately can predictions be made? Answers can be based on validity coefficients showing the strength of relation specified.

> Criterion-related validation provides evidence for job-relatedness. In other words, it is a technique for validating our relational inferences.

VALIDATION AS HYPOTHESIS TESTING

Criterion-related validation directly tests the hypothesis that criterion *Y* is a mathematical function of predictor *X*. It is not the only way to test a predictive hypothesis, but it offers a prototype. It specifies a criterion *Y* worth predicting and a way to assess a predictor *X*. It points out that a time lag is inherent in prediction, at least conceptually. The information on which predictions and decisions are made is available in advance—sometimes far in advance—of the time when the criterion information becomes available. A close look at the problems and procedures of criterion-related validation can help in understanding other ways to evaluate bases for personnel decisions.

The first essential requirement for good criterion-related validation is a well-chosen, well-measured criterion. It must be important to the organization and to the decisions to be made, have substantial variance, and be measured reliably and validly. Conceptualization and measurement seem obviously important, but the habit of using whatever criterion lies at hand is so strong that these obvious requirements are often overlooked. Statistical validation of a predictor should not merely assume that the criterion measure is valid. Its psychometric validity should be evaluated using the same principles used to evaluate other measures.

Generalizing from a research sample to an applicant population requires caution. A research sample hardly ever is a representative sample of an applicant population, which is a fact often overlooked. Only those selected can provide criterion data, so a research sample is usually a biased sample of an applicant population. Researchers should try to specify and match as well as possible the population to which their results should generalize, but they must also acknowledge some imprecision in the match.

BIVARIATE REGRESSION

Regression refers to the clustering of measures around a central point. A *scatterplot,* graphically showing a point for each pair of X and Y values, will show a distribution of Y values for any given value of X. Values of Y in each X column are distributed about a central point; usually, more of them are near that central point than are far away from it. It is convenient to think of the distribution as normal, around the column mean or some other designated central point.

If the two variables are related, then the central point in each column changes systematically with changes in the predictor variable. The pattern of change can be shown graphically with a smoothed regression line or curve that describes the relation. The pattern can also be described algebraically with a functional equation, $Y = f(X)$. Many functions are possible, but some may fit the data better than others. One can usually predict that, most of the time, performance of those who score high on the predictor will be better than that of those whose scores are low.

This general statement is based on the usually reasonable assumption that the relation is *positive* and *monotonic*. A relation is positive if higher predictor scores are associated with higher criterion scores. It is monotonic if that statement (or the converse negative statement) is true throughout the predictor score distribution. It is both positive and monotonic if the central points in the criterion distributions are consistently higher for successively higher values of the predictor—if the smoothed curve always goes up, even if only a little bit in some places.[2] If the functional relation is

---

[2]The emphasis on the smoothed curve is because random variations occur in the pattern of column means as central points; literally connecting them ordinarily yields a jagged pattern.

both positive and monotonic, then more of X implies more of Y throughout the X range.

If actual criterion level is to be predicted (rather than relative level), the regression pattern—the kind of relation between predictor and criterion—must either be empirically determined or assumed. Two different kinds of positive, monotonic relations are shown in Fig. 6.1. The equation for the linear (straight line) relation is $Y = 0.6X + 1.0$. In a linear relation, the incremental difference in predicted values of Y for adjacent values of X is constant throughout the range of scores in X. In the straight line in Fig. 6.1, a 1-point difference in X is always matched by a difference of .06 in the predicted value of Y.

The curve in Fig. 6.1 describes a different kind of relation. It is a simple freehand curve, drawn to represent a smoothed pattern approximating the mean values of Y (one definition of the central points) for narrow intervals of X. With such a curve, predicted values of Y differ very little for different scores in either the low or the high end of the X scale, but they differ a great deal in the midrange

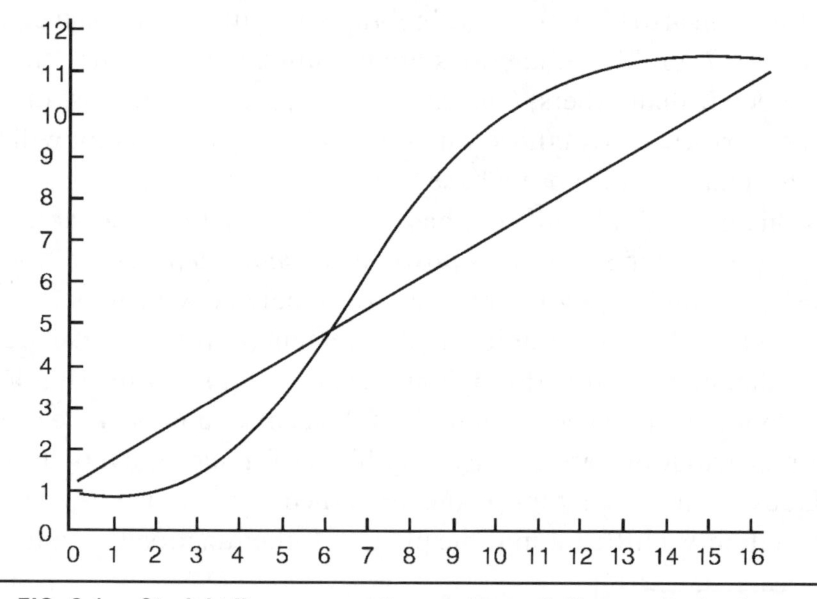

FIG. 6.1. Straight line or curve for use in predicting a criterion from assessment.

of the X scale. An equation could be computed for the curve, but it would have little practical value.

Linear Functions

The general linear regression is $Y = a + bX$. The constant b is the *slope* of the line, the incremental increase in Y with each unit increase in X, and a is the *Y intercept,* the expected value of Y when X equals zero.

WHY LINEARITY IS TYPICALLY ASSUMED

In personnel research, linear regression is typically assumed and rarely questioned, maybe because it is easily computed. Technically more important justifications for assuming linearity include:

1. In computations based on the same data set, the linear regression constants, a and b, and the associated statistics such as correlation coefficients, are more reliable than those in nonlinear equations. (A more reliable statistic is one with less variability from sample to sample.)

2. Linear regression is "robust"; its relevant statistics (a, b, r, etc.) do not seem to depend much on the fit of data to the basic assumptions.[3] To say a statistic is robust may suggest only that it is not particularly sensitive to violations of assumptions.

3. Evidence of nonlinear relations is relatively rare. Hawk (1970) and Coward and Sackett (1990) found them with about chance frequency in studies using the Generalized Aptitude Test Battery (GATB); similar results were found for the relation between conscientiousness and job performance (Robie & Ryan, 1999).

[3]The assumptions are, at least for linear correlation, linearity of regression and homoscedasticity, meaning equal Y variances in the different values of X. Homoscedasticity (and its opposite, heteroscedasticity) is defined more fully later in the chapter.

4. Departure from linearity can be statistically significant without being important.

5. Some nonlinear functions can easily be transformed (e.g., with logarithmic transformations) to linear ones.

6. Correlation coefficients based on the linear assumption are required in many statistical analyses following bivariate validation. Multiple regression, factor analysis, meta-analysis, and utility analysis are a few examples of procedures that usually need linear coefficients.

Despite the arguments favoring it, it is unwise to assume linearity automatically, without further thought. Scatterplots should be routinely examined for regression patterns and outliers. A nonlinear pattern may fit better and make more sense. Ghiselli (1964) reported a nonlinear regression that withstood several cross-validations. Where a specific form of nonlinear regression is superior to linear regression in repeated replications, there is little reason to use a repeatedly inferior linear regression, especially if the curve makes sense and makes substantially different predictions in the score ranges where decisions are made. This may be especially important for personality tests.

MEASURES OF CORRELATION

A coefficient of correlation describes how closely two variables are related. It is based on the tightness with which criterion values cluster around the central points that define the regression function. Various kinds of correlation coefficients describe degrees of relation; they may differ on the kinds of relation assumed, on data distributions, or on kinds of measurement scales, but they have important common characteristics.

Basic Concepts in Correlation

Any coefficient of correlation is based on a specified regression pattern. If the pattern does not fit the data very well, but is assumed in computing a coefficient, then the coefficient understates the relation. The degree of understatement can range from trivial to dramatic.

If correlation is perfect, then the research subjects have identical rank orders on predicted and actual scores, and the scale distances between measures of any pair of people is the same on both scales. Perfect correlation is rare; departures from perfection are expected. The lower the correlation, the greater the prediction error. Regression functions permit prediction; correlation coefficients permit inferences about the degree of prediction error based on the specified regression function.

Residuals and Errors of Estimate. A *residual* is the difference between the observed value of Y for an individual case and Y_c, the predicted criterion level for the value of X in that case; Y_c may be found from the regression equation or from a graph of it. If a less than optimal regression pattern is used, then the mean and variance of the residuals will be relatively large. When differences in Y are in fact related to those in X, the variance of the residuals is necessarily lower than the variance of Y itself. This is what is meant when it is said that X "accounts for" some of the variance in Y.

> It is often useful to think of *variance* conceptually, as well as statistically. Variance reflects differences in scores from person to person. How much of those differences on Y can be accounted for by differences on X? The *residuals* are the differences on Y that are not accounted for by X.

A Generalized Definition of Correlation. The basic defining equation for all correlation is

$$\textbf{Coeff} = \sqrt{1 - \frac{s^2_{res}}{s^2_y}} \qquad (1)$$

where "Coeff" is used in place of a more specifically identified coefficient to emphasize the generality of the equation, s^2_{res} is the variance of the residuals, and s^2_y is the total variance of Y. Most coefficients of correlation can range between 0 and 1.0; for monotonic relations, the range can be from +1.0 to –1.0, depending on whether high scores are associated with good or poor performance. (A negative slope can be changed to positive by the simple expedient of reversing the scale of one of the variables, so this discussion of basics is limited to positive values.) A coefficient of 1.0, then, indicates a perfect relation in which every data point falls directly on the regression line or curve with no residuals at all. The ratio of residual variance to total variance indicates the degree of imperfection in the strength of relation. If s^2_{res} equals $s^2_{y'}$, that ratio is 1.0 and the coefficient is 0.0.

Coefficients of Determination. If Equation 1 is squared (i.e., the square root is not taken), the result is called the *coefficient of determination*. It estimates the proportion of shared variance in the two variables, typically expressed by saying that the proportion of variance in one of them (usually *Y*) is "accounted for by" the variance in the other. This means common or associated variance, but the usual parlance includes terms like "variance explained by" or "variance accounted for" despite their unwarranted causal implication. Even the term itself, determination, inappropriately implies causation.

Validity coefficients of .30 are not uncommon. The coefficient of determination is .09, or 9% common variance. Expert witnesses and attorneys in litigation are fond of intoning in such a case that "less than 10% of the criterion variance is explained by the predictor," slurring over the word variance as if it were unimportant.

> The *coefficient of determination,* or r^2, is typically interpreted in terms of how much of the criterion variance can be explained by predictor variance; e.g., the amount of the differences from person to person in graduate school performance explained by their differences on the GRE.

Variance is an important statistical concept. Variances can be added together; standard deviations cannot be. The standard deviation is the closer description of variability because it is a kind of average of individual differences expressed in the same units as the measurement scale. However, it has limited mathematical usefulness. You cannot add (or subtract, multiply, or divide) the standard deviation of one measure to the standard deviation of another because standard deviations are square roots of other numbers. It is obvious that $3 + 3 = 6$; it is equally obvious that $\sqrt{3} + \sqrt{3}$ is not equal to $\sqrt{6}$.

A common variance statement is simply not a useful description of a co-relation; an unsquared correlation coefficient is directly useful. An even better descriptive statistic is the slope of the regression line; it is more meaningful because it gives the expected change in Y associated with a change in X. This is only the first of many caveats about bivariate coefficients of correlation and their derivatives. Historically, the validity coefficient was the end product, virtually the only product, of criterion-related validation. Researchers in psychometrics and personnel decisions are increasingly skeptical of a lone correlation coefficient as an index of the value of a predictor.

Third Variables. A second caveat is familiar: Correlation says nothing about causation. It is easy to presume that a variable obtained first somehow produces the second one. To do so is to forget the third variable problem. Both the X and the Y may be effects of some common third variable or collection of variables. Gulliksen (1950) gave a delightful example. He said that the number of storks' nests built each year in Stockholm correlated .90 with the annual birth rate there! Few people believe that storks bring babies, or vice versa, in Stockholm or elsewhere. If the correlation is reliable, then one might speculate about third variables that may explain it, such as economic variation or perhaps the coldness of winters. Other speculation is possible, but the only sure thing is that a causal interpretation of the correlation is wrong.

The Null Hypothesis and Its Rejection. To be useful for prediction, a predictor's correlation with the chosen criterion should be greater than zero—preferably substantially greater, but at least statistically significantly greater. The significance question is discussed later.

The Product–Moment Coefficient of Correlation

Nearly all statistical computer packages include procedures for computing product–moment coefficients, also known as Pearsonian coefficients. Different programs use slightly different equations, but all are derived from the basic product–moment definition:

$$r_{yx} = \frac{\sum z_x z_y}{n} \tag{2}$$

This basic equation looks simple but is too complex for practical purposes. It requires transforming every value of *X* and *Y* to *z* scores (once called the "moments" of a distribution), multiplying each pair of *z* scores, and finding the mean of the products. A useful computational equation uses raw scores:

$$r_{yx} = \frac{n\Sigma XY - \Sigma X \Sigma Y}{\sqrt{[n\Sigma X^2 - (\Sigma X)^2][n\Sigma Y^2 - (\Sigma Y)^2]}} \tag{3}$$

where r_{yx} is the product–moment coefficient for the regression of *Y* on *X*. *X* and *Y* are the raw scores, and *XY* is the product of the raw scores, for each person, and *n* is the total number of cases. Several things influence a product–moment correlation coefficient.

Nonlinearity. A product–moment correlation coefficient assumes linear regression. To the degree the assumption is violated, the coefficient will underestimate the degree of relation, but where evidence of nonlinearity is questionable or trivial, the linear assumption is still preferred.

Homoscedasticity and Equality of Prediction Error. It also assumes *homoscedasticity,* that is, equal residual variances in different segments of the predictor distribution. If the outline of the scatterplot is approximately an oval, the assumption may not be seriously violated. Serious violations, however, cause r_{yx} to understate the relationship seriously. Heteroscedasticity can be a more serious problem than usually recognized because it may result in correlation coefficients that markedly understate the value of a predictor. The average correlation may be poor, but if the lowest residual error is in that part of a distribution where the most critical decisions are made, the predictor may be more useful than the coefficient suggests. It may work the other way. If decisions are to be made at the extremes of the distribution (e.g., if only top candidates are to be accepted), and if residual error at the top scoring levels is great, then the predictor may not be useful despite generally high correlation.

Correlated Error. Measurement errors are assumed to be uncorrelated with each other and with the two variables. If the assumption is limited to random errors, violations have little effect on the correlation of reasonably reliable measures. Safeguards against major influences of correlated random error are maximizing reliabilities of both measures, and replicating studies in new samples.

Unreliability. As described in chapter 5, unreliability, in either variable, reduces correlation. The effect is systematic and therefore correctable. Predictor unreliability is simply a fact in the decision context as well as in research. Criterion unreliability, on the other hand, influences research findings but not individual decisions. Coefficients should therefore be corrected only for criterion unreliability. This estimates the population coefficient for the predictor as it is:

$$r_{y\infty x} = \frac{r_{yx}}{\sqrt{r_{yy}}} \tag{4}$$

where $r_{y\infty x}$ is the expected correlation between a perfectly reliable Y and the fallible predictor X.

Realism dictates two other actions. First, overestimate criterion reliability so that the resulting correction is an underestimate of the population value. Spuriously high corrections "may not only lead one into a fantasy world but may also deflect one's attention from the pressing need of improving the reliability of the measures used" (Pedhazur & Schmelkin, 1991, p. 114). Second, correct only coefficients that are statistically significant. Adjusting possibly zero correlations can be seriously misleading and is a bad practice. It is, fortunately, an uncommon practice, but it happens often enough to warn against it.

Reduced Variance. If variance on either variable is substantially less in the sample than in the population, then the sample coefficient underestimates population validity. Reduced variance is commonly called *restriction of range,* associated with truncation of one or both variables.

With a high correlation, the generally elliptical or football-shaped scatterplot in (a) in Fig. 6.2 is narrow relative to its length; if the correlation is low, the ellipse is wider, as in (b); if the correlation is zero, the scatterplot is outlined by a circle. Removing either end of the ellipse reduces variances and makes the remaining portion wider relative to its length, that is, reduces the correlation, as in (d) in Fig. 6.2.

The problem cannot be solved by meddling with the scale, such as turning a 5-point rating scale to a 9-point scale. The problem is not the measurement scale but the disparity in scale variance between the sample and the population. Anything that truncates the sample distribution reduces variance and, therefore, correlation. Several things can happen to produce a research sample with lower than population variance, and corrections are available for some of them:

1. The predictor distribution can be directly truncated, for example, by accepting all those above a cut score and rejecting

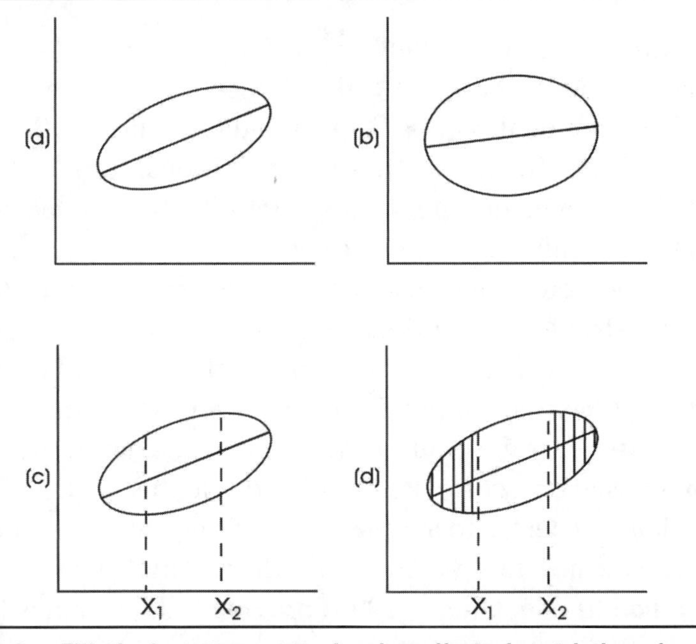

FIG. 6.2. Elliptical scattergrams showing effect of restriction of range on correlation: (a) scatterplot of high correlation, (b) scatterplot of low correlation, (c) plot of high correlation with X1 showing where low scorers tend to be lost to the research sample and X2 showing where high scorers are likely to be lost, and (d) the changed shape of the scattergram when the low and high scoring cases are in fact lost.

those below it. Variances are known both for the unrestricted group (an estimate of variance in the applicant population) and the restricted group (those hired), so the corrected correlation coefficient can be obtained by the equation

$$r_n = \frac{r_o \cdot \frac{s_{xn}}{s_{xo}}}{\sqrt{1 - r_o^2 + r_o^2 \cdot \frac{s_{xn}^2}{s_{xo}^2}}} \quad (5)$$

where r_n is the new estimate of the coefficient for an unrestricted sample, r_0 is the old (obtained) coefficient for the available restricted sample, and s_{xn} and s_{xo} are the predictor standard deviations for the unrestricted and restricted groups, respectively.

Sometimes the "old" standard deviation is not known. In this equation and the two that follow, an estimate can be based on available national norms. Sackett and Ostgaard (1994) recommended an estimate 20% lower than national norms.

2. The organization may accept all applicants on probation and then terminate or transfer people below some criterion cut point. Then a test may be given and concurrently validated. The direct restriction is on the criterion, not on the predictor, but the estimated unrestricted correlation coefficient can be found by reversing the roles of predictor and criterion in Equation 5.

3. Indirect truncation of the predictor occurs if prior selection is based on a correlated third variable. If selection has been based on one test, and another test is being validated, then variance on the new test is restricted to the extent that it is correlated with the old one. Guion (1998) provided the formulas for estimating the unrestricted coefficient, and for correcting simultaneously for unreliability and range restriction.

4. Sample variance may be lower than population variance just by chance. But one would not know, and no correction is available.

5. Unknown factors may have reduced variance indirectly. Again, no correction exists.

> Range restriction is *direct* when people are selected based on scores on the test being validated. It is *indirect* when people are selected based on some other predictor that happens to be correlated with the test being validated.

Correction equations can be used in cases of reduced variance even with no clear point of truncation. Instead of an explicit cut score, for example, there may be a region—a score interval with fuzzy boundaries—below which no one was hired, above which most applicants were hired, and within which decisions were mixed.

Distributions. Product–moment coefficients require no assumption about distributions, but some interpretations of them assume an underlying normal bivariate surface. Extreme skewness in one variable but not the other produces nonlinearity and consequent correlation reduction; in fact, any time the two distributions differ markedly in shape, correlation is markedly reduced.

Group Heterogeneity. A large sample sometimes seems like a Holy Grail people will do anything to find, such as combining small, disparate samples. Samples may then include groups of people that differ in systematic ways. Combining them may hide important differentiating characteristics. Subgroups in the overall sample may have different means on one or both variables or different correlations.

Questionable Data Points. Plotting data sometimes shows one or more *outliers*. An outlier is "an unusual, atypical data point—one that stands out from the rest of the data [and] may lead to serious distortion of results" (Pedhazur & Schmelkin, 1991, p. 398). An outlier can reduce correlation if it is included with the mass of data; in a small total sample, it could even turn an apparent positive relation to a negative one. Some outliers, on the other hand, would inflate the correlation.

A Summary Caveat. We have identified several things that can influence or distort a product–moment correlation coefficient. Sometimes the direction of error is plain, but some influences may lead to unknown or unknowable error. Some with knowable effects can be corrected, but many are like incurable aches and pains: You simply have to live with them. Living with them, however, should induce caution. One should not place undue faith in a single bivariate validity coefficient. It can offer some evidence—even good evidence—of validity, but potential distortions should be considered in evaluating that evidence. One may need to gather new data, either through replications or studies of possible explanations.

Statistical Significance

Research reports typically say something like, "the correlation was not statistically significant," or "it was significant at the 5%

level of confidence." These terms refer to the probability that the reported coefficient differs from zero only by chance; if it differs more than expected by chance, the "null hypothesis" of no relation is rejected. What researchers know, and how they behave, are not always the same. Too often they act as if, having rejected the null hypothesis, they can virtually equate the sample correlation coefficient with the population value, or as if mere rejection is enough to assure that the population correlation is usefully nonzero. Neither is so.

The Logic of Significance Testing. Statistical validation begins in a sample where both predictor and criterion data are known. Suppose $r = .20$. This is not a very strong relation, but it can be useful. Can a similar relation be expected in a later sample where decisions have to be made without prior knowledge of criterion performance?

Part of the answer depends on the quality of the research. We cannot have confidence in the generalizability of poorly designed or conducted research where research subjects are inappropriately chosen, data collection is haphazard and inconsistent, criteria suffer contaminations, or data recording or analysis is careless. However, any sample statistic is subject to error, no matter how carefully the research was conducted. Some error may be due to idiosyncratic characteristics of people in that sample. Part of the answer may lie in inevitable violation of statistical assumptions. Correlation analysis assumes that measurement errors are not correlated. In any given sample, however, the errors will in fact have some nonzero correlation, even if small. Part of the answer may lie in sampling error. The smaller the sample size, in absolute number or relative to the population, the greater the likely error.

Clearly, the unimpressive but potentially useful coefficient of .20 is to some degree in error, even if negligibly. Different samples from a common population would provide a distribution of different coefficients; the mean of a big enough set of them would match the population correlation. Can the population, and future samples from it, be counted on to give coefficients of about the same size as the one at hand? That is a useful question, but it is not the question answered by significance testing. Significance testing goes at it in a reverse process; it tests the null hypothesis that the correlation coefficient in the population is precisely zero. Now, rejection of the null hypothesis does not imply that the sample coefficient is a good estimate of the population coefficient, and failure to reject the null hypothesis does not mean that it is true. Literally, the null hypothesis "is *always* false in the real world" (Cohen, 1990, p. 1308). Specifically, it estimates the probability, p, that, if indeed the population correlation is zero, a sample would capitalize enough on error to provide a correlation as large or larger than that obtained, just by chance. Significance testing asks not what that probability is, but only whether it is lower than some prestated level. It answers with a yes or no dichotomy, not with a probability level.

Type I and Type II Errors and Statistical Power. In strict significance testing, a researcher either rejects or fails to reject the null hypothesis. If it is true and the researcher does not reject it, or if it is false and the researcher does reject it, the choice is correct. The choice is erroneous if the null hypothesis is true but is rejected, or if it is false but not rejected. These two types of errors are known as *Type I* and *Type II* errors, respectively. The chosen level of confidence is called *alpha*, α, the probability associated with Type I errors. The lower the α probability, the lower the probability of a Type I error.

The lower the likelihood of Type I error, the greater the likelihood of Type II error. Which is the more serious error can be determined only in the full context of a particular situation. As the probability of Type I error increases, so does the probability of hiring people on the basis of an invalid assessment. As the probability of Type II error increases, so does the probability that a valid assessment procedure will be discarded.

Statistical power "is the probability that a statistical test will lead to the rejection of the null hypothesis" (Cohen, 1977, p. 4). Power is a function of three things: the size of the sample used, the effect size (e.g., correlation) in the population, and the alpha level chosen. A judgment of significance, then, is made more likely by increasing sample size, by working with intelligently developed predictive hypotheses that are very likely to result in substantial correlations, or by relaxing α. Some ambivalence is justified; we like to reduce error, but we do not ordinarily like to lose power. The complement of power (1 – power) is the *beta* probability, β, the probability of Type II error—that is, the failure to reject a false null hypothesis.

> Published studies often report "*p*" values, such as $p < .05$. This means there is less than a 5% (the *alpha* level chosen) chance of a Type I error. *Power* is the probability of rejecting the null. One minus power (the *beta* level) is the probability of a Type II error.

Concepts of power and Type II error received little attention in early personnel research. Usually, failure to reach traditional levels of significance (i.e., .05) was not seen as a serious problem—if the results "approached" it, the sample was small, and the correlation was fairly large. If the predictor were badly needed, then an "almost significant" finding was likely to be used in decision making. It was not good science, and it was certainly not orthodox, but it might have made good business sense.

The advent of litigation under the Civil Rights Act of 1964 changed matters. Validity under the Uniform Guidelines became virtually synonymous with significance at the .05 level, and lack of a statistically significant validity coefficient was reason enough to abandon a predictor, regardless of other lines of evidence. Issues of statistical power became important; with insufficient power, one could lose the use of a good predictor; Type II error took on importance not earlier recognized.

A COMMENT ON STATISTICAL PREDICTION

In regression analysis, the predicted value is a specific point on the criterion scale, a central point in the *Y* distribution for the *X* value. More accurately, the prediction is that, on average, people with a certain score will perform at the predicted criterion level. A range based on the standard error of estimate can be specified within which the criterion value for an individual may be expected at a given probability. Identifying such a range acknowledges that most people are not going to perform at that precise point. Most researchers know these things, but in their statistical zeal, they tend to forget them. Together, these specifications are saying that the predictor variable itself leads us to expect a certain criterion performance, but chance or other things may intervene to lead any given person to perform at a better or poorer level.

Nearly all statistical analyses are based on assumptions that are rarely if ever satisfied in real data, can generally (on the average) be noticeably violated without seriously affecting results, but can be violated in any single situation with serious effects on results and their interpretations. One such assumption is the assumption of a normal distribution. There is no such thing in real data. Micceri (1989) examined 440 large sample distributions of test data and other distributions gleaned from published articles or reports of various kinds. All were in some respect nonnormal. He concluded that the normal curve, like the unicorn, is an improbable creature.

If the normal curve is improbable for one variable by itself, then a normal bivariate surface is more so. To be sure, statistical analyses based on the assumption of the normal bivariate surface have, on the average, been useful in analyzing real data. That fact is not enough, however, to justify the blithe assumption that violations of assumptions never matter, that a prediction has not been affected by them, or indeed that the prediction has not been affected by other considerations not in the equation. Statistical prediction, as surely as predictions without a statistical basis, are subject to informed professional judgment.

DISCUSSION TOPICS

1. Discuss the problems caused by restriction of range. Give examples of the problem, as well as steps you could take to correct it.
2. Come up with examples of predictors that would have non-linear relations with criteria. Be sure to consider criteria other than job performance ratings (e.g., turnover, sales).

7

Using Multivariate Statistics

Multiple Regression
Multiple Correlation
Validity Generalization

Most jobs are complex. Effective performance requires several traits, not just one. As performance is comprised of both abilities and motivation, multiple predictors will be needed to account for it. Predictions of performance require combining or sequencing predictors in some way. The method chosen should be based on both statistical considerations and professional judgment.

COMPENSATORY PREDICTION MODELS

Scores on predictors can be combined in any of several models. In a linear, additive model—the most common—scores are summed to form a composite, maybe with different weights for different variables. The several predictors are assumed to be linearly related in the composite, which is linearly related to the criterion. Summing scores is *compensatory*; a person's strength in one trait may compensate for relative weakness in another. For example, lower ability might be compensated for with more motivation. Consider Table 7.1. Candidate A has equal strength in all three traits. Candidate B is weaker than A in Trait 1 but may have enough added strength in Trait 3 to compensate. Candidate C is extremely deficient in Trait 2 but strengths in the other two may compensate. All three form the same composite score by adding the three component scores. If one trait is more important than the others, then its scores get more weight (i.e., multiplied by a larger value) than the others, as in the lower half of Table 7.1. If Trait 2 is considered so important that C's deficiency in it is unacceptable despite other scores, then an additive model is inappropriate.

Regression Equations

Multiple regression analysis finds optimal weights for the several predictors, multipliers that form a composite having the best possible correlation with the criterion in the sample studied. The composite of weighted predictors estimates the expected criterion value for each person. Those optimal weights are optimal only in

TABLE 7.1

Composite Scores for 3 Traits for Three Hypothetical Candidates

	Trait			
Candidate	*1*	*2*	*3*	*Sum*
Without different weights				
A	10	10	10	30
B	8	10	12	30
C	15	0	15	30
With different weights				
Weights	2	3	1	
A	20	30	10	60
B	16	30	12	58
C	30	0	15	45

the research sample. In a different sample, different optimal weights would be found. Ordinarily, the weights computed in one representative sample will approximate the optimal weights in most other samples.

A weighting method should be based on *rational* and *theoretical* grounds rather than on computations alone. Often, psychometric and statistical assumptions are not met in applied settings; it is not wise to take excessive pride in an impressive weighting system. It is wise to see if effective weights make sense.

Weights may be computed for either standardized or unstandardized scores. In conventional notation, the letter beta, β, stands for standardized weights used with standard z scores, and the letter b refers to unstandardized weights used with raw scores or deviation scores. Both kinds of weights depend on correlations with the criterion and other predictors. Unstandardized weights also depend on relative variances.

The case of two predictors illustrates more general principles. In raw score form (with simple subscripts), the 2-variable regression equation is

$$Y = a + b_1X_1 + b_2X_2 \quad (1)$$

where $a = Y$ intercept and $b =$ regression coefficients for multiplying predictors as identified by subscripts. If the composite score C is the sum of b_1X_1 and b_2X_2, then the equation can written in the familiar $Y = a + bC$ form, where $a = Y$ intercept and $b =$ slope of the regression of Y on the composite score C.

COMPUTING REGRESSION COEFFICIENTS

Regression coefficients can be computed directly from the relevant correlation coefficients and standard deviations:

$$b_1 = [(r_{yx_1} - r_{yx_2}r_{x_1x_2})/(1 - r^2_{x_1x_2})] \cdot (s_y / s_{x_1})$$

and (2)

$$b_2 = [(r_{yx_2} - r_{yx_1}r_{x_1x_2})/(1-r^2_{x_1x_2})] \cdot (s_y / s_{x_2})$$

where the values of r = a correlation coefficient, specified by subscripts, and s = a standard deviation of the criterion or of a predictor.

If $r_{x_1x_2} = 0$, the regression weight of either predictor is its validity coefficient reduced by the ratio of the criterion standard deviation to the predictor standard deviation. If raw score distributions are standardized, all standard deviations are 1.0, so standardized regression weights equal the validity coefficients. If $r_{x_1x_2} > 0$, then β weights are lower than the validity coefficient. If the two validity coefficients differ, then the predictor with the higher validity has the greater weight, and the disparity increases as the intercorrelation increases. If $r_{x_1x_2} = 1.0$, then one predictor is enough; the other adds nothing.

Multiple Correlation

Sometimes the size of the multiple coefficient of correlation, R, is of more interest than the regression equation. It is an index of the strength of the relation of the predictor composite and the criterion. It can be computed as a bivariate r, with the optimal composites as X, or from existing correlation coefficients. For the two-predictor case,

$$R^2_{y \cdot x_1 x_2} = \frac{r^2_{yx_1} + r^2_{yx_2} - 2r_{yx_1} r_{yx_2} r_{x_1 x_2}}{1 - r^2_{x_1 x_2}} \quad (3)$$

where $R^2_{y \cdot x_1 x_2}$ equals the squared multiple correlation for two X variables predicting Y; the various product—moment correlations are defined by the subscripts. The equation shows general principles of multiple correlation: the validity of the composite is proportional to the validities of the components, and the validity of the composite is inversely proportional to the intercorrelations among components.

The *multiple correlation, R,* will only equal the sum of the individual correlations when the predictors are uncorrelated (highly unlikely). If the predictors are correlated, then $R < r_1 + r_2$.

Suppressor and Moderator Variables

Suppressors. By those principles, each test in a well-developed battery is a valid predictor of the chosen criterion and has low correlations with other variables. A valid predictor may contain an invalid, contaminating variance component. A variable that does not predict the criterion but is correlated with the contamination may actually improve prediction. To see how this works, look again at Equation 3. If $r_{yx_2} = 0$, but if both of the other two correlations are not zero, then the numerator of that equation becomes simply r_{yx_1} (the other two terms being zero). The denominator is less than 1.0 (because $r_{x_1x_2}$ is not zero); therefore, $R_{y \cdot x_1x_2}$ is greater than the validity of the one valid predictor alone. The reason is that variable X_2 removes from the composite (suppresses) the unwanted variance in X_1 not associated with the criterion. In a regression equation, it has a negative weight.

Consider, for example, a case in which a paper-and-pencil test of law enforcement knowledge is used to hire security guards. This test is valid, but it requires a relatively high level of reading ability to complete—a level of ability not necessary for a security job. A reading ability test would correlate with the law enforcement knowledge test, but not with ability to perform the security job. The reading ability test would therefore receive a negative weight in the regression equation. Although it may slightly improve prediction to add a reading test to the security guard selection system, it would be hard to explain to the company (and the test taker) why a candidate is rejected for scoring too high on it!

Moderators. Moderator variables influence the relation between other variables; they are correlated with correlation. Frederiksen and Melville (1954) found prediction of academic performance from interests better for noncompulsive students than for those classed as compulsive. Although it is easier to think about validities in subgroups, validity should change systematically and continuously as the level of the moderating variable changes. A regression equation for one predictor and one moderator has the form

$$Y = a + b_1x + b_2z + b_3xz \tag{4}$$

where Y = the criterion, x = the predictor, z = the moderator variable, and xz = the product of x and z scores, the interaction or moderator term, weighted in the composite by b_3. In Equation 4, variables X and Z are expressed in deviation score units (e.g., $x = X - M_x$) with means of zero, unlike the linear Equation 1. Moderated regression is an additive (compensatory) model, but it is not linear because of the multiplicative term. A significant interaction term says that, for every value of z, there is a different slope of the regression of y on x, even though the difference may be small and gradual.

Like suppressor variables, examples of moderator effects for personnel decisions are rarely reported and rarely replicated. The initial surge of enthusiasm led to sweeping searches for moderators in whatever data pool was available; such reliance on exploration and serendipity was not often rewarded. Enthusiasm for demographic moderators (as solutions to fairness problems) was no more fruitful. Searches for moderators in the validity generalization paradigm have turned up only a few. As a result, many selection specialists have given up on moderators.

Such pessimism is unwarranted. Some failures to find moderators are methodological (e.g., use of raw scores). Many more are due to inadequate logic. Research agenda should abandon serendipity. Moderators seem more likely to be found after serious thinking, hypothesizing, and theory formation than after searches among variables for which there is no useful rationale. For example, Witt and Ferris (2003) hypothesized that, for jobs where interpersonal effectiveness is an important part of performance, conscientiousness would only predict performance for socially skilled people. Indeed, the authors found evidence across four studies that social skill moderated the conscientiousness–performance relation. The field of industrial and organizational psychology is big. Many activities and concepts, expected to influence a variety of work outcomes, have been studied and promoted extensively. A systematic consideration of such variables surely should be a rich source of reasoned moderator hypotheses.

Other Additive Composites

Multiple regression is but one way to form a composite, and reasons for forming composites are not limited to criterion prediction. Reasons might include, for example, weighting predictors to promote an organizational policy. Consider an organization interested in moving from a competitive to cooperative work environment; predictors that worked under the old competitive system might not work for predicting teamwork and cooperation. A weighting method should be based on rational, theoretical grounds rather than on computations alone. One important rational principle is simplicity. Studies long ago cast doubt on the value of weights determined by very sophisticated methods. Lawshe and Schucker (1959) reported predictions as good for sums of raw scores as for more formal methods, including multiple regression, which are supposed to maximize predictive accuracy. Often, psychometric and statistical assumptions are not met in applied settings; it is not wise to take excessive pride in an impressive weighting system. It is wise to see if effective weights make sense.

"Unit" weighting means simply adding scores or standard scores, literally multiplying by 1.0, as in the top of Table 7.1. Dawes and Corrigan (1974) insisted, and demonstrated, that use of more complex models offers no more than slight improvement over simple weights, whether equal or differential, in accounting for criterion variance; their finding held even with randomly chosen weights. Subsequent research has supported the finding. However, regression weights may predict better than unit weights if patterns of intercorrelations among the predictor variables differ, the regression-based multiple R is high, different predictors have substantially different weights, and the ratio of respondents to variables is large. In general, carefully computing weights to several decimal places may give only the appearance of precision; simpler nominal weights may do as well or better if variables are carefully selected, are positively correlated with each other and with the criterion, and do not differ greatly in validities or reliabilities.

NONCOMPENSATORY PREDICTION MODELS

A truly *noncompensatory* trait—one so vital to performance that no other strength can compensate—is unlikely. Psychologically, people learn to live with deficiencies and make up for them. Statistically, the idea suggests a discontinuous function with no functional relation on either side of the point of discontinuity. We know of no such finding. Even so, some researchers have found nonadditive, noncompensatory prediction models useful.

Multiple Cutoff Methods

A multiple cut (multiple hurdles) approach uses a cut score for each of two or more tests. An applicant scoring below the cut score on any of them is rejected; each test is a "hurdle" to clear. Two situations may justify the method: if each trait is so vital to performance that other personal strengths cannot compensate for weaknesses in them (e.g., good eyesight may be required of an airline pilot), or if their variance is too low to yield significant correlation.

Generally, however, objections to cut scores in bivariate prediction apply even more to multiple predictors, where even very low cut scores can result in rejecting too many candidates. More hurdles mean more rejections. Many of those passing all of the hurdles will do so with scores too low to suggest any genuinely useful qualifications at all. Cut scores high enough to assure people qualified on each trait may find no one qualified on all of them. A multiple cutoff approach is justified only when predictors are perfectly reliable. If practical considerations demand it, it can be modified by a partially compensatory model. Selection effects using compensatory, noncompensatory, and partially compensatory models are shown in Fig. 7.1; those selected score above (or to the right of) the lines applicable to both variables.

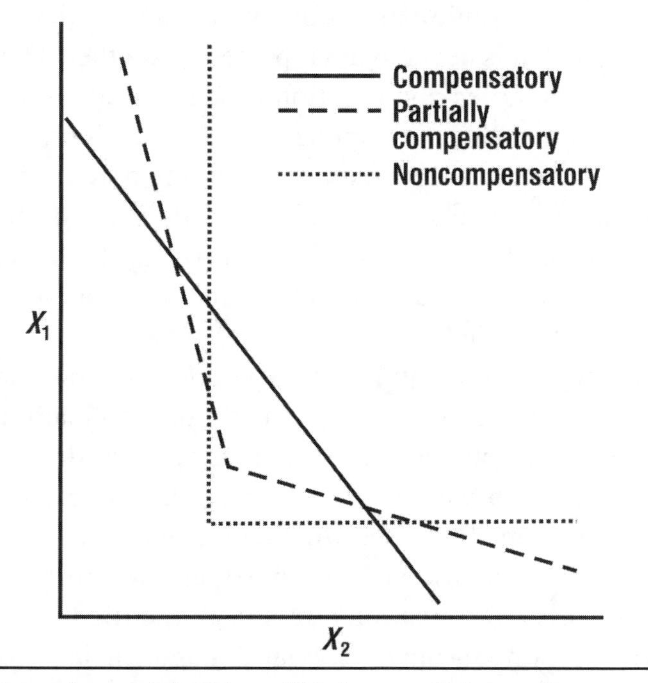

FIG. 7.1. Areas of decision within two-predictor scattergrams for compensatory, partially compensatory, and noncompensatory decision models; in each case, the area above or to the right of the line is the area within which selection is the appropriate decisions and those below and to the left of the line are rejected. From Guion (1965).

Sequential Hurdles

In a *sequential hurdles* approach, those who "pass" one or more preliminary steps are assessed later on other characteristics. The early cut scores are often intended to reduce the size of the group to be assessed by costlier methods. There may not be a fixed cut score; a fixed number of candidates more qualified than others may move to the next stage. Fixed cut scores transform scores to a dichotomy, 1 (*pass*) or 0 (*fail*). This is important in validating later assessments in a candidate population limited to those passing the earlier hurdles.

REPLICATION AND CROSS-VALIDATION

A simple additive combination can give a large validity coefficient in one sample that is never again repeated in another. The problem is worse with complex combinations, many variables, or peculiar nonadditive or nonlinear components. Because high validities encourage new personnel procedures promoting or requiring organizational change, it is unwise to rely on a one-shot coefficient that might have capitalized on errors. Results of validation, especially a multivariate one, need to be repeated—replicated—in a new sample when feasible.

Multiple regression requires *cross-validation*. Loose use of language sometimes treats cross-validation and replication as interchangeable, but they are different. Cross-validation applies multiple regression weights obtained in one sample to data obtained in a different one to see whether the multiple R found in the first sample holds up in a second or whether it was inflated by sample-specific error. Replication refers to a repetition of an original study, with or without some systematic change in measures or procedures, to see if independent results are similar.

Cross-validation is required in multiple regression studies because the composite-forming regression equation developed in one sample has the highest possible correlation with the criterion in that specific research sample. In another, independent sample from the same population, using the same equation, the new correlation is almost always lower. *Shrinkage,* the reduction in the size of the multiple coefficient of correlation, is expected. If shrinkage is negligible, then the weights are considered stable; if large, then the weights are not reliable and the composite is not recommended.

Double cross-validation combines replication with cross-validation. A regression equation is developed in each of two independent samples and cross-validated in the other. Predictors with strong weights in both equations have done well twice, and they can enter simultaneous regression analysis based on all cases, combining the two samples.

The logic of cross-validation calls for independent samples. A common but poor practice draws a sample and divides it, either into two equal samples or into one larger sample for research and a smaller "hold-out" sample for cross-validation. This practice may be better than no cross-validation at all, but it lacks independence. When a sample is randomly divided into two parts, any systematic error in one part exists also in the other, making similar weights more likely. Moreover, the research sample is smaller, so weights have more sampling error than if they had been obtained with the total sample.

The difference between the R^2 in the original validation sample, and the R^2 in the cross-validation sample is *shrinkage*.

Dividing a single sample is ill-advised, but it may not be feasible to draw two large samples. An alternative is to estimate shrinkage from a single sample by formula estimation. Formula estimates consider only sampling error, not measurement error, either random or systematic, but shrinkage from random error is lower in the large sample than in the smaller one resulting from dividing. However, it is a single sample; results should be replicated, if possible.

Wherry (1931) offered the most commonly used equation for estimating the shrunken coefficient from a single sample. As presented by Claudy (1978) but with notation used earlier, and in squared form, it is

$$\bar{R}^2 = 1 - [(n - 1)/n - k - 1)] \cdot (1 - R^2) \quad (5)$$

where $\bar{R}$ = the estimate of the shrunken coefficient, R = the computed coefficient, n = sample size, and k = the number of predictors in the equation. Given the option, replication is preferable.

VALIDITY GENERALIZATION

A replicated finding is better than one from even a good single study. Science wants to know what is generally (even if not invariably) so. Scientific generalization depends more on a chain of similar findings, from different settings and methods, than on an isolated one. Criterion-related validation tests the hypothesis that a given trait is dependably associated with a certain kind of outcome or criterion. A typical study is done in a single setting, with specific predictor and criterion measures. Supporting the hypothesis in that setting does not make it "generally so." Affirming the generality of a relation requires a research history supporting it in different settings with different details.

Validity generalization is a specific form of meta-analysis. Meta-analysis looks quantitatively for conclusions that have been generally so in independent research on the same basic hypothesis. Traditional literature surveys had the same objective but were verbal rather than quantitative, often imprecise, and subjective. Subjectivity remains in meta-analysis, primarily in coding information, but procedures are systematized and results are quantitative. Of the many approaches to meta-analysis, the one known also as validity generalization is the most directly appropriate to personnel testing.

Validity generalization (Schmidt & Hunter, 1977) assembles correlation coefficients from independent validation studies of the same hypothesis. The mean of the resulting distribution is an estimate of the mean in the population from which the samples came. The variance of the distribution exceeds zero only to the degree to which results in the samples come from different populations, stem from different systematic influences, or are subject to different sources of error.

The validity generalization approach begins with the idea that the criterion-related validity coefficient is the same in all tests of the research hypothesis—or would be if not for artifactual influences on the results of individual studies. Coefficients can be corrected statistically for some artifacts, such as sampling error, criterion unreliability, and range restriction; corrections for others are applied to the estimated variance of the distribution of corrected coefficients. If that variance can be explained largely by these artifacts, then validity is said to generalize across the diverse situations from which individual coefficients came. If not, then systematic characteristics of different studies are examined as potential moderating influences.

Validity generalization tests two hypotheses in addition to the substantive hypothesis. The *situational specificity* hypothesis is that criterion-related validity depends in part on unknown influences within research settings; it can be rejected if corrections substantially reduce the variance of the validity coefficient distribution. Corrections cannot be made for unknown or unreported artifacts, so Hunter and Schmidt (1990) advocated a rule of thumb that rejects situational specificity if 75% or more of the variance is explained by known artifacts. Unknown artifacts may account for the rest so that the corrected mean correlation may be treated as the population value across all studies.

The validity generalization hypothesis is not simply the obverse of situational specificity, although rejecting the hypothesis of situational specificity is a necessary first step. Validity generalization is supported when nearly all of the validity coefficients in the distribution are at or above a nontrivial level and in the same direction (all positive or all negative). Reports usually identify the point in the distribution above which 90% or more of the corrected validity coefficients lie. If validity generalizes, then the mean of the distribution of coefficients (after correction for statistical artifacts) is the best single estimate of validity in the job or job family sampled in the accumulated research.

Three different results occur in validity generalization research. A study may refute (or support) the situational specificity hypothesis by showing (or not) that the variance of the distribution of corrected coefficients approaches zero, support (or refute) the validity generalization hypothesis by showing (or not) that all or nearly all validity coefficients across diverse situations are nontrivial in size and in the same direction, and (if situational specificity is rejected and generalization is supported) give an estimate of population validity in the form of the mean of the corrected coefficients ($\bar{r}_c$). The quality of these findings depends on how many of the artifacts the analysis has been able to correct and on how well the corrections have been made. Research reports rarely give all the information needed for the corrections, but meta-analytic results are usually more dependable than single study results.

According to Schmidt and Hunter (1981), "Professionally developed cognitive ability tests are valid predictors of performance on the job and in training for all jobs" (p. 1128). This seems an overwhelming, even reckless, generalization, yet there is support for it, and it is important to note what it does not say. It does not suggest that all cognitive tests are equally valid predictors across all jobs, all criteria, or all circumstances. Validity in this sense means only that the correlation is nonzero across settings. For example, cognitive ability has been found to predict performance better for jobs higher in autonomy, versus jobs that are routine and structured (Barrick & Mount, 1993). Indeed, keeping workers happy and preventing turnover in boring jobs would seem to argue against a heavy reliance on cognitive ability in selection. Note that the criterion has shifted from performance to satisfaction and turnover. Considerable thought needs to be given to what outcomes are most important, given the organization's needs and priorities.

COMMENTS ON STATISTICAL ANALYSES

Chapters 6 and 7 have offered many equations relevant to the evaluation of predictors. Personnel researchers need extensive training in data analysis. A much wider variety of data analytic techniques is available to statistically well-trained people than described here, and different situations may favor different methods of analysis. The conventional statistics mentioned here are descriptive; they permit inferences of statistical reliability, but they are not well suited to seeing how well real data fit organizational needs or theoretical models. Research related to personnel decisions, perhaps due in part to the freezing of the field in the EEO era, has (like this chapter) given relatively little attention to newer, theory-confirming statistical methods. Those who will improve the empirical evaluation of assessment-based personnel decisions will surely develop a larger repertory of confirmatory techniques and models.

Researchers need an inclusive knowledge of statistical procedures, but there is an important caveat: Statistics is a tool, not a religion. Too often, researchers appear to have a blind faith in the results of statistical analysis. Statistics is a guide to judgment, not an alternative to it; results of statistical analysis merit thoughtful evaluation, not automated acceptance.

DISCUSSION TOPICS

1. When selecting weights to apply in a multiple-predictor situation, what are the advantages and disadvantages of relying on theory, regression?

2. Why is it important to cross-validate results in personnel research?
3. What are some problems associated with using a multiple hurdles process in selection?

8

Making Judgments and Decisions

Intuitive Prediction

Judgment Aids

Utility Analysis

The purpose of assessment is to provide a basis for decisions. Decisions about candidates are made by managers, not researchers. Good decisions depend on valid assessments. Whether the assessments lead to valid decisions, or are even considered in making decisions, depends partly on the way assessment data are presented. Decision aids help; managers should be trained in their use. Wise decisions require not only data and information, but the integration of them into a broader experiential framework of information and knowledge. Researchers and HR specialists should not merely pump data—assessment scores—to their managers; they should make sure the assessments are informative and fit into a broader scheme of managerial knowledge about people, jobs, the organization, and the position at hand.

JUDGMENTS OF VALIDITY

Validity of prediction is inferred, not merely computed. It is a judgment to be inferred only if the preponderance of evidence supports the intended prediction. A validity coefficient is accepted as evidence of valid prediction only if the data and analysis are judged adequate. If local validation is not feasible, and no relevant meta-analysis exists, then job-relatedness can be based on two sequential judgments in an option emphasizing psychometric validity. First, a trait must be judged related to performance of important aspects of the job—the predictive hypothesis. Second, the assessment device must be judged a valid measure of that construct (see American Educational Research Association, American Psychological Association, & National Council on Measurement in Education, 1999, Standard 14.12, p. 161). If logic and data support both judgments, then the assessment is judged a valid measure of a job-related trait.

EVALUATING A MEASURE

1. Did the developer of the procedure seem to have a clear idea of the attribute (construct) to be measured? Was development informed by at least a rudimentary theory of the attribute?
2. Do you consider the measurement methods—including presentation, procedures, response requirements—consistent with that idea?
3. Do you think the stimulus content is appropriate? Is the content domain unambiguous? Relevant to the measurement purpose? Was it properly sampled? Can responses be scored, observed, or evaluated reliably?
4. Can you infer care and skill in the development of the assessment instrument? Were pilot studies and item analyses done, and done well?

5. Is the score intended to reflect a single attribute or to sample a heterogeneous domain? If the former, are items internally consistent? If the latter, was the domain well defined and sampled systematically, and does it have at least a modicum of internal consistency?
6. Are scores stable over time?
7. Do the scores relate to other variables in a way consistent with the relations expected from the theory of the attribute?
8. Do relations disconfirm alternative hypotheses about the meaning of the scores?
9. Does the predictive hypothesis sensibly relate the attribute to job performance? Do job experts consider the attribute relevant? Is there prior research suggesting or even demonstrating its relevance?
10. Does a well-formed predictive hypothesis require other attributes of equal or nearly equal importance? If so, can the job-relatedness of the attribute at hand be evaluated on its own?
11. Is there any reason to suspect that a nonmonotonic relation exists? If so, is there any evidence suggesting the points in the assessment distribution where the relation changes from positive to zero to negative?
12. Are criteria measured validly and predicted with reasonable accuracy? The question assumes criterion-related validation, but requires judgments about criterion validity and possible contaminants, adequacy of research design, sufficiency of sample in size and composition, and others.

Answers to the first 8 questions in this list can be drawn from manuals or other documents or from local research. Favorable answers form a basis for inferring psychometric validity. Positive responses to the remaining items provide evidence of job-relatedness—even where the criterion-related evidence implied by Question 12 is missing. Answers to some of the questions are data based, but they require judgment, if only to judge the adequacy of the data. If an overall judgment of job-relatedness is based on good reasons for favorable responses to most of the first 11 questions, it is probably better than that based on a single, local, unreplicated criterion-related validity study.

MANAGERIAL USE OF ASSESSMENTS

Managers (not researchers, test developers, staff psychologists, or human resources specialists) make staffing decisions. Despite wanting the best people, they usually want to fill a vacancy satisfactorily as quickly as possible; testers generally want to maximize performance and compliance with government regulation. Most managers have no training in psychometrics or test theory, they may not understand the constructs assessed, and they may hold unwarranted views about tests. Some managers distrust tests and place little reliance on test scores. Perhaps worse is a manager who believes tests are great, who defers to test scores even when evidence shows them invalid, and who simply does not hear warnings or qualifications about them. To deal with both kinds of unwarranted views, some staff psychologists establish rules for using tests or other assessments in making personnel decisions. The rules might specify preferred score levels or patterns, circumstances to justify overlooking poor scores, or further information to consider along with test scores or other systematic assessments. Some managers may decide for themselves whether to use test information and, if so, how to use it. That seems an odd policy. Developing and validating systematic, standardized assessment programs requires an investment. It is strange to let individual whim determine how or whether the results of the investment will be used. Those responsible for the assessment programs should take active steps to gain program acceptance and to assure proper use of scores.

JUDGMENTS AS PREDICTIONS AND DECISIONS

Personnel decisions are judgments that imply prediction. Most often they have no research foundation and may follow no known plan. Typically, they are not seriously evaluated beyond vague statements like, "Joe really knows how to size people up." We can do better.

Statistical Versus Judgmental Prediction

Many judgmental predictions are not even recognized as such; that is, no clear statement identifies the basis for judgment or hypothesizes that it is somehow related to a predictable outcome. One might, of course, formally frame and test a hypothesis that a firm handshake, looking one squarely in the eye, or some other form of body language indicates that the candidate will work hard or be conscientious. More often, such cues are not even recognized as the basis for judging that "this person is a good bet."

Clinical and counseling psychologists make "clinical predictions," judgments, of likely future behavior. In evaluating a convict being considered for parole, a psychologist's duty may be to predict whether the person, if paroled, will be a repeat offender. Such predictions are not made lightly; the psychologist responsible for them gathers much data about the person, considers much data about recidivism in general, and gives these data much thought before making the prediction.

Likewise, the personnel decision maker may make informed judgments about candidates and the performance expected of them if hired. Candidates might be tested, interviewed, and evaluated in assessment centers; their backgrounds might be checked and people who have known them in various contexts might be interviewed for still more data. Much of the data about a candidate might be useless, and the decision maker may not know the value of specific pieces of information. Yet a decision must be made, it can be made on the basis of informed and explicit judgments, and those judgments are more or less well-informed predictions.

Statistical analysis can be misleading, too, particularly when data are poor or greatly violate statistical assumptions. Nevertheless, Meehl (1954) demonstrated that statistical prediction is consistently superior to clinical (judgmental) prediction. Later, he suggested six circumstances that might, perhaps, favor clinical prediction. Among them was the idea that optimal prediction might be based more on patterns of relations among predictors than on the linear, additive relations assumed in the multiple regression equations (the most common statistical prediction); perhaps well-informed clinicians (judges) could identify salient patterns better than could arithmetic processes. People making judgments might be using information in a "configural" way (i.e., using algorithms that may be nonlinear, nonadditive, or even noncontinuous). It was an interesting idea, but in subsequent research, it did not pan out. It has been a well-accepted view that statistical prediction is almost always, some even say necessarily, better than prediction by human judgment.

Prediction and Decision Without Statistics

Statistical prediction is feasible when common criterion and predictor data can be collected for a lot of people. In these cases, employment decisions can be evaluated in terms of mean performance of those selected. However, many decisions must be made without the luxury of research data. In the case of unusual jobs, high level jobs, or lower level jobs in small organizations many candidates may be assessed, but only one (or a few) may be chosen. The cost of error in these cases, and the reward for being right, may be greater than in those where statistical predictions are feasible. If only one person is chosen, then that person's performance is the crucial evaluation of the decision. In small or large organizations, the higher the organizational level, the fewer the incumbents. Even with dozens of keepers of accounts, there is but one comptroller. When that comptroller retires, moves to a different organization, gets fired, or dies, another person must be chosen to fill the position; perhaps a dozen people or more may be considered. There is no choice between judgmental and statistical prediction; judgment is the only option.

Combining Information for Overall Assessment

Ad hoc judgments and decisions in these low frequency selection decisions are usually inconsistent in procedure, unreliable in result, and difficult to explain by the people who make them. The predictions have unknown validity; they may not even be recognized as predictions. Matters can be helped by careful planning, and methods of consolidating information can be part of the planning.

> When an employer scans a resume and chats with an applicant to make a judgment, both the resume scan and the brief chat are considered *predictors,* subject to the same scrutiny as any other predictor (*Watson v. Ft. Worth,* 1988).

With common scales, several assessments of a candidate can simply be averaged, with or without differential weights (see chap. 7). The mean assessment, rather than the sum, is recommended to ease the problem of missing data. Noncompensatory combinations may also make sense.

JUDGMENT AIDS

Clarifying Judgments to Be Made

Those who are to make the judgments need a clear idea of the major responsibilities of the position to be filled and the qualifications required for it. The clarification serves to define and document the judgments required and the expected sequence in making them. Clarification is the first and perhaps most essential aid to reliable judgments, but it is not easily achieved.

Procedural Planning

Detailed plans for information and procedures can make the judgment process more systematic and therefore more reliable. The larger the pool of potential candidates, the greater the need for logistical planning. For wide-ranging search committees, we recommend planning both a sequence of judgments and the steps to follow in making them. For each candidate, at each step, the decision may be to move the candidate to the next step—which may mean getting new information or new assessments—or to drop the candidate from further consideration. The plan should clearly state the qualifications to be assessed at each step and the procedures to be used in assessing them. Procedural justice argues for a plan used as consistently as possible across candidates.

Developing Assessment Scales

Test scores are assessments; so are ratings in assessment centers or interviews, or from files. Some file information may be quantitative, some narrative, and both kinds can be useful. Information can be assessed on more than one dimension. Prior responsibilities, for example, might be assessed in terms of the cost of error, the scope of the responsibility accepted, or the quality of the achievement in fulfilling it—or something else. If the dimension is not specified, then different people may evaluate the same information on different dimensions, giving an unwarranted appearance of disagreement.

To assure procedural justice and reliability, the information to be used should be specified as unambiguously as possible and measurement scales developed. Some people want to have all assessments made on the same scale, whether based on test scores, interviews, or information in files or credentials.

At some point, at least some candidates are likely to be interviewed. A structured interview plan can standardize the interview and the related assessment scales. Interviews are notoriously lacking in evidence of validity—unless they are well structured. Predeveloped assessment scales help specify and standardize the nature of the judgments to be made. What kinds of information are wanted? Why is such information appropriate or relevant to the position to be filled? What is the nature of the dimension reflected by the information? How should it be evaluated? What relative weight should it have? Preparing the rating forms can provide answers to such questions ahead of time and assure a degree of procedural justice in turning from one file to another, from one interview to another, or from one evaluator to another. Procedural justice is important to candidates (Hausknecht, Day, & Thomas, 2004); its corollary, reliable judgment, is essential to the validity of the final decision.

Expectancy Charts

When tests are used but not empirically or locally validated, theoretical expectancy charts can be useful aids if an acceptable validity coefficient is available or can be estimated. They can be developed using a validity coefficient reported in a manual or other research report based on a comparable situation, estimated from an appropriate meta-analysis, estimated less formally from a body of prior research where each study fits only part of the situation at hand but the accumulated data fill it reasonably well, or estimated by panels of experts.

Expectancy charts show the percentage of those at given test score intervals who could be expected to be successful on the job. Expectancy charts are for decision makers, not for researchers. They provide a sense of the kind and strength of relation found but without the precision of a regression pattern or correlation coefficient. They do, however, promote understanding of the usefulness of predictors and help in making decisions about applicants. People with little statistical training can make predictions using expectancy charts.

Consider a situation where the assessment plan for a specialized sales position includes assessment by tests of two traits, general intelligence and surgency. Suppose that, for both psychometric and theoretical reasons, the Watson–Glaser Critical Thinking Appraisal (CTA; Total Score) and the Hogan Personality Inventory (HPI; Sociability Score) are used. Assume that no relevant validity coefficient was found for the CTA, but an expert panel linked component scores to job duties and concluded that a total score validity coefficient, appropriately corrected, would not be less than .35. A validity coefficient .51 reported in the Hogan manual (R. Hogan & J. Hogan, 1992) for advertising sales, a position making interpersonal demands similar to those in the position at hand, was rounded down to .50. These estimates permit theoretical expectancy charts for these two tests, shown in Fig. 8.1. Score intervals on the CTA were derived from the full norms for upper division

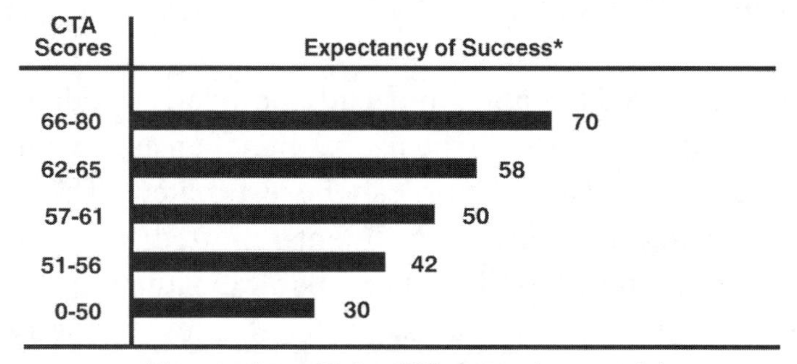

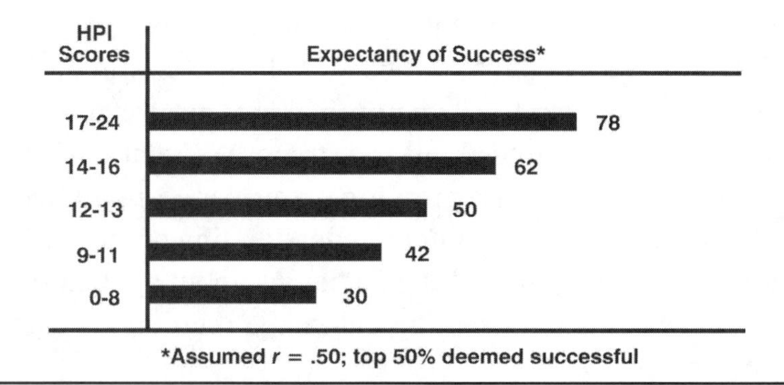

FIG. 8.1. Theoretical expectancy charts for two tests for a hypothetical specialized sales position.

college students; those for the HPI are based on total sample norms. Examination of Fig. 8.1 shows that someone who scores 63 on the CTA would have approximately 58% chance of success on the job, whereas someone who scores 23 on the HPI has approximately 78% chance of success on the job.

Expectancy Graphs

Theoretical expectancy graphs can be developed from empirical data by assuming linear regression and a normal bivariate correlation surface, the characteristic oval-shaped outline of a bivariate scatterplot when both distributions are approximately normal. If each distribution is dichotomized, as in Fig. 8.2, the proportion of superior workers above or below a specified score can be estimated. The proportion of the total area above the horizontal line (quadrants a and b) represents the proportion of employees classed

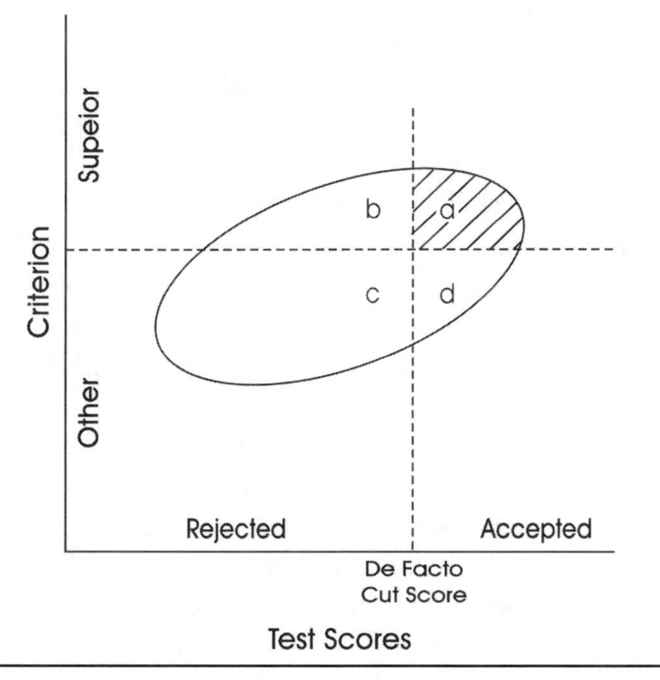

FIG. 8.2. Schematic diagram of relationship between validity, percentage superior without testing, and de facto cutting score.

as superior. The area to the right of the de facto cut score (a and d) represents the proportion of applicants who were hired: the *selection ratio*. The shaded quadrant a represents people who are both hired and superior. The proportion of those accepted who are also superior can be increased by relaxing one's definition of success (i.e., by lowering the horizontal line dichotomizing the criterion), by decreasing the selection ratio (moving the vertical line to the right) or by making the relation stronger (i.e., increasing correlation that narrows the elliptical outline of the data). Reducing the performance level defining success does little to improve organizational functioning. Raising the de facto cut score requires more recruiting.

The use of expectancy graphs can help to illustrate for managers the costs involved in moving the cut score up (more chance of overlooking a good applicant), and moving it down (hiring more people who will not succeed). It is also a way of demonstrating the impact of validity on the selection errors. Imagine if the oval-shaped outline of the scatterplot is changed to be much narrower (as happens with increased validity); the scatterplot goes from looking like a football to looking like a cucumber. Now the percentage of people who are hired and fail, along with the percentage of people who are overlooked, drops considerably. The graph demonstrates clearly how the selection ratio, validity, and definition of performance impacts the success of a selection program.

A staff psychologist's or researcher's responsibility includes assuring that decision makers are trained in the nature of the constructs being assessed, why they are important, the fundamental principles by which the assessment of them was evaluated, the nature of defensible and indefensible inferences from scores, and acceptable limits of individual judgments to override ordinarily defensible inferences. Expectancy charts and graphs can help. They help teach that prediction of either success or failure is rarely certain but is instead probabilistic. They usually show that the probability of success is greater at higher score levels. Good training would also teach the limits of predictions such as those imposed by the criterion chosen; an expectancy of a superior level of production gives no clue about probable performance on a criterion the decision maker might have preferred, such as a dependability or ingenuity.

Utility Analysis

Utility analysis is a formal, analytic study of usefulness that can serve as a decision aid when statistical information is available on predictor–criterion relations—even if only from meta-analyses or expert judgments of validity. Utility analysis can serve many organizational purposes; we mention just three. First, it can aid decisions about using a particular procedure, comparing the benefits of its use to the costs incurred in installing and using it. Second, it offers a means for choosing between alternatives. Many assessments are based on paper-and-pencil aptitude tests. An alternative might be a hands-on assessment of existing competencies. Utility analysis might determine the relative utility of each form of assessment. Where considerations like costs differ greatly, as they do in comparing paper-and-pencil tests with hands-on performance tests, utility analysis can be an important decision aid. Third, utility analysis is a tool for the internal marketing of a proposed program. Modern history includes many great ideas abandoned or never implemented because of a lack of compelling evidence of their worth. As a case in point, Johnson (1975), describing a book on the famous Hawthorne studies and subsequent counseling program, said that the Hawthorne plant had 5 counselors on the staff in 1936, reached a peak of 55 in 1948, and went down to 8 in 1955; "there came a time when new management … began to ask questions about justifying the cost of it. Under the impact of this questioning, the program declined" (Johnson, 1975, p. 275). Perhaps, but by no means certainly, utility analysis might have saved the program.

Utility analysis can help us determine the costs and benefits of implementing an assessment program. It can help identify which of multiple assessment procedures is most economical, and it can help sell the benefits of an assessment program to management.

Although many complex models of utility have been proposed, we present a highly simplified model here for illustrative purposes. The simplified equation, adapted from Brogden (1946, 1949) and Cronbach and Gleser (1957) is:

$$\Delta\$ = [(N)(\Delta r_{xy})(SD_y)] - [(A)(C)]$$

where Δ$ is the average dollar payoff as a result of using the selection procedure. *N* is the number of employees selected by the procedure. SD_y is the difference in revenue generated by average versus above average employees (commonly estimated at 40% of the average employee salary). Δr_{xy} is an estimate of how much the use of the procedure will improve the quality of hiring. This can be obtained by subtracting the effectiveness of the method currently in use from the method in consideration. For example, Table 8.1 shows validity estimates of selection methods used for hiring salespeople (Vinchur, Schippmann, Switzer, & Roth, 1998). If a company is currently using an unstructured interview and is considering the use of a measure of sales ability, Δr_{xy} would be found by subtracting the r_{xy} for the unstructured interview from the r_{xy} for the sales ability measure (.45 – .20 = .25). *C* is the estimated cost of the proposed selection method (see Table 8.1), and *A* is the number of applicants tested. Using this example for a situation in which 100 salespeople will be hired from 500 applicants at $40,000 starting salary would yield:

$$\$375{,}000 = [(100)(.25)(\$16000)] - [(500)(\$50)]$$

Estimates from utility equations have sometimes been staggering and even incredible. It may be that the individual level of analysis typical of most utility studies ignores the system that is the organization and therefore exaggerates expected utility. People seeking to convince others of the value of specific programs must

TABLE 8.1

Validity and Estimated Cost of Selection Methods for Hiring Salespeople

Selection Method	r_{xy}	*Estimated Cost*
Random	.00	0
Graphology	.00	$75
Unstructured Interview	.20	$50
Biodata	.50	$75
Sales Ability Inventory	.45	$50
Potency (Extraversion)	.28	$75
Achievement Orientation	.25	$75
Cognitive Ability	.30	$50

be as conservative as possible to make their estimates seem realistic to managers who have seen other projections of potential savings go sour. Utility analysis may be most useful in considering the relative utilities of available options.

The greatest challenge, however, in utility research may be ir overcoming the perceived complexity of the method. In a survey o members of regional associations of applied psychologists anc HR professionals, Macan and Highhouse (1994) found that man agers did not respond well to utility procedures, and the profes sionals themselves found the equations complex and difficult t understand. Highhouse (1996) argued that researchers need to fo cus on the utility estimate as a *communication device,* and factor such as ambiguity, credibility, and latitude of acceptance deserv attention. It seems that other disciplines have been far more effec tive in communicating the utility of such things as an improve diet, increased exercise, and wearing set belts. Personnel psychol ogists should follow their lead in determining simpler and cleare methods of communicating utility.

CONCLUDING COMMENT

We have tried to argue that judgmental and statistical prediction is not an "either/or" choice (Westen & Weinberger, 2004). Indeed, judgmental prediction can easily be transformed into statistical prediction by transforming impressions into scale scores and combining these scores with test scores using a judgmentally based formula. It is the *consistency* of the mechanical formula that accounts for its accuracy on average. People have a great resistance to formulas. Why is this so? One reason is that people know that formulas blindly applied are bound to lead to prediction errors. For example, a graduate program that simply selects applicants based on a combination of scores will occasionally overlook those "diamonds in the rough" who would have been successful if given the chance. The graduate program, therefore, is closing its eyes to mistakes that could otherwise be avoided. What people fail to consider, however, is the even greater number of errors that would be made without use of the mechanical formula. As Hogarth (2001) observed, people find it difficult to understand that you must accept error to make less error. This does not mean that the decision maker should always ignore information that cannot be formalized into an analytical procedure (e.g., the job candidate makes a racist comment at dinner). Ganzach, Kluger, and Klayman (2000) showed that expert fine-tuning of mechanical combinations of employment interview scores resulted in more accurate predictions than using the mechanically-combined scores alone. People can recognize important information that formulas will never consider. The challenge is to recognize when this information is truly job relevant, versus a personal theory with no validity.

DISCUSSION TOPICS

1. What is meant by the statement *you must accept error to make less error?* What implications does this statement have for selection?

2. How can people doing selection be better trained to judge what is job relevant? How can interview impressions be standardized and compared with test scores?
3. Why do people have such a hard time understanding utility analysis? What could be done to simplify it?

9

Analyzing Bias and Assuring Fairness

Unfair Discrimination
Item & Test Bias
Test-Score Banding

Fairness and freedom from bias are not the same thing, but there is some overlap in meaning. Bias is technical; fairness is more a matter of opinion, policy, and power. During the U.S. civil rights debates of the late 1950s and early 1960s, words like bias, fairness, discrimination, and prejudice seemed to be used almost interchangeably; definitions and distinctions are still not universal.

Bias refers to systematic group differences in item responses, test scores, or other assessments for reasons unrelated to the trait being assessed. Bias is more easily alleged than demonstrated; it is easier to imagine the various kinds of third variables that may bias scores than to show their influence. If a test item requires knowledge common in one group but not in another, and if that knowledge is irrelevant to the trait, then the item is biased. It is *culturally biased* if an acceptable response depends on skills or information common in one culture but not in another. Cultural bias can be expected across countries in multinational organizations, but it is less certain for subcultures (e.g., Black and White) within a single national experience where the same media of mass communication (movies, television, print media, school curricula, etc.) give subcultures much in common despite some profound differences.

Discrimination means making distinctions. It is not always pejorative; to call someone a "discriminating person" has a favorable connotation. Assessment procedures are supposed to help their users make distinctions—to discriminate between those with much of a trait and those with less (or those with even more), or to discriminate between those who can do the job acceptably and those who cannot (or who can do it better). The word has an unfavorable connotation when distinctions are based on prejudice, stereotypes, procedures, or policies unrelated to the trait or to the performance it predicts. Such discriminatory (not discriminating) practices are poor organizational policies, and many are illegal.

In employment, fairness refers to the job relevance of a potentially biasing or discriminatory practice. An item in a job knowledge test for decorators or furniture finishers may ask about japanning; answers may distinguish those with prior understanding of the activity from those without it, fairly and without bias: It discriminates precisely on the basis of knowledge relevant to the job, and that is the intent of the test. The item is not relevant to a house painter's job.[1]

In short, fair discrimination distinguishes those highly likely from those less likely to achieve a performance standard. *Unfair discrimination* exists "when persons with equal probabilities of success on the job have unequal probabilities of being hired for the job" (Guion, 1966, p. 26).[2] Analysis of bias tries to ferret out instances of unfair discrimination.

---

[1]"Japanning" refers to coating an object with a hard, black, glossy varnish or lacquer of a sort originally associated with Japan.

[2]The definition is somewhat ambiguous and was later cleaned up by Einhorn and Bass (1971).

DISCRIMINATION

Discrimination Based on Group Membership

It is illegal in the United States to discriminate against any person on the basis of race, color, religion, gender, or national origin. Groups of people identified on such bases (different laws identify various bases) are called protected groups.

> The term *protected groups* does not mean that some people are not protected under Title VII law, only that some *group characteristics* are not. Gay people as a group are not protected from discrimination under Title VII, but each person in that group, as in many other undesignated groups, remains protected from discrimination on the basis of the explicitly protected categories (e.g., race or religion).

Discrimination need not be intentional to be illegal. A procedure (e.g., tests or interviews) with the effect of unfairly discriminating against people in a protected group is discrimination under the law, even if inadvertent. Procedures with only a "chilling effect," discouraging applications, may also constitute illegal discrimination. Organizational decision makers must be alert to inadvertent or chilling discriminatory practices—even if only to avoid litigation—and be aware that unfair discrimination that is legal is nevertheless unwise.

In the United States, group-based discrimination is so entangled with legal issues that groups defined in other ways are often overlooked. Socioeconomic groups, groups defined by cultural or intellectual habits, and other kinds of groups without legal or political protection may be discriminated against with no threat of litigation. Such discrimination is nevertheless poor management; it can rob the organization of people with excellent qualifications. Many kinds of people are, perhaps routinely, discriminated against on grounds not protected by law: people with unusually long or short hair, people who are unusually tall or short, people who are not well-dressed or are too well-dressed—in short, people with characteristics that displease the decision makers. Focusing on valid, job-related assessment can reduce such instances of bias in decisions.

Distributional Differences

Statistical analysis of bias and discrimination is necessarily group oriented. Analyses can examine group differences in score distributions, in validity, or in predictions. Unfortunately, the only commonly considered distributional difference is the difference in mean scores. This is not enough; differences in variance, skewness, other distributional characteristics, and psychometric differences that influence the distributions should also be considered in analyses of bias.

Group Mean Differences. A lower mean test score in one group compared to another is not by itself evidence of bias, nor is use of test scores with group mean differences evidence by itself of discrimination. Nevertheless, too often a mean difference is the only basis for allegations of discrimination. Markedly different mean scores can occur for many possible reasons other than bias. Consider just four of them:

1. The two groups are biased samples of their respective populations. One group is among the best in its population, the other from those in the lower tail of its population distribution.
2. The two groups are representative samples of populations that actually differ on the trait being measured.
3. Many of the test items require background experiences not common in the lower scoring group.
4. Conditions of test administration differed in the two groups.

The first of these is plausible if the higher scoring group was subjected to stringent screening and the lower scoring group came from extensive, uncritical recruiting. If the second is plausible, then different means may not indicate bias at all. The experiences in the third may be job related. The fourth may describe an error in administering a test in one of the groups. The many reasons for mean differences are extremely difficult to evaluate. A conference on civil rights reached agreement on this if on little else: "Average group differences in test scores do not necessarily reflect bias arising from test construction or use.... Average group differences in test scores may remain in tests even if all bias is removed" (U.S. Commission on Civil Rights, 1993, p. 7). Referring to mean differences as bias, without even thinking about nondiscriminatory potential causes, is simplistic and misleading; citing mean differences as bias and denying a genuine possibility of true differences is dishonest.

Many textbooks sidestep the issue of group mean differences in test scores, such as the rather substantial differences in average cognitive ability test scores between Whites and Blacks. The reason for this is unclear, but it could be that people fear raising an issue that is believed to be inherently racist. In other words, people may fear that group differences in cognitive ability are due to race, and not some third variable. Certainly, we know that cognitive ability does have a heritability component. It does not follow, however, that the group differences themselves are based on heredity. A trait can have a heritability component and show group differences having nothing to do with heritability.

Differences in Other Distributional Characteristics. Distributions may differ in variance. Protected groups may include people from disadvantaged, even dysfunctional, backgrounds—and also people with more education and higher socioeconomic heritage. A plausible hypothesis is that minority groups have higher variance on tests of occupational skills and information influenced by personal background experiences, as illustrated in Table 9.1. The group means are different, but the difference in variability is greater. If it were possible to hire all people with scores of 16 or

TABLE 9.1

Hypothetical Distributions for Two Groups Differing in Test Score Means and Standard Deviations

	Group A		*Group B*	
Raw Score	*f*	*cum f*	*f*	*cum f*
20	1	80	1	40
19	2	79	2	39
18	3	77	1	37
17	9	74	1	36
16	21	65	2	35
15	23	44	2	33
14	10	21	5	31
13	6	11	6	26
12	3	5	7	20
11	1	2	6	13
10	1	1	4	7
9			1	3
8			1	2
7			0	2
6			0	2
5			1	1
M	15.3		12.6	
SD	1.7		3.6	

more, with top-down selection, 50% of Group A would be hired but only 22.5% of Group B. However, at a smaller selection ratio, the effect may disappear or even reverse because of the differences in variance; if only the top-scoring 10 of the 120 candidates are hired (those with scores of 18 or more), then the proportions hired are 7.5% in Group A and 10% in Group B. If Group A has a higher mean, less variance, and less skewness than Group B, then is the test biased against either group? Only if these differences stem from causes unrelated to the trait being measured. Nothing in the distributional statistics, however, speaks clearly to that point; the only clarity is that the relative proportions receiving favorable decisions is affected by a combination of these statistics and the selection ratio.

Discrimination as Systematic Measurement Error. Distributional differences may stem from true differences or from systematic sources of measurement error related to group membership. The latter can happen when groups are defined or influenced by unmeasured third variables such as test-taking habits. If the influence of a third variable is greater in one group than in others, then it can be a source of unintentional, unknown, and unfair discrimination—even if not illegal. A test user who was too cheap and unethical to buy her tests used poor quality photocopies instead. It was easy to show that this user not only violated copyright laws but also reduced the validity of her intended inferences; visual acuity was a strong influence on the scores. Scores were biased against people with even mild visual disability, which constituted unfair discrimination. The incident occurred long before ADA, so using the scores for decisions was unfair and unwise, but not yet illegal. Unfair discrimination denies jobs to qualified people and denies the services of qualified people to organizations. Unfair discrimination due to unknown and unmeasured third variables, may reduce both psychometric validity and job-relatedness.

ANALYSIS OF BIAS AND ADVERSE IMPACT IN TEST USE

Test bias is a psychometric term referring to distortion from different unwanted sources of variance in scores from different groups. *Adverse impact* is a social, political, or legal term referring to an effect of test use. Table 9.1 illustrates adverse impact if the test is used to select a lot of people, but none for filling only a few positions. The group means are different, but the difference in variability is greater.

Test Bias as Differential Psychometric Validity

Test bias produces scores with systematically different meanings for people who are alike on the characteristic being measured. To define bias more precisely, the interpretation of test scores is biased for or against members of a group if groups of people matched on the trait measured have different scores because of one or more sources of variance related to group membership. Several features of this definition merit attention. First, it is the meaning inferred from scores that may or may not be biased, not the test per se, although intrinsic test characteristics may contribute to biased inferences. Second, it is group related. The score of an individual test taker may be invalid, but bias is only one possible source of invalidity. A score can lead to a wrong inference if the person misunderstands the instructions; bias exists only if the instructions are presented so that many people in the group have a common misunderstanding. Third, the definition requires reason to believe that the groups of people being compared are equal with respect to the trait being measured. A measure of bias that does not disentangle itself from genuine group differences is not interpretable. Finally, the definition places the emphasis on sources of group variances, not on group means. Sources of variance are potentially identifiable. Variance is supposed to be due to the same source—the characteristic being measured—in all groups. Bias exists when other sources of variance influence scores in one group but not in another. An example offered by Steele and Aronson (1995) is *stereotype threat* (e.g., the degree to which Blacks or females are vulnerable to general stereotypes about their abilities and to which that vulnerability affects scores in testing where consequences are important). Recent attempts to find evidence for stereotype threat in the field have not been successful, suggesting that one should be cautious in linking this phenomenon to subgroup test score differences in employment settings (Cullen, Hardison, & Sackett, 2004; Stricker & Ward, 2004).

A definition of bias offered by N. S. Cole and Moss (1989) treats it as "differential validity of a given interpretation of a test score for any definable, relevant subgroup of test takers" (p. 205). This definition of bias, and its accompanying call for discriminant and convergent validity evidence "within a hypothesis-generating orientation that requires the examination of plausible rival hypotheses" (N. S. Cole & Moss, 1989, p. 205) might be called *differential psychometric validity.* Investigation of bias from this perspective includes much more than merely comparing correlation coefficients. Test developers and users must think carefully through the maze of complexities, contradictions, and ambiguities possible in any evaluation of psychometric validity. These requirements are exacerbated when one subgroup is to be compared with all others to decide whether the construct inferences from scores in that group differ from the inferences from scores in the others.

A given research setting may involve several groups, but it is easier to think of bias analysis as comparing them two at a time. The convention in bias analyses refers to a *focal group,* potentially a victim of bias, and a *reference group* (often all others) used for comparisons by any of a variety of statistical tools. Simple factor analysis can be used, but simultaneous factor analysis comparing factor structures in different groups simultaneously is more directly relevant. Analysis of variance methods have been in use for many years. And, of course, the item response theory (IRT) models, particularly at the item level, are widely recommended and appropriate for the differential validity context.

Adverse Impact

Under some circumstances, test scores have adverse impact—a legal term, not a statistical or psychometric one. Although adverse impact ratios are often cited, along with mean differences, as if they provided evidence of bias, they do not. They may be confused because adverse impact is a term with an attitude problem—a negative attitude forcing adversarial roles. It is "fraught with inferences and implications that there is some kind of inherent biasing characteristic of tests that accounts for different selection ratios among candidate subgroups" and "instead of selecting a neutral term (e.g., 'pass–fail' ratio), the agencies chose 'impact,' which carries the clear connotation that tests intrinsically have an impelling or compelling effect on candidates from one subgroup" (Lawshe, 1987a, p. 493).

Adverse impact can occur for several reasons, of which bias is but one. Other reasons include chance, measurement problems inherent in the test, the nature of test use, differences in distribution sizes, reliable subgroup differences in general approaches to test taking, or true population differences in distributions of the trait being measured. Adverse impact may be said to be due to bias only if one or more of the first five of these reasons is shown (except the first, which is not systematic) and if the sixth one can be rejected.

> *Adverse impact* is only due to bias if the groups are truly the same on the trait being measured. If there are true differences between the groups, then adverse impact reflects real differences on test scores and can be defended as a business necessity.

The use of an adverse impact ratio depends on changing candidate sample characteristics and is therefore unstable (Lawshe, 1979, 1987a). And again, adverse impact ratios do not consider true population differences. Table 9.2 illustrates the problem. If we knew true ability levels, then we would know that Group 1 has a higher proportion of qualified candidates than does Group 2, that is, that selection ratios based on true abilities are truly different, although the impact ratio would be greater than 80%. What we have, however, is two different methods of measuring the ability that give fallible results. Use of Method A results in adverse impact under the 80% rule; use of Method B does not. But is Method B truly superior? Observed selection ratios under either method differ only trivially, yet only Method A implies adverse impact. In fact, it can be argued that Method B adversely affects employment opportunities in Group 1 because it fails to recognize Group 1's greater likelihood of having truly qualified members.

TABLE 9.2

Selection Ratios and Adverse Impact Ratios for a Hypothetical Case

	Proportion Selected[a]		
Basis for Decision	*Group 1*	*Group 2*	*Adverse Impact Ratio*
True ability	.72	.62	.86
Method A	.76	.58	.76[b]
Method B	.67	.67	1.00

Note. From "Adverse Impact From a Psychometric Perspective," by G. H. Ironson, R. M. Guion, & M. Ostrander, 1982, *Journal of Applied Psychology, 67,* pp. 419–432. Copyright by the American Psychological Association. Reprinted with permission.
[a]Assume all "qualified" candidates are selected. [b]Adverse impact under the 80% rule.

Criterion Bias

In criterion-related validation, the criterion should be reliable, valid, and free from third variable biases. It is amazing how easy that sentence is to write and how difficult it is to accomplish. Reliability is often exceedingly difficult to ascertain for criterion measures; sometimes nothing short of a generalizability analysis will do it, and often such analyses are not feasible in working organizations. A serious attempt to assess criterion validity may in itself be a way of assessing criterion bias. Evidence of valid measurement of the intended criterion construct is the sort of evidence most appropriate; a major question in psychometric validation is whether extraneous sources of variance influence the measures. If so, and if the numbers of cases allow, it should be possible to determine if the extraneous sources are related to subgroup composition.

DIFFERENTIAL ITEM FUNCTIONING (DIF)

Some litigation has centered on a concept of bias in individual items. Psychometricians prefer the term *differential item function-*

ing (DIF) to *item bias* (Holland & Wainer, 1993). Traditional item statistics, such as the proportion of the sample giving a correct answer, are inappropriate for studies of DIF because of their dependence on the trait distribution in the sample studied. Because they reflect group differences in that trait, they cannot disentangle genuine differences from bias. Some litigants, however, have called tests biased merely because of group differences in item pass rates. Drasgow (1987) described out-of-court settlements of two court cases on the basis of this simple-minded item difficulty statistic. In one case, *Golden Rule Insurance Company v. Washburn* (1984), the settlement stipulated that, on future tests, group item difficulties should differ by no more than .15. The second, *Allen v. Alabama State Board of Education* (1985), was more restrictive, specifying a maximum difference of .05.

Item difficulty differences on a widely used test exceeded the .15 maximum of the Golden Rule agreement on 90% of the items when responses of Black males and Black females were compared to those of White males, which is one of those apparently interesting facts that is without meaning, because genuine group differences in these statistics are confounded with bias. An item response theory method, however, identified fewer than half of the items as biased—and inconsistent in direction of effect; the numbers of items harder for minorities nearly equal the numbers of items easier for them. In short, the canceling effect of these differing directions made the cumulative effect on total test scores very low. With similar findings for other subgroups, Drasgow concluded that no measurement bias existed in total test scores in the six groups studied. This is not an unusual research finding.

ACTING ON THE FINDINGS

Despite the problems, researchers attempt to analyze for bias or fairness, especially if there is adverse impact. The Guidelines continue to call for evidence of differential validity, and professional judgments have to be made, even with flawed data. What should be done when it is reasonable to suppose that test scores are biased against a group? Before anything else, clarify needs. Is the top priority to maximize criterion performance or to avoid even the appearance of discriminatory practice? Is either of these the only priority, or is a balancing trade-off needed? The answer is neither universal nor self-evident; it depends on many things, including the costs of error in the situation at hand.

CORRECTIVE ACTION UNDER THE UNIFORM GUIDELINES

Guidelines Provisions. The Guidelines recognize adverse impact as prima facie evidence of discrimination, and a discriminatory procedure is treated as biased. Four options are available under the guidelines:

1. *See if the procedure can be justified by law, such as the business necessity argument*. A large body of case law has developed over the years, modifying some aspects of the Guidelines and supporting others.
2. *Abandon the procedure*. This eliminates one possible source of discrimination (or of litigation), but it begs the question of how to choose among candidates. Ideally, choices are based on valid assessment with no adverse impact. The ideal is hard to find.
3. *Modify the procedure to reduce adverse impact*. One modification uses compensating procedures so that the bottom line is absence of adverse impact. Another adjusts scores to eliminate adverse impact. These options are no longer available.
4. *Offer convincing evidence of job-relatedness*. Valid testing is not discriminatory under the Guidelines, although different levels of validity are balanced against different levels of adverse impact.

Personnel decisions often require resolving conflicting values and predictions. Employers and the larger society may have competing objectives. Employing organizations want their personnel decisions to improve, or even maximize, performance and productivity. The larger society wants personnel decisions to increase employment of people who, historically, were excluded systematically from consideration. Inconsistent objectives should be faced frankly and the competing values balanced openly, according to policies and procedures clearly acknowledging required trade-offs. It is, in fact, silly to consider these objectives as competing. Dropping old policies of exclusion and competently assessing the qualifications of all candidates, including those formerly excluded, can yield genuine benefit, both in jobs for those otherwise not considered and in enlarged pools of well-qualified job candidates.

Moreover, hiring people formerly excluded can contribute to overall utility in ways not usually included in the criteria for test validation. Consider, for example, a metropolitan police force in which community political leaders have decreed that police will spend much of their time walking a beat. The objective is to reduce crime and improve the quality of life in the neighborhoods through catching and arresting criminals, a watchful presence, and knowing the people on the beat. Knowing the people implies more than knowing their faces or even their names. It implies knowing the common values and experiences of people in the neighborhood, and beyond that, knowing those of neighborhood leaders. Neighborhoods in a city are diverse, creating a real, not just ideological, requirement for police force diversity. Hiring policies might require hiring to fill gaps in the kinds of community insights currently available. One police class might need overrepresentation of low income ethnic neighborhoods; another might need recruits who know and understand those with affluence. Hiring should not follow rigidly the traditional top-down policy required in most civil service jurisdictions, even though it would maximize criterion utility.

In short, three concepts are too often confused in arguments related to EEO and personnel decisions: *psychometric concepts,* which include the reliability and validity of scores; *statistical concepts,* which include the predictive utility of scores as well as the predictions themselves; and *social policy concepts,* such as affirmative action. If organizational and social goals are to be met, then these concepts must be kept as distinct, well-defined, unconfused, and balanced as possible.

Substantially different score distributions for different groups of candidates, a low selection ratio, and a psychometrically sound predictor with good criterion-related validity can combine in effect to shut out members of a smaller group with a lower distribution. To whatever extent policy rejects shutting out groups of people, alternative or adjunct procedures may be necessary. Policies should be explicit so they can be debated and their implications thoroughly understood. The alternative or adjunct procedures should be evaluated in terms of their effectiveness in balancing differing policy values. We distrust ideological declarations that a favored procedure will virtually assure high validity and very nearly get rid of adverse impact, bias, or general unfairness. Understanding the effect of a procedure on each objective should precede advocacy.

Score Adjustments

Adjusting scores to give preference to a group of candidates is not a new idea. Civil service laws have long provided for adding points to the test scores of veterans. Although adding points to the scores of those in an adversely affected group is one way to reduce adverse impact, doing so is illegal in the United States. Section 106 (1) of the 1991 Civil Rights Act provides: "It shall be an unlawful employment practice for a respondent, in connection with the selection or referral of applicants for employment or promotion, to adjust the scores of, use different cutoff scores for, *or otherwise alter the results of,* employment related tests on the basis of race, color, religion, sex, or national origin" (italics added).

Race-Norming in the U.S. Employment Service. The prohibition is the direct result of controversy over "race-norming" in the use of the General Aptitude Test Battery (GATB) in the U.S. Employment Service (USES). The GATB was developed as a job counseling and job referral tool. The controversial procedure (as described by Hartigan & Wigdor, 1989) was based on factor analysis and validity generalization (Hunter, 1983). It reduced scores on 10 individual subtests to 3 aptitude scores: cognitive, perceptual, and psychomotor composites. These scores were added with weights derived independently (based on regression analysis) for each of five job families. The composite scores were expressed as percentile ranks in the applicant's population group: Black, Hispanic, or other. A given score in a group with a lower distribution of scores would have a higher percentile rank than it would if based on all three groups combined. In effect, the separate norms added points to scores of minorities.

Employment Quotas. The USES procedure was denounced in many quarters, including Congress and the executive branch, as a quota system. It reduced adverse impact, and its effect was that of a quota. In an area where the labor market is 20% Black and 10% Hispanic, and nearly all the rest White, a true proportional quota would call for hiring two Black applicants and one Hispanic applicant for each seven White applicants hired. Such a quota need not be filled at random. Many employers have used within-group, top-down selection to avoid adverse impact; applicants are listed in rank order within groups according to their scores, and those hired are the most qualified in their respective groups.

Quotas have long been anathema in American society, where the prevailing view has been that individuals should be considered for opportunities on the basis of their own merit.[3] Those who used group norms to fill quotas did so less for ideological reasons than

[3]An embarrassing chapter in American history is the now nearly forgotten period when colleges and universities used quotas to restrict admissions of Jews.

to avoid litigation. It was considered the surest way to reduce adverse impact; moreover, it is the ultimate group parity fairness method. Is its effect on mean performance level detrimental to the hiring organization? There is no strong evidence that it is, although finding people who would admit to having the requisite data may not be easy.

"Ranges of Indifference" in Test Score Bands

One procedure uses *score bands,* which are intervals within which score differences are in some sense trivial, or *ranges of indifference.* Within a band, selection decisions may consider diversity. The procedure is often considered a means of compensating for adverse impact. It has been introduced in that context, but it can serve much broader purposes.

The practice of banding has been needlessly controversial. Arguments favoring or opposing banding are based partly on psychometric grounds (e.g., assessment reliability) and partly on statistical grounds (e.g., statistical significance levels). Framing arguments in these terms is a distraction. The purpose is to transform a raw measurement scale into one that groups unit raw score intervals into larger ones where raw score differences do not matter; within such an interval, choices can be based on other, perhaps competing, considerations. In a sense, all score use involves banding. The raw measurement scale has bands, albeit of unit width; for example, statistical analyses consider a raw score of 10 to be the midpoint of the 9.50–10.49 score interval, or band. Use of a cut score creates two bands, one passing, the other not. Most banding is between these extremes. Generally, banding sets score intervals greater than raw scores but smaller than the entire region above or below a cut score. Whatever the size of the interval, the same two problems must be faced: how to define band width, and how to choose within a band where candidates outnumber openings.

Band Width. Scores contain error. Two people with the same raw scores may differ in ability, and two people of the same ability may have different scores. When faced with two candidates of somewhat (but not dramatically) different scores, it is reasonable to ask whether the scores differ significantly, statistically. The standard error of the difference, s_d, between two scores may be defined as $s_d = s_m \sqrt{2}$ where s_m is the standard error of measurement. A band interval might be defined as 1.96 s_d, within which a score difference is not (at the 5% level) significantly different from 0. A broader interval might be defined as $2 \cdot s_m$. Or one could use the standard error of estimate, s_e, to define an interval of scores within which differences in predicted criterion values might be considered trivial.

The basis does not have to be statistical; a score distribution might be divided arbitrarily into four or five or a dozen intervals with nearly equal frequencies and these might be treated as bands. Statistical definitions of band limits provide an appearance of scientific objectivity, but appearance masks the arbitrariness involved. Even with statistical definitions, arbitrary choices determine whether band width is based on predictor unreliability or on unreliability of predicted criterion performance and the level of confidence used.

The definition might be based on managerial judgments of how much loss in utility (a band width greater than 1.0 does involve some loss) can be sacrificed to other considerations. Managers might agree in conference on a band width they consider about right. They may decide that band width is not constant, making bands narrower (or broader) in the middle of the distribution than at the extremes. All of these are arbitrary, but no more arbitrary than the choice of statistical definitions.

Decisions Within Bands. Within a band, decisions can be based on other information. They might be based on information not routinely available, on assessments of traits not part of a general or common predictive hypothesis, or on affirmative action or diversity goals. Contextual criteria, not used in test validation or implicit in the predictive hypothesis, could be considered within bands. Choices could be based on additional assessment; one may have a very desirable selection procedure that is not cost-effective if used for all applicants, but is cost-effective if used only with those applicants within a band. Choice could, of course, be random, but we do not recommend it.

> Although the Supreme Court has not ruled on the legality of *banding,* lower courts have upheld its use (Henle, 2004). The practice is less likely, however, to survive scrutiny when minority preference is the only factor used to make decisions within bands (*Officers for Justice v. Civil Service Commission of San Francisco,* 1991).

Fixed Bands. Table 9.3 shows a plausible distribution of scores. It has a plausible mean and standard deviation (79.7 and 5.14, respectively), it has some gaps (but not many), and it comes fairly close to a normal curve—a little flatter, not quite smooth, not quite symmetrical, but fairly close. Arbitrarily, without recourse to any statistic, it has been marked off in intervals of 4 points on the score scale. The top band has a top score of 98. There is only one such score, and no one scored 97, 96, or 95 (the remaining three values in the arbitrary interval). The next interval would include values of 91–94, also with only one case, so we start over (again, quite arbitrarily) with 91 as the top of the second band. That band has four cases; the third band has eight cases, and so it goes. How should selection from bands differ from selection according to raw scores?

Let us accept as given that the top scoring person gets hired. That score is substantially higher (better) than any other, so barring some disqualifying fact, the predicted performance of the person with that score is surely good enough to get the job. What about the four people in the next band? Suppose there are only two openings. Which two get hired? The decision might be based on a random draw; it might be based on information not included in validation because it is not routinely available. Perhaps the candidate scoring 91 has a history of repeated felony convictions. That per-

TABLE 9.3

A Hypothetical Frequency Distribution Marked Off in Bands

Score	*f*
98	1
91	1
90	1
89	2
87	3
86	2
84	3
83	4
82	6
81	10
80	12
79	7
78	8
77	9
76	5
75	2
74	3
72	2
70	2
67	1
60	1

son might be rejected despite the high score if repeated convictions are considered a disqualifying characteristic. (Disqualifying characteristics, of course, can also operate in top-down decisions.) If one of those people scoring 89 is a minority person, and if the organization has not hired very many minorities, then the offer may go to that person. If that person accepts, which of the two remaining people in the band will fill the one remaining vacancy? Without a strong reason to prefer one over the other, the decision may be made with a coin toss. One person remains in the band. If the next opening does not occur for several weeks, then that person may no longer be available, and the next opening may be filled from the third band. Otherwise, that person must be considered before others; hiring options stay limited to the band until everyone in it has been hired, disqualified, or otherwise withdrawn from consideration—that is, until the band has been "exhausted."

By this practice, it is hard to see that banding differs in any practical way from top-down selection. It is also hard to see, if each band must be exhausted before going to the next lower one, that banding leads to quotas or does much to reduce adverse impact unless band intervals are very wide and bands near the top of the total distribution have many more people in them than there are openings. With reasonably narrow bands, most decisions are based on scores on the presumably valid, demonstrably job-related assessment predicting a valued criterion; a smaller number of decisions are based on other considerations.

The discussion so far may seem to imply that everyone is assessed at the same time, but that is not necessarily the case. As new candidates are assessed, they can be placed in the band in which they score. In Table 9.3, for example, after the first two bands have been used up, a new examinee might get a score of 90 and enter the second band. Unless there is a disqualifying characteristic, that candidate would be virtually assured of the job regardless of subgroup identification. Neither of these patterns of use fits the way banding tends to work in organizations. Bands are typically chosen to increase minority hiring; within a band, minorities get preference, either totally or by quota. Nevertheless, the band must be used up; nonminorities in the band eventually are selected.

Sliding Bands. Sliding bands differ from fixed bands in that they more or less slither down the distribution rather than going down in jumps. As with fixed bands, the highest scoring person is deemed the candidate most likely to perform well on the criterion; an interval can be defined, with that score at the top, in which score differences are trivial. When the highest scoring person is out (selected, disqualified, or refused offer), the sliding band concept notes that there is now someone else at the top of the distribution, and the next step is to identify the people whose scores differ only trivially from the one now on top.

The distribution in Table 9.3 can also illustrate sliding bands. Instead of the 4-point band width, however, we arbitrarily choose the s_m as the basis for definition. Assuming a reliability coefficient of .85 (neither very good nor very bad) and a 5% alpha level, the band width can now be rounded conveniently to 5.5. Assume that predictive validity is high and the job is technical and requires supervision of less well-trained technicians. Table 9.4 provides some imaginary information about the 17 people at the top of the score distribution. The top band, with a 5.5 band width, would extend down from 98–92.5; it is still home to just one person who surely seems likely to be hired. Then the band slides down to the second person; he scored 91. This is now the highest score, so the band extends down to 85.5 and includes nine people whose scores on a highly valid test differ only trivially. There is one opening; one of these nine people must be selected. It will not be the one who scores 91 as long as the policy frowns on repeat felons. Not many women study in this technical area, and there are few minorities in this company and in this job. The White male scoring 89 may be passed over on that basis alone, but his apparent brashness and relative inexperience may also argue against choosing him. Another White male and a Hispanic male, both scoring 87, have relevant technical training and experience but lack supervisory experience. Without behavioral evidence, pro or con, about the effect of the White male's family status on his work, it is not a relevant consideration—and it may not be in any case. The two White females may have more relevant work experience; one has some supervisory experience. The Black male with a score of 86, while taking a relevant course of study and getting further study after graduation, was not a very good student. It does not say why not—and finding out why not would surely be useful. The best that can

TABLE 9.4

Characteristics of Top Scoring Candidates in Distribution in Table 9.3

Score	*Ethnic Group*	*Gender*	*Further Information*
98	White	M	BS + special seminars in the field; handled self well in interview, good impression; known to company official as expert in the field.
91	White	M	BS + special study in the field; seemed very sure of self in interview, too cocky; has repeated felony convictions; has relevant experience in the field.
90	White	F	BS, good GPA; no problems in the interview; has some limited but appropriate experience; school and experience came after children (2) were in college.
89	White	M	Currently in last year of 3-year technical school program; seemed brash to interviewer; getting some part-time experience on current day job.
89	Black	F	Some college, relevant, and fairly good GPA; seemed nervous in interview, not self-confident; useful but limited experience; has grown in job responsibilities.
87	Asian	M	Graduate degree in history; diffident during interview; no relevant job experience; active volunteer in community organizations.
87	White	M	Technical school diploma and 12 years technical experience in reputable company; expressed clear goals in interview; divorced, single father.
87	Hispanic	M	Technical school diploma and 11 years technical experience in reputable company; expressed clear goals in interview.
86	White	F	Graduate degree in art; no interview problems; has had some technical and supervisory experience in commercial computer art and sculpture.

Score	*Ethnic Group*	*Gender*	*Further Information*
86	Black	M	BS + special seminars; marginal GPA; clear goals in interview; extended experience but in company not known for quality.
84	Black	M	In 2nd year of 3-year tech college program; apparently doing well according to faculty reference letters; did not communicate well during interview; no relevant experience.
84	Black	F	BS, good GPA, went to school 6 years while working full time; lacked social skills in interview; has 7 years relevant experience, moving up from labor pool to supervision.
84	White	F	BS, good GPA; understood importance of technical questions in interview; 3 years experience; excellent performance ratings.
83	White	M	BS + special seminars; was an undergrad lab assistant; no problems in interview; reputation as technical expert known to company officials; 12 years experience in different companies.
83	Hispanic	M	BS + graduate courses in South America; interview went poorly because his English is inadequate; some relevant experience but unevaluated.
83	Asian	F	BS + graduate courses; interview rating of "promising"; 2 years experience under technically excellent supervisor.
83	Black	M	High school drop-out, GED diploma; interview failed to learn much about early work experience, but uncovered major work achievements during last decade, including the last 3 years with good experience in this field.

be said at this point is that the choice will be from one of these five, but more information is needed before a nonrandom choice is made. Calls to listed references with explicit questions, perhaps a better, more structured interview with each candidate, and possibly additional testing of constructs deemed important to the work might provide important information required for a satisfying decision.

When the choice is made, it will not be the top scoring person; he was considered disqualified. Therefore, the band slides again, just as if the top scoring person had been hired. Disqualified is a key term. Procedural justice demands that reasons for disqualification be clear and consistently applied. Some decisions can be based solely on predicted job performance; some can be based on policies that reasonable people would be likely to accept (e.g., unwillingness to hire people repeatedly convicted of felonies). There is danger, however, of disqualifying for reasons that are ad hoc, prejudicial (not necessarily a proscribed prejudice), and invalid.

In most practical situations, sliding bands seem no more likely than fixed bands to promote increased minority hiring. The only real difference is in defining a "used up" band; the sliding band shifts when the top score is taken out, and all scores must be removed before shifting a fixed band. Either procedure can allow consideration of other information; the decision process calls for judgment. The role of judgment in decision making has already been emphasized, and the quality of judgment is not a unique consideration. Use, or possible abuse, of the judgment opportunity is to be evaluated where it exists. The question of banding, sliding or otherwise, is whether the exercise of managerial judgment is a good idea. We believe it is necessary.

DISCUSSION TOPICS

1. Discuss different methods of score adjustments (i.e., race norming, banding, quotas) and identify the pros and cons of each approach for reducing adverse impact.

2. Compare and contrast the concepts bias, fairness, discrimination, and prejudice.
3. When would it be advantageous to use one type of banding procedure versus another?

III

Choosing the Right Method

10

Assessing Via Tests

Paper & Pencil
Work Sample
Situational Judgment
Computer Adaptive

A *test* is an objective and standardized procedure for measuring a psychological construct using a sample of behavior. A test is objective in that responses can be evaluated against external standards of truth or of quality—correct or incorrect, or better or poorer than a standard. Measuring implies quantification. Tests are scored quantitatively, with measurable precision, on numerical scales representing levels of a construct to be inferred from the scores. A *construct,* as we use the term, is a fairly well-developed idea of a trait; most constructs in testing are abilities, skills, or areas of knowledge. Tests use a standardized procedure with the same stimulus component for all test takers.[1] *Standardization* refers primarily to controlling the conditions and procedures of test administration, that is, keeping them constant,

[1]"Stimulus component" may, but does not necessarily, mean "item." Computer adaptive testing, and some other test procedures, do not require the same set of items for all takers.

or unvarying. If scores from different people are to be comparable, then they must be obtained under comparable circumstances. If people tested in one room have 30 minutes in which to complete a test, and those in another have only 20 minutes, neither the circumstances nor the scores are comparable. Any circumstances of test administration potentially influencing scores should be standardized. More than anything else, it is attention to standard procedure that distinguishes testing from other forms of assessment. The distinction is fuzzy. This chapter describes a variety of procedures for assessing KSAs, ranging from highly standardized tests to assessments with little or no standardization, with no clear line distinguishing tests from other assessment procedures.

Defining a test as a sample of behavior means the examinee is not passive but does something. In other kinds of testing (e.g., blood tests), the object of measurement sits passively while something is done to it. In psychological tests, the examinee responds to test stimuli by writing answers to questions, choosing among options, recognizing or matching stimuli, performing tasks, ordering objects or ideas, or producing ideas to fit requirements—and this is not an exhaustive list.

NORM-REFERENCED AND DOMAIN-REFERENCED TESTING

Test scores are often *norm referenced*, that is, interpreted relative to the scores of people in a comparison (norm) group. Whether a score is considered good or poor depends on the distribution of scores in the norm group. Figure 10.1 shows percentile ranks associated with raw scores in three hypothetical distributions. An examinee with a score of 12 has answered half of the items correctly. It is a magnificent score compared to those in Group C, better than more than 99% of the scores in that group. Compared to those in Group B, it is about average—not very good or very bad. It is not good at all (in the bottom quarter) in Group A, which is the group with the best set of scores.

Raw Score	Percentile Rank in Group A	Group B	Group C
24			
23	99.9		
22	99.4	99.9	
21	97.7	99.6	
20	94.3	98.5	
19	88.4	96.4	
18	79.9	93.0	
17	70.2	88.6	
16	60.0	83.1	
15	50.0	76.9	
14	40.8	69.9	
13	32.3	62.1	99.9
12	24.6	54.0	99.2
11	18.1	45.5	97.2
10	12.7	36.7	94.1
9	8.5	28.2	89.3
8	5.4	23.9	82.6
7	3.1	16.7	73.9
6	1.7	10.6	63.2
5	.8	5.7	51.0
4	.3	2.5	37.5
3		.7	23.7
2		.2	11.9
1			4.0
0			.4

FIG. 10.1. Differences in interpretations of a given test score with different norm groups; a raw score of 12 is in the bottom quarter of the distribution in Group A, slightly above average in Group B, and outstanding in Group C.

Norm tables are rarely consulted in employment testing. Expectancy tables are more useful, but they too are norm-referenced, comparing candidates with each other. In a set of candidates, those with higher scores at any level are preferred over those with lower scores. Hiring the best of a poorly qualified lot, however, is poor management. In a test of prerequisite job knowledge, if every examinee should have a very high score, then it is not helpful to say that someone with a very low score is less ignorant than a lot of other people and should therefore be chosen.

An alternative to normative interpretations was originally called criterion-referenced interpretation. In it, scores are interpreted relative to the content domain being tested; we prefer domain-referenced interpretation.[2] Under either term, the basic idea is that a domain of accomplishments is identified and defined. It should be defined clearly enough that people, even those who disagree about the domain, can generally agree on whether a specified fact or achievement is in or outside of it. Measures of the domain should fit the definition, and scores should be explicitly interpretable in terms of it.

In *domain-referenced* testing, the domain, not a point in a score distribution, is the criterion for referencing or interpreting an obtained score. A score of 12 on a 24-item test may mean knowledge of half of the content, but a better, fuller interpretation can identify the half not known. Content domains are rarely homogeneous, a fact permitting diagnostic uses of domain referencing.

> An example of a *norm-referenced* test might be a test of mechanical aptitude. Those with higher scores would be seen as better candidates for mechanical careers than those with lower scores. An example of a *domain-referenced* test might be a test designed to certify a mechanic as competent to work on a certain automaker's vehicles—there is a well-defined domain of knowledge that the person must master.

In theory, any test can be used for either norm- or domain-referenced interpretation. In practice, tests may be developed differently for these differing purposes. Clarity of test purpose, always important, is especially so in domain-referenced testing. It is not

---

[2]Not everyone shares this preference. Linn (1994) considered "domain-referenced" to require domain specifications too rigid to be feasible for any but extremely narrow, finite domains; he said that "criterion-referenced" refers to "broader, fuzzier, but more interesting achievements" (p. 13). Glaser (1994), who introduced criterion-referenced testing (Glaser, 1963; Glaser & Klaus, 1962), preferred the original term, pushing aside the barnacles of misinterpretations of his idea that occurred over the years.

enough to say that a test's purpose is to measure knowledge of computer repair procedures. Defining "knowledge of repair procedures" requires clarity about component content areas; components should be assigned relative weights, and the kinds of items to be used for each component should be specified.

Internal consistency, and the reasonable assumption of transitivity it permits, is a basic requirement in norm-referenced testing; people being compared should be compared on a common basis. It is less important in domain-referenced testing; in fact, if it is very high, the content domain may be too restricted. Of course, without some minimal internal consistency, scores have no meaning. Components of a content domain that are uncorrelated, or negatively correlated, should be separately scored. Evaluating the validity of a norm-referenced test is primarily correlational, either in the sense of criterion-related validation or of confirming and disconfirming construct interpretations. Evaluating the validity of a domain-referenced test calls for expert judgment of the match of items to the specified content domain.

TRADITIONAL COGNITIVE TESTS

Cognitive tests allow individuals to show what they know, perceive, remember, understand, or can work with mentally. They include problem identification, problem-solving tasks, perceptual (not sensory) skills, the development or evaluation of ideas, and remembering what one has learned through general experience or specific training. They include intelligence tests, achievement tests, and job knowledge tests, among others.

Most tests now used are called paper-and-pencil tests, but materials do not define traditional tests. The defining features of traditional tests are that they are well-standardized, their items can be reliably scored, and they can be administered to groups of people. Commercial tests of cognitive ability are commonly used and, within 12 minutes or so, can provide reliable scores that predict as well as measures that take hours to administer. One such test, the

Wonderlic Personnel Test, has been used to screen NFL recruits since 1970. Table 10.1 shows the average Wonderlic score for professional football players, along with average scores in other professions. The overall average Wonderlic score for adults is 20.

An example item on a test of general cognitive ability:
Which number in the following group of numbers represents the smallest amount?
a. 11 b. 1 c. .111 d. .011

Off-the-Shelf Tests. It is almost always cheaper to buy a test than to develop one, but a commercial test may have less face validity than a locally developed test that refers explicitly to specific jobs or sets of jobs within the organization. Job-specific local tests developed by people well-trained in psychometrics can be as reliable and valid as commercially available ones. One study paired three subtests of the *Differential Aptitude Test Battery* (DAT) with related job-specific tests (Hattrup, N. Schmitt, & Landis, 1992). For example, the DAT Verbal Reasoning test, a measure of the verbal compre-

TABLE 10.1

Average Wonderlic Personnel Test Scores of Various Occupations

Occupation	*Average WPT Score*
Chemist	31
Programmer	29
Newswriter	26
Sales	24
Bank teller	22
Professional football player	21
Clerical worker	21
Security guard	17
Warehouse	15

Note. From "Taking Your Wonderlics," by J. Merron, 2002. Retrieved February 27, from http://sports.espn.go.com.

hension factor, was paired with a technical reading test based on manuals used on the job. Confirmatory factor analysis showed that the same constructs were measured in each of the three pairs of tests. Hattrup et al. (1992) concluded that test users do not gain much, psychometrically, by building homemade, job-specific tests, even good ones, but that they do not lose anything either, and may gain considerably in testing program acceptance. No matter how much a test developer tries to make particular tests highly specific to particular uses, general cognitive constructs still account for most of the variance. Those who think they are doing things that are new or highly specific may only be fooling themselves.

PERFORMANCE TESTS

Performance testing in the workplace means assessing proficiency in some aspect of job performance. Performance tests may be cognitive or noncognitive, paper-and-pencil or "hands-on," and anywhere from the most to the least constrained kinds of responses. They may be criteria or predictors intended to predict no further than the immediate future. An applicant who does well on a welding test may be expected do good welding the first day at work; situational variables like equipment, materials, supervision, coworkers, or personal traits like motivational level, may determine whether a good beginning is continued. Although prediction is always implied, performance tests are used mainly to assess proficiency, skill, or knowledge at the time of testing—here and now, not at some future time. Unlike low aptitude candidates, those lacking knowledge or skill may acquire it through special training and reapply when ready.

Performance tests can be used to predict performance on a higher level job requiring similar kinds of proficiency, to identify outside candidates who need no training beyond a general orientation, to identify training needs, as a criterion in validation, to provide proficiency-related interpretations of predictors, and in performance evaluation. Only the first of these has a strong future orientation; the principal orientation of all the other purposes is here and now. Use as a criterion should be more common than it is, but its value as a criterion can be overstated. Performance testing usually describes how well tasks can be performed when the individuals are doing their best. Where testing is intended to predict actual performance, not a hypothetical maximum level, performance test scores may be inappropriate criteria. Again, the method of assessment should fit its purpose.

Work Samples and Simulations

The most common "hands-on" performance tests may be work samples. They are well-established as predictors. Their criterion-related validity is consistently shown in reviews (e.g., Schmidt & Hunter, 1998).

A work sample test is a standard sample of a job content domain taken under standard conditions. Aspects of the work process, the outcome, or both may be observed and scored. In a flight test for a pilot's license, the focus is on process; a check pilot has a checklist of required maneuvers and evaluates how well each is performed. A candidate for an office job may be given a typed manuscript with many scribbled changes on it, be seated at a word processor, and told to prepare final hard copy; perhaps only the result is observed and scored. In either case, the work sample is a *standardized abstraction* of work actually done on a job. There are degrees of abstraction. A work sample might be faithful reproductions of actual assignments, sanitized simulations of critical components, or the extreme abstraction (measures of isolated skills used on the job).

Simulations imitate actual work but omit its trivial, time-consuming, dangerous, or expensive aspects. They may imitate a task almost exactly, as in some simulations of aircraft cockpit tasks. They may imitate only the general flavor of reality, as in assessment center management exercises.

Other possibilities carry abstraction still further. Performance tests might use *talk-through* interviews (Hedge, Teachout, & Laue, 1990) to describe the steps, tools used, and decisions made in doing the job. A work diary might be used. A collection of product examples (a "portfolio") may be evaluated. Even a multiple-choice test may abstract from overall performance the knowledge and understanding of processes, tools, and choices that make up performance on the job. Simulations that are not highly abstracted are known as *high fidelity* simulations; the greater abstractions may be *low fidelity* simulations (e.g., Chan & Schmitt, 2002).

Developing Work Samples. Work sample development begins with job analysis, although not everything the analysis identifies is included. A complete job analysis identifies a job content *universe*. The part of the universe to be assessed is a job content *domain*. Related assessment possibilities (including scoring methods) make up a test content universe, and the choices among them define the intended test content domain.

Proficiency is the construct measured by a work sample, but it takes many forms. For a criterion, it should identify all tasks critical for overall performance. For selection, it omits critical tasks learned on the job. Ordinarily, tasks defining proficiency should be those that many, but not necessarily all, workers are likely to perform well. Most work samples use only frequent tasks; rarely performed tasks might be in the domain to identify those who can handle unusual job situations.

Equipment or material used should match that actually used on the job. Tolerances and procedures for monitoring equipment should be established; if holes into which things are inserted get larger over repeated testing, monitoring hole size may be an important aspect of standardization. As always, pilot studies should evaluate the clarity of instructions, scoring procedures, and characteristics of test components (e.g., items), as well as overall reliability and validity of scores.

SCORING WORK SAMPLES

Scores are usually ratings. An overall rating of process, product, or component part can be dichotomous (e.g., satisfactory or unsatisfactory) or a scale point. A work sample product might be matched to one of a set of samples previously scaled from very poor to excellent; the score being the scale value of the sample it most closely matches. More objective measures can be used. A score on machine set-up might be the time required to do it. The score can be the pounds of pressure required to break a weld. A computer might count the number of corrections made in a sample word processing task. Ratings predominate, however, and their associated problems (see chap. 11) can be helped with procedures like the following:

1. Job experts should choose work sample content, specify desired performance, and provide at least a preliminary scoring key or protocol.
2. Scorers should be trained to use the protocol: what to look for and how to evaluate specific events or product components.
3. The same performance or product should (if possible) be evaluated by two or more independent observers; impermissible differences in ratings should be defined and the procedures for reconciling differences prescribed.
4. All possible procedural safeguards of reliability should be built into the scoring system.

Situational Judgments

An important challenge when selecting candidates for a position is predicting how potential employees will respond to important tasks and problems they may encounter in the workplace. Some problems are difficult, although not impossible, to recreate in a work sample. Situational judgments are low fidelity simulations of important work tasks, presented in a multiple-choice format. Typically, the situational dilemmas are related to core job competencies, such as responding to irate customers for service-oriented jobs (McDaniel & Nguyen, 2001). Candidates are presented with a series of job-relevant scenarios and a set of possible responses to each situation. They are then asked to indicate which of the responses they would be likely to employ if confronted with the situation. In this sense, situational judgments are very similar to situational interview questions discussed later.

> An example item from the *situational judgment* portion of the FBI Special Agent Selection Process:
>
> You are shopping when you notice a man robbing the store. What would you do?
>
> a. Leave the store as quickly as possible and call the police.
> b. Try to apprehend the robber yourself.
> c. Follow the man and call the police as soon as he appears settled somewhere.
> d. Nothing, as you do not wish to get involved in the matter.

An alternative to the "what would you do?" item stem is one that asks respondents to choose the "best response" to the situation presented. McDaniel and Nguyen (2001) argued that this approach is less susceptible to faking. Ployhart and Ehrhart (2003), however, found that the "would do" approach showed more favorable item characteristics than the "should do" approach. This is consistent with the idea that intentions concerning what you would do are more predictive of behavior than is knowledge about what you should do (Ajzen, 1991).

It appears that situational judgment tests can be developed that correlate with performance over and above job experience, cognitive ability, and personality (Chan & N. Schmitt, 2002). Like any other testing method, what is measured by situational judgment tests (SJT) is dependent on their construction. SJTs that are, in essence, proxies for general cognitive ability can be constructed, or tests emphasizing creative problem-solving or personality variables can be developed, depending on the content of the scenarios presented and which of the response options is determined to be correct. It is important, therefore, to distinguish between situational judgments as item-development *method,* and situational judgment as a *construct.* If the goal is to measure good judgment, then this approach holds much promise (Brooks & Highhouse, 2006). But researchers need to focus more on defining what good judgment is, and specifying the nomological network of relations to other constructs.

Noncognitive Performance

Physical Abilities. Measuring strength, muscular flexibility, stamina, and related abilities usually requires equipment and individual testing. Equipment needs described by Fleishman and Reilly (1992b) are often simple. Assessing stamina may use an electronically monitored treadmill with an accompanying electrocardiograph, but a simple step-climbing test can also assess stamina, although with less precision.

Fitness Testing. Task performance, physical fitness, and health may be related. Task performance, as measured by a work sample, may be supported by physical abilities (e.g., stamina). Abilities are supported by biological systems (e.g., cardiorespiratory systems), which may be impaired by health problems. A person with emphysema suffers cardiorespiratory impairment, resulting loss of stamina, and difficulty in tasks like climbing stairs. Poor fitness is a problem for both the person and the employer.

Medical and physical testing should have higher than typical priority, if for no other reason than protection from litigation. Litigation can spring from many directions (including getting hurt in fitness testing). An organization may be legally liable for hiring unhealthy or physically inept employees (under the concept of negligent hiring); there is an opposing liability for discrimination against the disabled. Employees who hurt themselves or develop health problems because of physically demanding jobs add to worker's compensation costs. Performance errors or accidents stemming from fatigue or clumsiness may bring suit from fellow employees, customers, or the general public. Rejected or underplaced applicants may sue under civil rights laws.

The potential cost is too great, both in the risk of litigation and the risk of physical pain, to continue using arbitrary, poorly assessed standards of fitness or physical skills. Some perennial questions must be faced. For example, a physically demanding task may not be performed often but, when it is, injury might result. Should employment decisions be based on the ability to perform that task? Because of its infrequency, a worker may have little opportunity on the job to develop or maintain the necessary physical skill. On the other hand, infrequency may give time for rest and recovery between occasions. Should the job be redesigned with the rare but risky task assigned to another job with similarly demanding tasks regularly done? Or should such tasks be spread around? Sometimes there is no option. In police work (sometimes defined as boredom occasionally interrupted by panic), the need to meet unusual physical demands is always present. Should physical fitness testing look at the job as a whole or at its maximum requirements? Should it be assessed periodically?

In many jobs, recurring personnel decisions may be made almost daily on employees' here-and-now readiness to work; for example, is this pilot fit to fly today? Is there an impairment that would make this construction worker's job especially dangerous today? Temporary proficiency impairments may be due to medication or drugs (including alcohol), fatigue, illness, or preoccupation with nonwork sources of stress. Drug testing is increasingly widely used, but drug tests or tests for blood alcohol level or body temperature do not assess impairment. It may be more useful to use performance tests of the specific proficiencies required, or perhaps physiological measures of performance impairment.

Sensory and Psychomotor Proficiencies. Work combines cognitive, muscular, sensory, and attitudinal components; a useful work sample might focus on the sensory component. Requisite here-and-now job performance may include sensory proficiency such as correct identification or distinctions of distant shapes, colors, musical pitch, or unseen but touched objects. Except for some classic studies (e.g., occupational vision; see Guion, 1965; McCormick & Ilgen, 1980), little research has addressed the assessment of sensory skill for personnel decisions. Fleishman and Reilly (1992b) identified assessment methods for a few sensory abilities; more importantly, perhaps, they identified some important skills (e.g., night vision) for which no existing measures were identified; these, too, are ripe areas for research.

Psychomotor skills, especially dexterity and coordination, are more widely tested. Especially common is the use of dexterity tests, often requiring examinees to insert pegs or pins in holes. Scores can be the number of pins (or assemblies) inserted within a time period or the amount of time required to fill the board. Examples of tests for other psychomotor skills are provided by Fleishman and Reilly (1992b). Commercial psychomotor tests are available, but sometimes manipulations imitating those required on a job should form the test. Job analysis can identify the recurring stimulus patterns and the kinds of coordinated responses required.

High skill levels in some sensory or psychomotor areas may compensate for deficiencies in others, in work as in more general life skills. The compensatory development of unusual auditory skills among the legally blind is one example; the extraordinary skin and muscle sensitivity of the deaf and blind Helen Keller is legendary. Examples need not be so dramatic to have implications for personnel management. Rehabilitation counselors tell about people lacking certain sensory (or motor) skills performing well on jobs many employers would have denied them. Hope for finding compensatory skills is based more on anecdotes than on research. Evidence does not yet lead to general propositions about genuinely compensatory patterns.

COMPUTERIZED TESTING

Technological change can make tests obsolete (e.g., stenographic tests used circa 1940) or create opportunities. Computerized technologies offer new ways to do conventional testing and new ways to do unconventional testing.

In large public jurisdictions, several thousand candidates might be tested simultaneously in different locations with different test administrators. Beyond logistics challenges, mass testing may pose psychometric problems only for tests requiring rigid time limits; differences among examiners in timing accuracy are a source of error. Even appropriate speeded tests are avoided because a timing error may unfairly disqualify or give unfair advantage to examinees in at least one location.

Computerized testing can solve the practical problem of controlling instructions and time limits. There are other psychometric advantages as well. By controlling the time for individual items, rather than an overall time limit, all subjects can attempt all items, and internal consistency analysis is feasible. Individual item characteristics can be changed, such as changing item difficulty by changing the item's exposure time.

Computers also allow for the visual projection of items and even visually presented episodes. Video tests have been reported for assessing situational judgment in customer service jobs, among others, with gratifying validity coefficients (e.g., Chan & Schmitt, 1997; Dalessio, 1994).

A major advantage of computerized testing is that Item banks can be created and calibrated according to stable item characteristics (either those of classical test theory or IRT). Computers can draw items according to specifications to make up unique test forms for each examinee, permitting a large number of psychometrically equivalent forms to be generated from the bank. Item banking therefore offers a potential advantage for both test security and the common problem of retesting. Two different candidates may see some common items, but item differences would be substantial enough to reduce the test security problems associated, for example, with item memorization.

Computerized Adaptive Tests (CAT)

Conventional testing is also known as *linear testing*; all items are presented one after another to all examinees. A high ability person flies through the easy items; only hard items show just how able that person is. Linear testing is therefore an inefficient use of testing time.

Adaptive testing, on the other hand, uses a branching algorithm and, therefore, fewer items. It begins with one item of moderate difficulty; the next one chosen depends on the response given to the first one—and so on until a predetermined criterion for stopping the test has been reached. If the first item is answered correctly, then the next one may be more difficult. If the next one is answered incorrectly, the third item may be between the first two in difficulty. Adaptive testing has long been used in individually administered ability tests, but it required the combination of modern computers and the development of item response theory to bring it to its current level of sophistication.

The discussion of CAT procedures has been brief, partly because of uncertainty about its relevance to personnel assessment and decisions. Adaptive testing can maximize the precision of ability estimation at any point on the ability scale. In personnel decisions, however, precision is important mainly at that part of the scale where most decisions are made. If about 20% of those who apply for a job will actually be hired, and most of those offered a job will accept, then precise measurement would not be very important below the 75th or above the 90th percentile. With good item parameter estimates, a brief conventional test can be developed that distinguishes well within that narrow region, but not in the low or very high scores where such differentiation amounts to little more than a nice psychometric exercise.

ISSUES AND CONTROVERSIES

Setting Cut Scores

A cut score effectively dichotomizes a score distribution, loses information, and, if not near the mean, substantially reduces validity. Dichotomization is rarely recommended. The following situations, however, justify and even require a cut score:

1. Civil service jurisdictions commonly give a test to masses of candidates at one time and do not test again for a year or more. Candidates are listed in an "eligibility list" ordered from those with the highest score to a minimum score. The minimum is a cut score below which examinees may not be listed and no one will be hired.
2. Licenses or certification are intended to certify a useful level of knowledge or skill, a degree of competence presumed to protect the public against incompetence. Certification is not limited to governments. Private organizations, including trade associations, may elect to certify the competence or knowledge of salespeople, technical advisors, repairers, or others whose work affects customers or the public.
3. Hiring may be cyclical. For example, if there is a policy of hiring new graduates from high schools or colleges to work as trainees, most hiring will be done at about graduation time in the spring. Openings may arise at any time through the year. By forecasting the number of openings likely to be needed before the next hiring phase, and with a fairly accurate notion of the score distribution, one can establish a cut score that will provide the necessary number of trainees who can then be assigned to more permanent positions that become available.
4. Assessment may be sequential; an assessment may be scored on a pass–fail dichotomy to decide who gets to the next step. Where many candidates compete for one or a few positions, preliminary screening may be used for all candidates, sav-

ing complete assessments (e.g., assessment centers or complex simulations) for the most promising ones. For some jobs, the preliminary assessment may look for intrinsically disqualifying considerations (e.g., poor spelling among proofreader candidates).

Cut scores are too often established merely for convenience. With them, managers getting a candidate's test score do not need to make any judgment more taxing than whether or not it exceeds the cut point—and no HR person needs to explain more valid decision processes to the managers. This bad habit would not be worth mentioning if it were not so common, so unnecessary, and so costly in terms of assessment usefulness.

The Predicted Yield Method. Distributions of candidate qualifications fluctuate from week to week. Availability of openings also varies. The two may not coincide; the best applicants may present themselves when there are no immediate openings. One large company in a small town had such a problem in hiring skilled clerical workers. The best applicants graduated from high school and community colleges in the spring and usually moved away. The solution was to hire good applicants when available, place them in clerical pools, and promote or transfer employees as positions opened up.

The plan required fairly accurate prediction of the number of openings likely over the coming year and knowledge of the probable distributions of qualifications. A cut score could then be found to permit hiring enough people at graduation to meet the organization's needs for that year. This kind of cut score is not a costly dichotomization; it is based on a top-down policy. In effect, it is an answer to, "If all these people were available when we wanted them, and if we hired from the top-down as positions opened up, how far down the distribution would we go?"

R. L. Thorndike (1949) termed this the *predicted yield policy*. There is no need to hire only in the spring to use the predicted yield method, and the time span need not be so long. The need is for reasonably accurate forecasting of positions to be filled and of score distributions. These require good record keeping and research. Number of openings is estimated by knowing of planned retirements and transfers or promotions. Records of past experience with turnover due to sickness, death, or family-related resignations can help. Reasonably accurate forecasts are more likely if informed by research on subsamples; reasons for turnover, for example, may be related to age or gender. Expected organizational changes must also be considered.

Estimating the number of available applicants requires knowledge of economic and employment trends. Local influences should be considered, such as the possible closing of a major business or arrival of a new one. Such factors influence not only an overall number of applicants but the pattern of applicant flow. Test score distributions may be different for different groups of people; they may differ substantially in different local communities. Setting useful cut scores requires realistic knowledge of local distributions, requiring reliable local norms. As time goes by, the original cut score may prove too high or too low to provide the predicted yield—or the predicted number of openings is too high or low—and adjustments may be appropriate.

Regression-Based Methods. Figure 10.2 shows four kinds of relations. Panel *a* shows a positive, linear regression. Panel *b* shows a positive but nonlinear monotonic regression. In either case, top-down selection is appropriate; a critical score can be based on predicted criterion level.

Panel *c* is a positive monotone up to a point, after which the curve levels off and differences in X have no associated differences in Y. Above that point, people with different scores should all be considered the same.

Panel *d* (relatively rare) is nonmonotonic. The curve is positive up to a point, after which increases in X are associated with criterion decreases. In such a case, both low and high critical scores

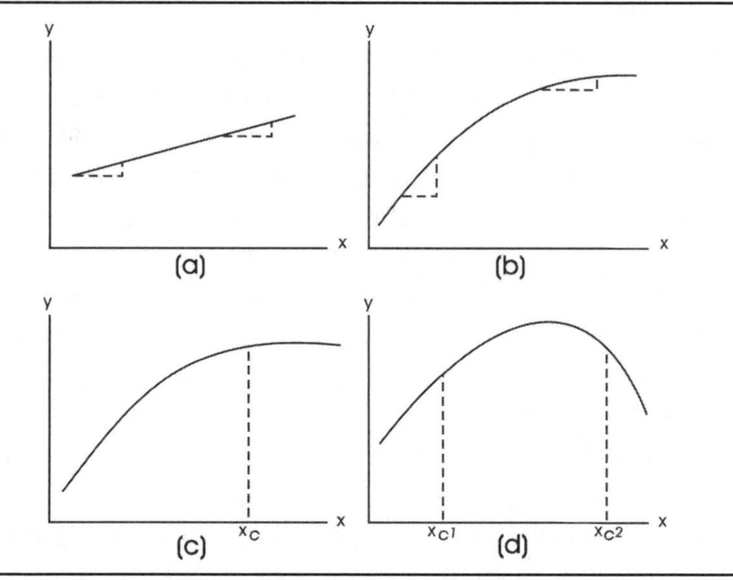

FIG. 10.2. Kinds of relationships of test scores to performance.
From Guion, R. M. (1991). Personnel assessment, selection, and placement. In M. D. Dunnette & L. M. Hough (Eds.), *Handbook of industrial and organizational psychology* (2nd ed., Vol 2, pp. 327–397). Palo Alto, CA: Consulting Psychologists Press.

might be set to screen out extreme scorers likely to be unsatisfactory. Such patterns seem more likely with personality than with cognitive tests.

In any of these cases, it is possible to base a cut score or two on predicted levels of performance. If a criterion level can be identified that is too low, such as not being able to keep up with a work flow and resulting in lost time for others, the regression equation can be used to identify an associated critical test score or minimum qualification.

Cut scores can be established by working *backward* through a regression equation. Thus:

$$Desired\ Performance\ Score = a + bX$$

A manager can specify a performance level that is desired of all new hires. The equation is then solved for X, the score needed on the predictor to achieve the desired performance level.

Translations of Psychometric Instruments

Multinational organizations, and some within a single country, face a special problem in testing people who speak different languages. Mere translation is not the simple matter it would appear. Literal translations, even if possible, may not have the same psychological meaning in two languages; score equivalence is unattainable with literal translation. Translation by "centering" (getting the gist of the meaning) and acceptable back-translation into the original language seems to give equivalent meaning, but that does not assure equivalence in inferences from scores; centering may change psychometric properties dramatically, including constructs measured. Cultural differences can influence scores and their interpretation at least as much as language differences. Cross-cultural testing faces at least three kinds of problems: differences in approaches to tests, problems of test administration, and score equivalence.

Two psychometric considerations should govern test translations. First, test item parameters must match in the original and translated versions. Item matching is best done by IRT. Perhaps not every item would be translated to achieve precisely the same parameters in a 3-parameter model, but the distributions of item parameters could be kept comparable. Second, the two versions should be pretty much equally valid measures of the same constructs. Do various antecedent and subsequent correlates behave similarly? Do both versions escape the same contaminating sources of variance? Positive answers say that the tests are measuring the same constructs.

Instead of translating a test developed in one country into the language of another, Schmit, Kihm, and Robie (2000) described the development of a "global" personality measure. The idea behind their approach was to develop the measure globally, beginning with item writing, through to item translation and data analysis. Alternatively, multinational companies can treat operations in each country as independent and develop locally valid assessment procedures. With this option, the entire test development process can take place within the culture, cultural factors influence construct definition, item writing, instruction development, and all of the developmental research. This option makes sense only if "home country" and local personnel are not competing for the same opportunities, such as promotion to a specified position. Whether a construct important to performance in one culture is also important in another is a problem cross-cultural staffing needs to address.

Tests and Controversy

Testing, and personnel assessment generally, is and has been controversial. There are controversies among psychometrically trained experts, among people trained in different test-using disciplines, between psychometric professionals and people outside of these professions, and in society generally. In the face of all the fuss, it is strange that testing remains an important basis for so many kinds of decisions. Few people would want to get rid of various kinds of licensing exams, despite their sometimes serious deficiencies. The cry for educational proficiency exams has been translated into law in many states. Government civil service procedures using merit examination concepts grew out of disenchantment with less objective bases for selection.

In the face of controversy, it is well to remember that tests have compiled a good track record. They have successfully predicted performance on jobs and other kinds of criteria as well. Put together in a battery of tests measuring different things, groups of tests have even better records.

They are good, they are useful, but they are imperfect. Perfection cannot reasonably be expected; too many other things influence criteria for test scores to predict them perfectly. Even so, there is room for improvement. Many things we do well with tests can be done better and with greater understanding. Things we do not do so well with tests provide still greater challenges. The search for new and better ways to measure candidate qualifications, and for new and better definitions of the nature of the qualifying traits, should go forward. However, a lot of bright new ideas, once thought promising, have been tried and have withered. Psychometric history is strewn with the remnants of once grand new ideas. Many tests that were supposed to measure more important constructs than those traditionally measured have gone out of print with only negative findings resulting from their use. Item types once hailed as panaceas have left the scene in ignominious defeat. Enthusiasm for new ways, commendable as it is, is no substitute for data.

New ideas usually build on old ones. In a new century, there is strong urging for new approaches to measurement and assessment, approaches that do not build on old principles but seek to replace traditional testing with new constructs and methods. Many new ideas are not as different as their enthusiastic proponents assume. Proponents should amass data to show that the expected merits of the new ideas do in fact obtain, that they match or exceed those of the old ones, and that the substitution of the new for the old does not result in losing valued merits of the old without compensating new merits. In short, new ideas in measurement should be sought, articulated, and tried. But we should not allow them to be embraced, adopted, and swallowed whole without competent trial and empirical comparison with the old.

DISCUSSION TOPICS

1. What is the difference between typical and maximal performance? How is this distinction relevant to choice of tests for selection?
2. Should test makers strive for high "fidelity"? What are the advantages and disadvantages?
3. Is there ever a good reason to use a cutoff score?

11

Assessing Via Ratings

Rating Formats
Rater Training
Evaluation Process

Ratings are ubiquitous. Ratings of job performance are common; they are also used in many other assessment methods. Raters may be peers, superiors, or subordinates; they may be outsiders used for special purposes or used because of their special expertise. One person or several, working independently or as a panel, may do the rating. Ratings may be criteria or predictors. More research has been done on ratings of job performance than on ratings for other purposes, but it is relevant to other purposes and settings. This chapter emphasizes *performance ratings*. The focus is on *ratings as assessment methods,* not on their use in performance management.

Performance rating predates scientific psychology. Robert Owen, an early 19th-century English industrialist and Utopian, developed a "silent monitor," which was a tapered wooden object about 4 inches long painted and numbered on the four sides. Each day, the supervisor would turn one side forward for each employee to indicate conduct the day before. Conduct consisted of hard work, being on time, producing well, and so forth. The black side, numbered 4, was shown for "bad" conduct. "Indifferent" was blue and numbered 3, "good" was yellow and numbered 2, and "excellent" was white and numbered 1. A rating could be appealed to Mr. Owen; after time for appeal elapsed, the rating was recorded in a "book of character" (M. Cole, 1953, p. 56).

Rating requires at least three things: a *source* of information, preferably observation or records; *organizing* and *remembering* that information in preparation for rating; and quantitatively *evaluating* what was remembered according to some rule. Remembering observations is central. In rating a product, the time from observation to evaluation is a few minutes; for annual job performance ratings, it might be a full year.

Whatever the use, ratings are psychometric measurements, even if not very precise. Ratings are often held in low esteem as measurements. They are victim to countless forms of error, both random and systematic. Kane (1987) claimed the field of personnel psychology is stagnant because it cannot adequately measure its major dependent variable, work performance. However, J. P. Campbell, McCloy, Oppler, and Sager (1992, p. 55) said, "Although ratings generally have bad press, the overall picture is not as bleak as might be expected," and claimed that ratings are more likely to be explained by actual ratee performance than by contaminants. Yet, they agree that there are problems. Ratings need all the help they can get, and most of the attempts to help have come mainly in three forms: to improve rating formats, to train raters, and to influence the evaluation process.

RATING METHODS

Ratings can be based on scales, comparisons, or checklists. They can be used for overall assessment or for assessment of more specific dimensions. Sometimes diagnostic ratings of relative strengths and weaknesses are made. Some predictive hypotheses specify that a predictor should be related more to some aspects of work rather than others. Some call for a global, overall rating. Methods and formats should fit needs.

Graphic Rating Scales

Graphic rating scales are the most common of all rating methods. They can be used for overall ratings, but they are used more often to rate different aspects or dimensions of overall performance. Variants of graphic rating scales are shown in Fig. 11.1. The basic form is *a*, with *b* showing how ratings become numbers. Some users prefer to give more structure to the scale by using verbal phrases instead of numbers, as in *c*. Numbers or words anchor the scale points.

The number of scale divisions varies widely; it is usually an odd number with "average" occupying a central position in the scale. More discrimination may be needed at the "above average" levels, so scales like *d* can put average somewhat off center. Eliminating the basic line, as in *e*, eliminates problems in knowing where a rater means to put a sometimes hasty check mark, as does scale *f*, which includes verbal anchors and more definition of the performance trait being rated. The numerical and verbal anchors are combined in *g*, which also uses more and finer gradations from the low to the high end of the scale. How many response categories is an optimal number? Little discrimination is possible with only two or three (although this may be enough when several ratings are added for an overall rating). It is probably absurd to ask raters to make distinctions along a 25-point range (although scale *g* simplifies the task by asking, in effect, for sequential judgments identifying first a group of 5 units). The 5-point scale is so widely used that it seems as if it had been ordained on tablets of stone. Some writers put the limit at 9 scale points, but it is an arbitrary decision; there is little evidence that the number of scale units matters much, and the choice comes down to the researchers' preferences.

Scale *h* also combines verbal and numerical anchoring for eight possible responses. Numerical values of the responses can be

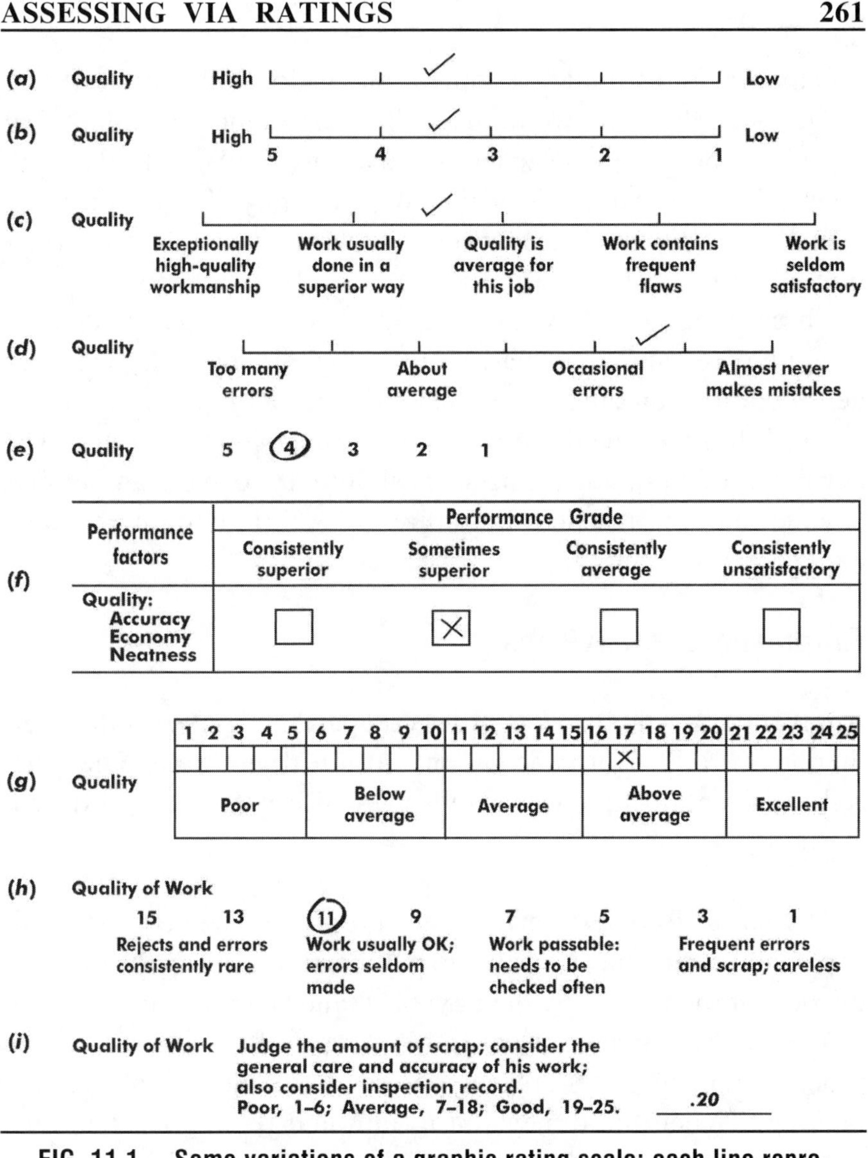

FIG. 11.1. Some variations of a graphic rating scale; each line represents one way in which a judgment of the quality of a person's work may be recorded. From Guion (1965).

changed according to the relative importance of the dimension being rated. In the example, "quality" has been prejudged to be worth a maximum of 15 points; other dimensions might have a maximum value of 8 or 10 or 30 or more points in a differential weighting scheme. If, for example, "cooperation" is deemed to be worth 25 points, then the scale would have different numerical values, but would still be placed in 8 response positions. Scale *i* entirely abandons the visual scale; it does not aid the rater by dividing the scale visually into 5 broader categories. It does, however, further structure the rating task by defining more clearly what is to be rated.

These variations show that the rater's task can be changed by changing the nature and clarity of the anchors that define the values at points along the scale, the nature of the required response, and the clarity of the definition of the dimension to be rated. The developer of a graphic rating scale should try to avoid ambiguity; beyond that, the research literature gives little help in choosing one format over another.

Employee Comparisons

Another well-established practice compares the ratee to others, either on overall performance or on multiple dimensions. The usual result is a ranking of ratees, achieved in different ways by different methods.

Method of Rank Order. Ratees might be listed on a sheet of paper, and raters may be asked to put the number 1 by the name of the best of the lot, a 2 by the next best, and so on through the list. Names might be placed on cards to be arranged. A more systematic procedure, using cards presented in random order, is "alternation ranking." When the dimension to be rated (e.g., conscientiousness, or overall job performance) is understood, the rater first identifies the best of the lot on that dimension and then the poorest. Cards with these names are pulled and the sorting has begun. Of the remaining names, the rater again selects the best and the poorest and places those cards accordingly. The process of alternating from best to worst continues until all have been ranked. The task gets progressively harder; extreme judgments are easy, but differences near the center of the distribution are harder to identify.

Method of Forced Distribution. When many people are to be rated and fine distinctions are not needed, gross ranking can be done with a *forced distribution*. This is a variant of graphic rating scales in that each person is assigned to a category in frequencies that mimics the assumption of a normal distribution. A number of categories is chosen (typically 5, rarely more than 9), and proportions of distributions (translated into frequencies) to be placed in each category are specified. A 5-category example is shown in Fig. 11.2. A rater with 38 names to rank writes the names of the 4 top people in Column A, the names of the next best 8 people in Column B, and so on.

Method of Paired Comparisons. Each ratee can be compared to each of the others in a set. For each pair of names, the rater indicates the better one on some specified dimension; the top of the rank order is the one chosen most frequently. The same name should not appear in two consecutive pairs; each person should be listed first and second equally often. There might be a lot of pairs;

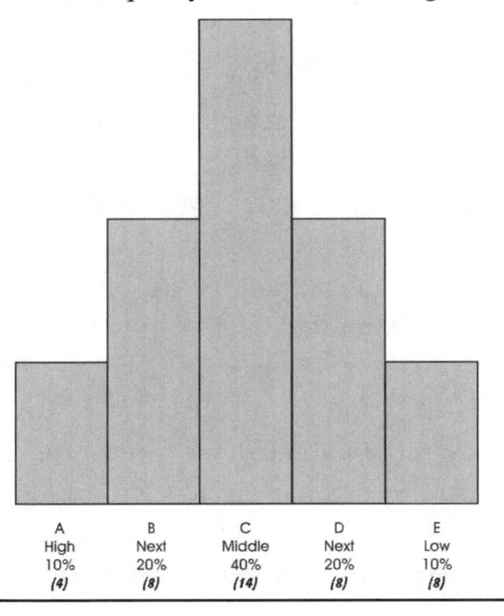

FIG. 11.2. A sample form for forced distribution ratings; numbers in parentheses show how a rater with 38 people to rate should distribute them. From Guion (1965).

if 5 people are to be compared, then there are 20 pairs of names. Ten people require 45 pairs, and 20 people require 190 pairs.[1] Lawshe and Balma (1966) provided tables for setting up such pairs. The number of times a given name is preferred can be transformed into a standard score scale, often with a mean of 50 and standard deviation of 10. With a long list of people to be compared, the amount of time required can get out of hand. Reasonable people disagree about how long is too long. Guilford (1954) put the limit at about 15, but Lawshe, Kephart, and McCormick (1949) reported that a list of 24 names (276 pairs) was rated reliably in 30 minutes—not an excessively wearying task, and one that could be shortened using modern computers.

Behavioral Descriptions

It seems reasonable to assume that raters can offer better assessments if they avoid glittering generalities or ambiguities and describe specific on-the-job behavior or outcomes.

Behaviorally Anchored Rating Scales (BARS). P. C. Smith and Kendall (1963) described a logic of rating and a procedure for developing a rating system. Many rating scales have been said to follow the Smith and Kendall approach, but they do so only if using a full system of supervisory observation, recording, and rating of behavior. It was the form, and its use of scaled behavioral anchors, that attracted attention and resulted in the generic term *behaviorally anchored rating scales* (BARS). The many rating methods called BARS, and some criticisms of BARS not relevant to the procedures recommended by Smith and Kendall, called forth a clarification by Bernardin and P. C. Smith (1981). They pointed out that the Smith–Kendall approach was a sequence beginning with observation followed in order by inference, scaling,

[1]These numbers assume that each pair is compared only once; the number of pairs is $n(n-1)/2$, where n is the number of people to be ranked. Every pair can be listed twice using both orders of presentation, but this requires twice as many pairs.

recording, and summary rating.[2] We provide only a rudimentary summary here.

Table 11.1 outlines the general steps in developing a BARS. First, the behavioral anchors were not intended to describe behavior a rater had actually observed; they were descriptions of behavioral *expectations* at different levels of performance on specified dimensions—examples that might be anticipated or "expected" of a ratee at any of these levels, even if they did not actually occur. They were "expectations" in the sense of "That's just the sort of thing you come to expect from Joe."[3]

TABLE 11.1

General Steps in Developing a BARS

Step #	*Description*
1	Convene one or more groups of potential raters.
2	Develop a list of the performance dimensions that should be evaluated.
3	Develop definitions of high, low, and acceptable performance for each dimension.
4	Develop lists of behavioral examples of high, low, and acceptable performance.
5	Give the lists of behavioral expectations and the dimension definitions to one or more new groups of potential raters not included in the first groups.
6	Designate judges among potential raters to identify the behavioral examples, within each dimension, that describe a worker whose performance is outstanding and another whose performance is unsatisfactory.
7	Give statements that survived the preceding steps to judges from another group of potential raters for scaling by the method of equal appearing intervals.
8	Develop and distribute a final rating form to raters before ratings are due.

[2]Some say that the method has evolved, and evolution accounts for the variety. It can be said more accurately that it has been distorted by treating it merely as another rating format, without treating the form as part of a system.

[3]Expectations, in the Smith–Kendall sense, are anticipations of reality, not idealistic dreams of job demands or obligations.

The second key provision is *retranslation,* which is a procedure to assure that behavioral statements originally written for a certain dimension are seen by others as illustrations of that dimension. The procedure is analogous to that in translating a passage from one language into another. A first group of judges writes behavioral expectations to fit each dimension. A second, independent, group of judges reads statements for all dimensions, mixed together in random order, discusses definitions of the dimensions for a common understanding, and then independently allocates each statement to a dimension. A "good" item is allocated by most judges to the dimension for which it was developed. If there is no modal agreement about where it belongs, then the statement is dropped.

The third key provision minimizes ambiguity of scale value by having judges sort statements on a range from extremely unfavorable to extremely favorable. The variance of judgments is a measure of the ambiguity of the statement; high variance statements are eliminated.

A fourth feature of the Smith–Kendall procedure is usually ignored. It permits raters to give at least one example of ratee behavior actually observed for each dimension rated. It could be inserted at that place on the scale that appropriately identifies its position relative to the defining anchors.

The term *BARS* has come to mean a kind of rating scale format that uses only some of the Smith–Kendall procedures. Figure 11.3 illustrates a BARS format; it used the Smith–Kendall procedures for scale definitions and for generating, retranslating, and scaling behavioral expectations. It does not illustrate a procedure for getting continuous observations and recording them as part of the rating process. Note, however, a difference in the form from traditional graphic scales: The scale separation marks are not the scale points that are anchored. True, there are very general descriptions apparently anchoring the top, bottom, and midpoint of the scale (shown on the left). Instead, the scale values anchored are those of the behavioral examples, shown by the arrow pointing from the statement

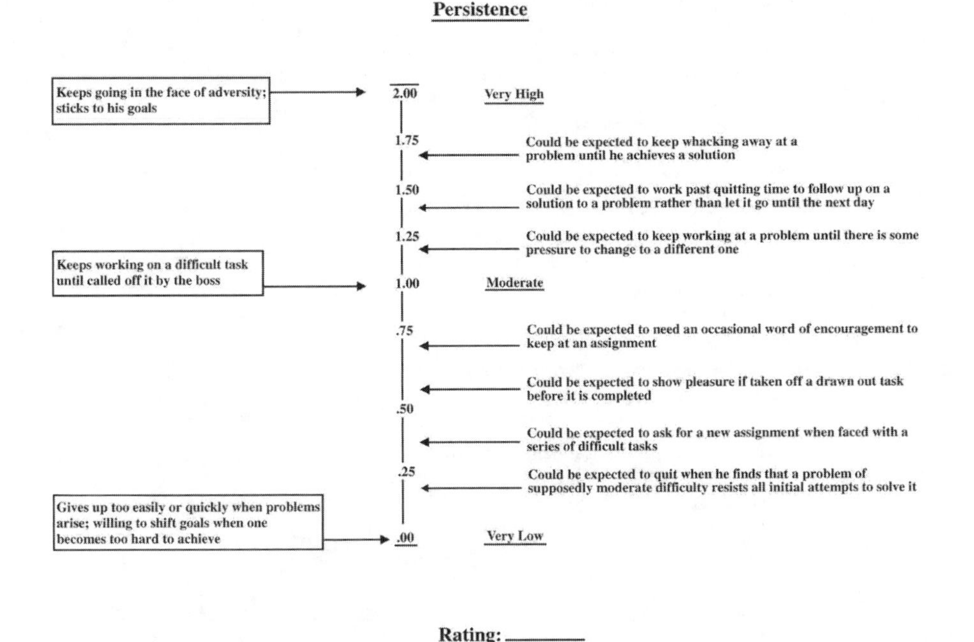

FIG. 11.3. One example of a behaviorally anchored rating form devised using some key features of the retranslation of expectations; it is a form for measuring an aspect of motivation, work persistence, in a group of engineers.

to the scale. A rater can decide which statements exemplify the kinds of behavior one might expect from the ratee.

Behavioral Observation Scales (BOS). Instead of largely unobserved behavioral expectations, Latham and Wexley (1981) rated actually required job behaviors, grouping them for specific job dimensions. Their scales are called *behavioral observation scales* (BOS). The response scale is *frequency* of observation, a 5-point scale ranging from 1 (*almost never*) to 5 (*almost always*) as shown in Fig. 11.4. The five points are defined in terms of the percent of the time the behavior is observed. Latham and Wexley (1981) suggested percentages of 0%–64% for (*almost never*) through 65%–74%, 75%–84%, 85%–94%, and 95%–100% (*al-*

1. Overcoming resistance to Change*

(1) Describes the details of the change to subordinates.
Almost never 1 2 3 4 5 Almost always

(2) Explains why the change is necessary.
Almost never 1 2 3 4 5 Almost always

(3) Discusses how the change will affect the employee.
Almost never 1 2 3 4 5 Almost always

(4) Listens to the employee's concerns.
Almost never 1 2 3 4 5 Almost always

(5) Asks the employee for help in making the change work.
Almost never 1 2 3 4 5 Almost always

(6) If necessary, specifies the date for a follow-up meeting to respond to the employee's concerns.
Almost never 1 2 3 4 5 Almost always

Total = ______________

Below Adequate	Adequate	Full	Excellent	Superior*
6-10	11-15	16-20	21-25	26-30

*Scores are set by management.

FIG. 11.4. A behavioral observation scale for assessing a manager's skill in overcoming resistance to change.
From Latham, G. P., & Wexley, K. N. (1981). *Increasing productivity through performance appraisal.* Reading, MA: Addison-Wesley. Reprinted with permission.

most always); they have also reported using a straightforward 20% increment for each scale point.

BOS can be developed in less time than BARS because prior item scaling is not needed. If job analysis is well done and well organized, behavioral statements should be prepared with minimal effort and time. Job analysis surveys may be too elemental; if so, job experts may consolidate elementary items into broader, more comprehensive statements. Items are usually considered equally weighted, but differential weights could be assigned by expert judgment. The job relevance of the ratings is obvious.

An important feature of the BOS is that the evaluation takes place in scale development, not during the rating process itself. In other words, the developers of the rating instrument determine what behaviors should be engaged in frequently. The rater, therefore, is merely an observer and reporter, rather than an evaluator.

Although the BOS is aimed at minimizing rater involvement in the evaluation process, by simply asking the person to report frequency with which the behaviors occur, we suspect that rater evaluation is commonly injected into the frequency reports. Certainly, a supervisor can see which behaviors lead to a positive evaluation, and which lead to a negative. Moreover, prototypes of effective employees are likely to influence frequency reports as much or more than the actual behavior of the ratee. An advantage of the method, however, is that it clearly communicates to the ratee which behaviors should be engaged in frequently, and which behaviors should be avoided.

Behavior Summary Scales (BSS). Assume a rating scale like Row *h* in Fig. 11.1, where each of a few descriptors covers a range of scale values. Now replace those relatively vague descriptors with a set of behavioral statements, each of which consolidates or summarizes a larger number of highly specific behavioral examples. The result could be a behavior summary scale (BSS) like that shown for Navy recruiters in Fig. 11.5 (Borman, 1986).

To develop these scales, expert recruiters generated hundreds of examples of specific behavior in a two-day workshop; others were derived from stories told by recruits about experiences with recruiters. Content analysis resulted in nine performance categories. Eliminating redundancies and retranslating the remainder resulted in a pool of 352 examples. In BARS development, a few of these with the least variance in scale values, with scale values scattered nicely throughout the range, would be used. Instead, the group described by Borman tried to write more general summaries so that the summaries would represent, as much as possible, the

Establishing and Maintaining Good Relationships in the Community

Contacting and working effectively with high school counselors, newspaper editors, radio and TV personnel, and others capable of helping recruiters to enlist prospects; building a good reputation for the navy by developing positive relationships with persons in the community; establishing and maintaining good relationships with parents and family of prospects; presenting a good navy image in the community.

9 or 10

Extremely Effective Performance

Is exceptionally adept a cultivating and maintaining excellent relationships with school counselors, teachers, principals, police, news media persons, local business persons, and other persons who are important for getting referrals and free advertising.

Is innovative in informing the public about the navy; actively promotes the navy and makes friends for the navy while doing it; always distributes the most current navy information.

Volunteers off-duty time to work on community projects, celebrations, parades, etc.

6, 7, or 8

Effective Performance

Spends productive time with individuals such as police, city government, or school officials; may lunch with them, distribute calendars, appointment books, buttons, etc., to them, and/or invite them for cocktails.

Arranges for interested persons such navy activities as trips to the Naval Academy; keeps relevant persons informed of navy activities.

Encourages principals, counselors, and other persons important to a prospect to call if they have any questions about the navy.

3, 4, or 5

Marginal Performance

Contacts school officials only sporadically; keeps them waiting for information they want; relationships with counselors, teachers, etc., and persons important to an applicant or recruit are distant and underdeveloped.

Is not alert to opportunities to promote the navy; rarely volunteers off-duty time to promote the navy and is unenthusiastic when approached to do something for the community; rarely accepts speaking invitations.

Is, at times, discourteous to persons in the community; for example, sends form letters to persons who assisted him or other navy recruiters; is not always alert to the family's desire for more information about the navy and the program in which their son or daughter enlisted.

1 or 2

Ineffective Performance

Does not contact high school counselors; does not accept speaking engagements; drives around in car instead of getting out and meeting people.

Alienates persons in community or persons important to an applicant by ignoring them, not answering their questions, responding rudely, demanding information, encouraging high school students to drop out of school; sometimes does not appear at recruiting presentations for which he or she is scheduled.

Presents negative image of the navy by doing things like driving while intoxicated or speeding and honking impatiently at other drivers; may express dislike for the navy or recruiting.

FIG. 11.5. A behavior summary scale to rate navy recruiter performance. From Borman, W. C. (1986). Behavior-based rating scales. In R. A. Berk (Ed.), *Performance assessment: Methods and applications* (pp. 100–120). Baltimore: Johns Hopkins University Press. Reprinted with permission.

content of all 352 examples. It took two steps. First, all examples were grouped into four levels (as shown in Fig. 11.5); then, three statements were written describing the content of examples at each level.

Forced Choice Scales. Sisson (1948), finding at the outbreak of World War II that performance ratings used by the U.S. Army did not help distinguish officers ready for promotion from others, developed a new, more differentiating system known as *forced choice ratings*. The method used tetrads of four descriptive statements, each with two statements about equally favorable and two equally unfavorable. Prior research determined, for every statement, a preference index (P) for favorability and a discrimination index (D) of how well the statement distinguished between those independently identified as superior and others. Let + indicate high preference or discrimination and – indicate low; every tetrad had statements described as P+D+, P+D–, P–D+, and P–D–. The rater chose one statement as most descriptive and another as least descriptive, without knowing the scoring key (which was limited to discriminating items). The method gave valid ratings, but raters resisted use of a system they could not control.

PSYCHOMETRIC RESEARCH ON RATINGS

Regardless of purpose or quality, ratings are measures. Questions and issues in the psychometric evaluation of tests and other assessments apply also to ratings, with added ones as well.

Measurement implies individual differences in the trait measured, and they imply variance and the evaluation of possible sources of variance in the resulting measures. Variance in ratings (or "scores") should, of course, be mainly associated with variance in the actual performance of ratees. Variance in the ratings also stems from influences of the measurement procedure, irrelevant worker characteristics, characteristics of the situation in which performance is measured, and characteristics of the raters. In short, common psychometric problems are exacerbated in ratings.

Constructs Assessed

Constructs rated are rarely well defined, so psychometric validation of ratings is difficult. Factor analyses has been used with sets of ratings to identify underlying dimensions, and other forms of correlational analysis have been used to see whether different ratings of presumably the same constructs correlate well with each other but not with ratings presumed to assess dissimilar constructs. One serious problem with this approach is that so-called convergent validity, or of interrater reliability, may be little more than evidence of converging biases.

Agreement, Reliability, and Generalizability

Interrater agreement is often treated as a form of reliability, but agreement and reliability are different. Judges agree if they make the same ratings; they are reliable if they put ratees in roughly the same relative order. The distinction is clear in Table 11.2. Reliability can be high without agreement about the degree to which the characteristic being judged describes the ratees (Case 2). It can be low without necessarily meaning much disagreement among raters (Case 3). Both agreement and reliability are useful information about a set of subjective ratings.

Which statistic do you want? The answer depends on the intended use. If the ratings are used as validation criteria, then interrater reliability (or "rate–rerate" reliability of a single rater) is more important because reliability limits validity. If the ratings are to be used for decisions based on level of proficiency, or if they are to aid interpretations of correlated test score levels, then agreement is more important.

TABLE 11.2

Hypothetical Ratings Illustrating Different Levels of Interrater Agreement and Interrater Reliability for Interval-Scaled Data

	Case 1: High Interrater Agreement and High Interrater Reliability			*Case 2: Low Interrater Agreement and High Interrater Reliability*			*Case 3: High Interrater Agreement and Low Interrater Reliability*		
	Rater			*Rater*			*Rater*		
Ratee	*1*	*2*	*3*	*1*	*2*	*3*	*1*	*2*	*3*
A	1	1	1	1	3	5	5	4	4
B	2	2	2	1	3	5	5	4	3
C	3	3	3	2	4	6	5	4	5
D	3	3	3	2	4	6	4	4	5
E	4	4	4	3	5	7	5	4	3
F	5	5	5	3	5	7	5	5	4
G	6	6	6	4	6	8	4	4	5
H	7	7	7	4	6	8	5	5	4
I	8	8	8	5	7	9	4	5	3
J	9	9	9	5	7	9	5	5	5
M	4.8	4.8	4.8	3.0	5.0	7.0	4.7	4.4	4.1
SD	2.7	2.7	2.7	1.5	1.5	1.5	.5	.5	.9

Note. "Interrater Reliability and Agreement of Subjunctive Judgments," by H. E. A. Tinsley and D. J. Weiss, 1975, *Journal of Counseling Psychology, 22,* pp. 358–376. Copyright by American Psychological Association. Reprinted with permission.

ESTIMATING RATER AGREEMENT

With two raters, each rating all ratees, and only a few rating categories, an easy index of agreement is the percentage of ratees assigned to the same categories by both raters. Suppose, for example, that the manager and assistant manager of a restaurant independently classify every candidate for entry-level work; a candidate might be considered further for kitchen work, dining area work, or neither;

assume the pattern of agreements and disagreements in Table 11.3.

Summing actual proportions in the diagonal cells shows 46% agreement. Is 46% substantial, reasonable, or poor agreement? To answer, consider the expected (chance) proportion of agreement. The corresponding sum based on marginal proportions is 38%. Is 46% agreement enough greater than chance (38%) to justify further this way to assess candidates? The answer to this, too, is a judgment call, but several indices of rater agreement have built in consideration of chance agreement. An early index was *kappa* (Cohen, 1960), κ, appropriate for the case with two raters and nominal ratings:

$$\kappa = (p_a - p_c)/(1 - p_c)(1)$$

where p_a = actual proportion of agreements, and p_c = expected or chance proportion of agreements. For Table 11.3, κ = .13. For perfect agreement, κ = 1.00, so this is not at all a pleasing level of agreement, quite apart from questions of statistical significance.

TABLE 11.3

A Matrix of Agreements, Expressed as Proportions

		Manager			*Marginal*
		K[a]	*D*	*N*	*Total*
	K	.06 (.02)[b]	.10 (.08)	.04 (.10)	.20
Assistant	D	.04 (.04)	.15 (.16)	.21 (.20)	.40
Manager	N	.00 (.04)	.15 (.16)	.25 (.20)	.40
Σ Margin		.10	.40	.50	1.00

[a]Raters indicated that the candidate should be considered further for kitchen work (K), that the candidate should be considered further for dining area work (D), or that the candidate need not be considered further for either area (N). [b]Actual proportions of assignments to a cell are given first; proportions in parentheses are expected proportions based on the marginal totals.

As part of the Job Performance Measurement Project in the military services of the United States, Kraiger (1990) studied experimental performance ratings in each of four Air Force specialties. The major source of variance in all four specialties was not ratees, but the interaction of ratees with rating sources. Increasing the number of raters, if they are reasonably independent and parallel, will increase reliability; Kraiger (1990) concluded, on the basis of his full data, that the generalizability of these ratings (unlike their classical reliability estimates) can best be improved by averaging ratings from more sources. Raters with different perspectives will see different pieces of information about any given ratee; averaging across these perspectives can give opportunity for more relevant information to influence composite ratings.

Validity of Ratings as Predictors

Performance ratings are often criteria but can be predictors. Ratings are incorporated in interviews, assessment centers, work samples, portfolios of past achievements, auditions, or free-response tests; note that the predictor in these assessment methods is not the interview, assessment center, or whatever; it is the rating summarizing someone's judgment based on observations. Evaluation of job-relatedness of ratings is done just as it is for other predictors.

Psychometrically, validity describes inferred meaning. Ratings are too often accepted uncritically as meaning whatever the rating scale label says, even when raters, if challenged to define the label, would not agree. Competent evidence of psychometric validity is rarely sought; in fact, most often, no psychometric evaluation occurs at all beyond possible checks on interrater agreement or reliability.

Bias as Invalidity

Ratee characteristics not being rated are sources of bias if they influence ratings; they reduce validity. In a widely cited meta-analysis, Kraiger and Ford (1985) found that raters gave higher ratings to ratees of their own race. Later, however, Sackett and DuBois (1991) compared the Kraiger and Ford (1985) findings with those in gigantic USES and Project A data sets. In the USES data, and in the Army technical proficiency and personal discipline ratings, both White and Black raters gave higher mean ratings to Whites. For military bearing, Blacks received higher ratings from both Black and White raters. Why did these big studies differ from that by Kraiger and Ford? Sackett and DuBois (1991) wondered and looked at the studies by Black raters in the Kraiger–Ford meta-analysis. Two were lab studies, four used peer ratings; of the eight supervisory ratings studies, four were done before 1970. They concluded that the finding of higher ratings within same race rater–ratee pairs were premature. The Sackett and DuBois (1991) comparison of pre- and post-1970 studies suggests that research findings, particularly when major social issues are involved, are specific to the times, to the zeitgeist, in which they are obtained—as Cronbach (1975) warned. Perhaps this presumed interaction is another example where social change—greater acceptance of diversity—has resulted in a change of what is scientifically demonstrable.

THE RATER IN THE RATING PROCESS

The Classical Psychometric Errors

Central Tendency. Some raters cluster all ratings around a central point on the scale, a midpoint or a subjective average, resulting in low variance. Central tendency seems to indicate raters who avoid unpleasant consequences by avoiding extreme ratings.

Leniency or Severity. Some raters are easy, some hard; some lenient, others severe. Early discussions of the leniency error described it as giving higher ratings to people the rater knows; the more general idea of habitual leniency or severity in rating has long been included in the definition and is now dominant. Raters with very high mean ratings are considered systematically lenient; those with low means are systematically severe.

Halo. E. L. Thorndike defined *halo error* as a "marked tendency to think of the person in general as rather good or rather inferior and to color the judgments of the [specific performance dimensions] by this general feeling" (E. L. Thorndike, 1920, p. 25, as quoted by Balzer & Sulsky, 1992, p. 975). According to Balzer and Sulsky (1992), his work used contradictory definitions of halo: correlations of ratings on specific scales with overall ratings, and intercorrelations among dimension scales. The one operational definition assumes that a general impression influences ratings on dimensions; the other assumes that raters simply fail to distinguish dimensions. Both assumptions of halo lead to spurious intercorrelations.

Dimensions to be rated are ordinarily not orthogonal, so some observed correlations are not errors. The decades of research have "provided documentation that the phenomenon is ubiquitous. More recently, a great deal of effort has been expended on reducing halo, a modest amount on articulating the sources of halo, and surprisingly little on whether haloed ratings are inaccurate" (Cooper, 1981, p. 219). Intercorrelations may be influenced by reality or by the rater's implicit theory of personality or performance; they may also be due to error.

> A simple example of *halo error* is the widespread perception that tall people are better managers than short people. Research has shown that height is more strongly related to *subjective* ratings of performance than to *objective* performance measures (Judge & Cable, 2004).

Other Psychometric Errors

Although prior information about a ratee may have a biasing effect, this effect seems to diminish over time. *Prior impressions* may be based on knowledge of prior ratings. An experiment by Murphy, Balzer, Lockhart, and Eisenman (1985) found that knowledge of a ratee's previous performance rating influenced ratings of subsequent performance. This well-replicated finding has important implications in assessment centers where ratings are made on several dimensions, then discussed in sequence by the panel of raters. A similar concept, called *escalation bias,* was studied by Schoorman (1988). Raters had prior information about ratees; some had participated in decisions to hire them; some had agreed, some did not. The bias effect of participation and agreement with the hiring decision accounted for fully 6% of the rating variance.

Individual Differences in Ability to Rate

Rater Qualifications. Some raters are more qualified to rate than others. The main qualification is relevant knowledge, including knowledge of demands on the ratee as well as understanding ratee behavior. It may include knowledge of the work process and of both desirable and flawed product characteristics. Qualifying knowledge comes from observation or experience, not from hearsay, prejudice, or stereotypes. Typically, although not always, immediate supervisors are more qualified to rate job performance than second level supervisors who are more removed from the person and the work being rated; the relevance of the contact, not merely its frequency, seems to be the key qualification. For some work samples, the most qualified raters may be people who have demonstrated a high level of skill at the work, although highly skilled people may have automatized their skills too thoroughly to observe clearly.

Training. Minimal rater training should include instruction in the meaning of words used on the rating form, the procedure to be followed in making the ratings, and aspects of the judgment process such as avoidance of rating errors. Much can be added.

Borman (1979, p. 418) suggested that rater training might produce, and be evaluated by, three kinds of outcomes: reduction in classical rating errors; improved psychometric validity, including interrater agreement; and improved accuracy. Of these, we think the most practical efforts are those to increase psychometric validity, but most research emphasis has been placed on the other two. According to Bernardin and Buckley (1981), efforts to replace classical errors have amounted to little more than trading in one kind of response set for another. They advocated training that emphasizes observation of behavior, such as:

1. *Diary keeping,* in a formal system, with support at all higher organizational levels assuring that supervisors are themselves evaluated on how well they keep diaries.
2. *Frame of reference (FOR) training,* which involves identifying raters whose ratings are peculiar and helping them develop a common understanding of the dimensions to be rated and of the observations that support different levels of ratings.
3. *Training raters how to be critical.* Many raters hate to give negative ratings. Training might increase ability to handle encounters resulting from negative appraisals (Waung & Highhouse, 1997). Increased self-efficacy in giving feedback is likely to reduce rating errors such as leniency, yet this topic has not received much research attention

Different people may observe a worker's performance from different perspectives, or frames of reference. Usually there is a dominant, modal frame of reference in an organization, maybe not deliberately. With a common frame of reference, raters can define levels of performance effectiveness for different performance dimensions with a common language. To see if there is one, raters can be asked to rate the relative effectiveness of each item in a list of critical behaviors and the importance of job dimensions. Raters who do not agree with most other raters are considered idiosyncratic and targeted for FOR training. They are brought together to consider the job description, to discuss the important performance dimensions, and to understand the differences between "correct" (modal) evaluations and various idiosyncratic ones. Such training uses a conference method of group problem-solving techniques to arrive at a consensus about how rating should be done. Day and Sulsky (1995) considered FOR training the most promising of all rater training methods.

Organizational Level. Self, supervisory, and peer performance ratings typically do not correlate well. People at different organizational levels may have different qualifications to rate. Oppler, Peterson, and McCloy (1994) found that peer and supervisory ratings were predicted by different things and were not interchangeable. They attributed the differences to the greater exposure of peers to fellow trainees, especially in Army settings. These results might also be explained by differences in the constructs most salient at the different levels. Research on supervisory ratings may not apply to other rating problems; self or peer ratings may work better (i.e., be more valid) for some purposes. In assessment centers, assessors are not necessarily supervisors, but they do occupy a hierarchical position of authority; peers may be in a better position to rate some kinds of assessment center performance. Peers may be better judges of certain traits (e.g., work motivation). For some purposes, self ratings may be more valuable, such as self ratings of confidence. For other purposes, other raters may be better: Customers can rate service; experts can rate work sample results; or professional people can rate readiness for something (e.g., readiness to return to work after trauma or to profit from specific training).

Rater Motivation. Poor, invalid ratings may be expected from a rater who lacks confidence in the purpose of the ratings, distrusts the researcher, or simply "has other fish to fry." Understanding and acceptance of purpose is crucial; supervisors who see the request for ratings as "still more paperwork" are likely to look on the request more as an infringement on their time than as a positive means of achieving personal or organizational goals.

Rater motivation might differ for different rating purposes. A rater might be more highly motivated to rate people where a "deservedness" decision is to be made, where the ratings may determine who gets merit pay or special recognition, or where "designation" decisions are the outcome, such as picking out one ratee among others for promotion or a special training opportunity. We have only begun to scratch the surface in understanding the effects of the social context on performance ratings (Levy & Williams, 2004).

Aids to Observation and Memory

Records. In many settings, daily production records are kept. Review of such records can jar the rater's memory and point out aspects of performance such as level and consistency of production, recorded errors, and related facts. If the problem is to assess performance quality, and if such factual information is available, then why rate? A part of the answer is that information in the files may be uneven in quality and relevance. A simple thing like the number of widgets produced each day may be tempered by a rater's knowledge of the specific equipment a ratee uses; some pieces of equipment are more prone to breakdown, slower in function, and so on. The best assessment may still be a subjective judgment—but it must be an informed judgment reached by getting and considering an array of factual information.

Incident Files or Diaries. Some appraisal forms list job duties on one side of the page and require the rater to write an anecdote or critical incident illustrating a ratee's performance of each of them. The principle is similar to that in the Smith–Kendall BARS approach of assigning ratee behavior examples to appropriate points in the scale: The rating given is supported with specific behavioral evidence. A problem with this is that the evidence recalled at the time of rating may not be a good summary description of the ratee or ratee behavior. The rater is more likely to remember the dramatic, salient example of a single brilliant achievement or major blunder than more typical incidents (of these the blunder is more likely to be remembered). Recent events are more likely to be recalled than those that happened earlier.

Bernardin and Buckley (1981) recommended diary keeping as a training method, but only if it is systematic and has support from the top of the organization. Top support for diaries implies that supervisors themselves are evaluated on how well they keep diaries. Diaries, however, offer no panacea. In an experiment, Balzer (1986) found that a diary system can slip badly for those who have good impressions of the ratee but do not see the rating task as very important; it will work best for those who have good impressions and see the task as central to their jobs. This field testable hypothesis deserves testing.

Bernardin and Beatty (1984) offered recommendations for training people to maintain such records, for example: Tie training in recording observations to scale familiarization training so that observations are recorded relative to the behavioral dimensions to be rated. (b) Record objectively, not evaluatively. (c) Record a predesignated minimum number of observations per scale. (d) Make the diary-keeping system a formal part of organizational policy and practice. (e) Require the rater's supervisor to monitor the diary keeping.

Comments

The best procedures for one rating purpose may not fit a different one. Rating people on behavior shown only during the course of an audition or interview is different from rating performance over the span of a year; rating aspects of objects, such as work samples or portfolios, is different from rating people or aspects of their behavior. They may differ in time span of observations or of memory, in complexity of dimensions rated, in organization of data, in opportunity to reconsider, and in many other details. Effects of such differences have not been studied.

Although much remains to be learned about cognitive influences on ratings, ratings will not be accurate if the rater is afraid to give feedback, or is concerned about the negative impact of poor ratings on a raters' willingness to work hard. It is certainly important for a rater to know how to rate accurately, but it is equally important for this person to see some positive outcomes (and few negative ones) associated with accuracy.

DISCUSSION TOPICS

1. What factors might reduce a rater's motivation to provide accurate ratings? Which rating errors are due to motivation, and which are due to cognitive limitations?
2. How would you provide evidence for the validity of a performance rating system for use in making promotion decisions?

12

Assessing Via Inventories and Interviews

Self-Report
Biodata
Unstructured & Structured Interviews

Testing and scaling (including rating) are two basic psychometric procedures; other kinds of assessment procedures are derived from one or both of these approaches. Some of the less constrained constructed response tests are derivatives of both, developed like tests and using rating scales in scoring. Others evolved from the two psychometric foundations and also from forms of assessment that developed outside of the psychometric tradition. Commonly used approaches to assessment, derived both from testing and rating traditions, include inventories and interviews.

INVENTORIES

Inventories are usually self-report measures of interests, motivation, personality, and values. Most of them are developed using test construction principles and, like tests, are scored by summing scores for item responses. Unlike tests, responses are based on opinions, judgments, or attitudes, not on externally verifiable information. Responses may be dichotomous (e.g., agree or disagree), multiple choice, forced choice, constructed response (as in sentence completion tests), or on rating scales with three or more levels (e.g., agree, uncertain, disagree).

Varieties of Inventories

Checklists. Lists of words or phrases can be assembled, and people can be asked to check those that describe them and leave blank those that do not. Items might be chosen to fit a theory. Alternatively, panels of experts may judge whether or not an item fits a designated trait, and a decision rule (e.g., 80% agreement or more) may be set for retaining items.

Scaled Response Inventories. Choosing from three or more categories in an ordinal sequence is a response. The Minnesota Multiphasic Personality Inventory (MMPI) may be the oldest of these measures still in use; its response options are "true," "false," and "cannot say." Such a scale amounts to little more than a dichotomy with an escape clause. Many commonly used scales have more categories, such as a 5-point scale ranging from low to high in appropriateness as a self-description of the respondent.

Multiple-Choice or Forced Choice Instruments. Many inventories are multidimensional; items may have multiple response options each reflecting a different construct (e.g., Sixteen Personality Factor Questionnaire). Options may be responses to a question or simply sets of words or phrases arranged in sets of three or four from which respondents choose one that is the most (or least) descriptive.

Alternatives to Inventories. Common alternatives for personality assessment were (and are) *projective* techniques. These consist of ambiguous stimuli ranging from ink blots and vague pictures to cartoons and picture arrangement tests to sentence completion forms. Figure 12.1 shows an example of an item from the Tomkins–Horn Picture Arrangement Test, one of the few projective tests developed for use in industry. Applicants would be asked to arrange the pictures into a story that makes sense, and then to describe the events in the story. Although Kinslinger (1966) concluded that this was one of the more promising projectives for personnel assessment, the measure never garnered much attention, and is no longer commercially available.

Most projective devices do not measure specific traits, making psychometric validation difficult. They are based on the idea that individuals will "project" their own personality characteristics on

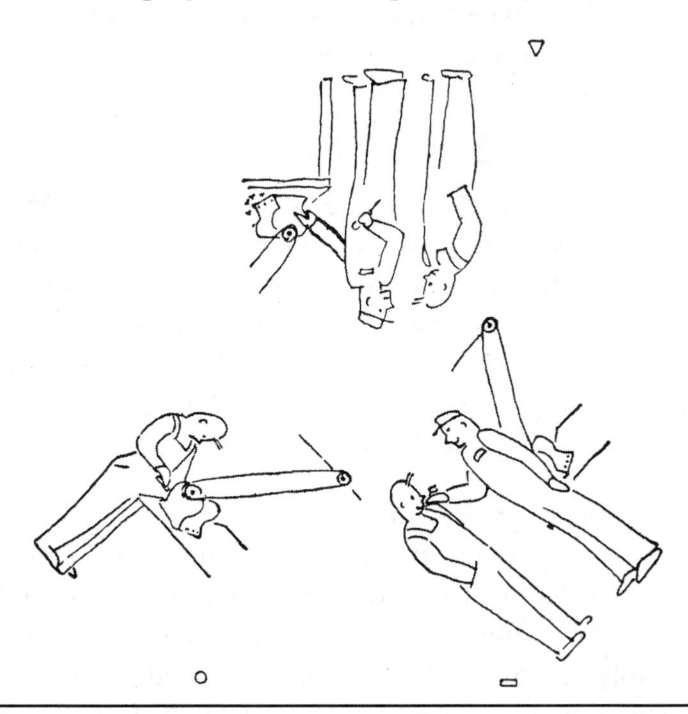

FIG. 12.1. The Tomkins-Horn Picture Arrangement Test (PAT; Tomkins & Miner, 1957) consisted of a number of pictures arranged in random sequence. The candidate's task was to arrange each sequence and write a short sentence describing it (Highhouse, 2002). The PAT is no longer commercially available.

an ambiguous stimulus. The usefulness of the tests for assessing personality continues to receive lively debate (see Lilienfeld, Wood, & Garb, 2000; Viglione & Hilsenroth, 2001), but there is meager evidence for their usefulness in making inferences about occupational success (Highhouse, 2002).

Distorting Responses

The accuracy of self descriptions can be questioned. When applying for a job, people like to make a good impression. Sometimes they are not very truthful in describing themselves, deliberately faking to make a favorable impression. Sometimes people lack real insight into their own behavior.

Faking. A *response set* (also called *response style* or *response bias*) is a tendency to follow a particular habit in responding to such stimuli as inventory items. A very common example is a *social desirability* response set, the tendency for people to say things they think others want to hear, the tendency to try to look good to other people. Candidates for a job usually want the job; they are motivated to present themselves favorably during interviews, when taking tests, or when completing inventories. A social desirability set can slip into a deliberate attempt to look good known as *faking*. Faking has been a particular concern in employment offices. It would not be remarkable if an applicant for a position requiring much alertness were to respond "no" to the question, "Do you daydream frequently?" An applicant for a sales position is unlikely to say "yes" to the question, "Do you dislike talking to other people?"

Some inventories have special scales to try to detect faking. The MMPI has a "Lie scale." Hough and Tippins (1994) had a similar scale they called "Unlikely Virtues." With high faking scores, and maybe very low ones as well, there is a loss of confidence in inferences drawn from personality scores. Often scores on faking are used for score adjustments on the trait scales, but the adjustments rarely enhance prediction of job performance (Goffin & Christiansen, 2003). If a candidate understands the demands of a job well enough to fake appropriately, then it is quite possible that on-the-job behavior will be appropriate, regardless of the person's behavior away from work.

James (1998; James, McIntyre, Glisson, Bowler, & Mitchell, 2004) presented an innovative approach to personality assessment based on *conditional reasoning*. The notion is to reduce faking by indirectly measuring unconscious cognitive biases that people rely on to justify or rationalize their behavior. Individual differences in these biases are assumed to relate to different motives or traits. For example, an item measuring aggression might present respondents with a list of reasons for why Americans prefer foreign cars. A more aggressive respondent might prefer a reason that describes American car makers as greedy and unconcerned with quality. A less aggressive personality might choose a more innocuous reason. Put simply, respondents with different motives are assumed to pick different solutions to the reasoning problems. Although this approach has attracted a lot of attention among personality researchers, it is still too early to say if it has promise for assessment in employment settings.

Another attempt to reduce faking uses *forced choice* items, or those in which choices must be made between equally desirable or favorable options. Bernardin (1987) presented a forced choice method for measuring job-related discomfort. The logic of the method is that everyone has things that they dislike, but some people's dislikes are more job related than others. Thus, Bernardin and his colleagues (Bernardin, 1987; Villanova, Bernardin, Johnson, & Dahmus, 1994) developed items that put job-related discomforts (e.g., sitting for long hours) up against everyday discomforts unrelated to the job (e.g., standing in long lines). The logic is that applicants who repeatedly choose the job-related discomforts as most uncomfortable are less likely to fit with the job in question. This is a very promising approach that remains under-researched.

Several personality inventories have used forced choice principles. Some offer a choice between equally attractive alternatives, each assessing a different trait. Some offer a choice between equally attractive alternatives for the same trait but differing in item discrimination indices, somewhat like forced choice performance ratings. The logic is that social desirability contributes no variance to the trait scores. This logic has not worked as well as anticipated in practice. The most effective way to discourage faking of personality inventories may be to simply warn test takers against it (Dwight & Donovan, 2003).

Acquiescence. The tendency to accept or agree with an item regardless of what it says, the *acquiescent response set,* has been well-documented (e.g., Jackson & Messick, 1958). Suppose a set of positively stated inventory items were rewritten in a second form as negatively worded statements. Responses to the positive and negative forms should logically be negatively correlated. Agreement with any positively worded item should ordinarily predict disagreement when the item is reversed and worded negatively, for example, when the positively worded item is "I like my job" and its negatively worded counterpart is "I do not like my job." A person who agrees with the first statement is generally expected to disagree with the second. However, for many inventories, such reversals of item content often result in the same responses for both and, over several items and several people, the correlation of scores is positive, not negative. That is, no matter whether the item is worded in one direction or its opposite, people tend to respond in the same way—to acquiesce, however it is worded.

Applicant Reactions

An applicant for a position as cashier is unlikely to object to an employment process using an arithmetic test including items on addition and subtraction. The same applicant may be bitterly offended, however, if the process includes an inventory intended to measure trustworthiness or asks questions about religious background. The example shows one of the kinds of reactions that concern people using inventories for employee selection; it is the "What business is this of yours?" reactions. Civil liberties and civil rights groups are wont to support offended applicants, contending that many interest and personality inventories contain material that is prurient, illegal, and an invasion of privacy.

People may feel offended by personality inventories for other reasons. Certain words—some more than others—may be offensive to some people and especially to some groups of people. Some research suggests that the problem may not be large. There was much concern in the 1980s about integrity tests (which are better described as inventories) and the reactions of those who take them. However, Ryan and Sackett (1987a) found that participants in an experimental trial generally (with a few exceptions) considered integrity testing an appropriate management tool. In general, there appears to be no differences in reactions to selection procedures based on gender, age, or ethnic background (Hausknecht, Day, & Thomas, 2004).

Applicant reactions to tests can be a problem when candidates see no relevance of the inventory items to the job sought. Some very personal questions may be relevant to some jobs, and the relevance may have been verified by competent research. Perhaps candidates should be told in advance that some questions may seem irrelevant to the job but have been shown to differentiate between those who succeed and those who fail. It seems likely that a candidate who wants a job, and is given the courtesy of an explanation of an inventory's relevance to that job, will be less likely to take offense at individual items. If so, such courtesies may further safeguard validity.

Although applicant reactions remain a very popular area of research, their influence is likely very minimal when compared with all of the other factors that go into choosing a place to work. It is also doubtful that reactions to a selection procedure are likely to have long-term effects on things such as job satisfaction or organizational commitment. Researchers may be better off considering *employer* reactions to selection devices (e.g., Lievens, Highhouse, & De Corte, 2005; van der Zee, A. B. Bakker, & P. Bakker, 2002), considering the general preference for hunches and intuition over more structured approaches to assessing applicant qualifications (see e.g., Gladwell, 2005)

PERSONAL HISTORY ASSESSMENT

The best predictor of future behavior is past behavior—a cliché, to be sure, but generally true. Students who skip a lot of lectures in one semester are much more likely to skip lectures the next semester. A candidate who performed well on a job in the past is likely to perform well on a similar job in the future. The assessment problem is to learn about and evaluate past behavior of candidates. An internal candidate might be known by others in the organization. In an earlier, less litigious era, one could learn about an outsider's past behavior from reference checks; such queries now produce little more than verification of dates of enrollment or employment—if that. Candidates can be asked about their own past behavior, performance, or experience. Whatever the source, the first problem is to get information that is not distorted or unreliable. The second problem is to turn the information into a useful assessment. Information can come from answers to questions of limited scope, whether asked of candidates (the usual way) or others who have known them. It can become an assessment method by treating answers like inventory responses.

Weighted Application Blanks

In many organizations, scoring keys were developed for what became known as *weighted application blanks*. Several were developed and described in publications in the 1950s and 1960s; a variety of methods for assigning weights to responses was described in

Guion (1965). The use of weighted application blanks has waned, but they remain a useful method for trying to understand and reduce turnover for lower level jobs. A small company experiencing high turnover might examine the applications of employees hired over the last year or so, and separate them into *stayers* and *leavers*. How do the applications of the two groups differ? Table 12.1 shows the scoring of three application items for a small supplier to the automobile industry. This company was experiencing turnover of as much as 100% per year! The 100 "stayers" were identified by obtaining application forms of the last 100 employees hired who stayed more than 6 months. The 100 "leavers" were identified by obtaining application forms of the last 100 employees who stayed less than 6 months. As Table 12.1 shows, the leavers were more likely to be higher skilled and higher educated. Thus, higher scores given on these items would indicate high risk for turnover. As this example shows, reducing turnover begins by understanding the profiles of people who are staying and leaving.

TABLE 12.1

Scoring of Three Application Items

Application Response	*Stayers*	*Leavers*	*Difference*	*Score*
Age				
Under 26	20	40	–20	0
26–39	50	35	15	0
Over 39	40	15	25	0
Self-reported skills				
More than 3	14	84	–70	2
Education level				
Some high school	21	11	12	0
High school graduate	50	57	–7	0
Some college or trade	15	46	–31	1

Note. Scores derived from tables in *Development and Use of Weighted Application Blanks* (pp. 27–28), by G. W. England, 1971, Minneapolis Industrial Relations Center, University of Minnesota.

Biodata

Biodata includes items about prior events or behaviors, but is it a biodata item or a personality inventory item if it asks about prior feelings or attitudes? An item such as "How did you feel when ...?" may be found in either type of inventory. There is a substantial overlap in the kinds of constructs measured with biodata and those measured by personality inventories, but there are differences, too. Both reflect personality attributes, but biodata is the larger domain, reflecting interests, attitude, skills, and abilities in a single set of questions. If a biodata form includes all of these, then the meaning of its scores is obscure. Too often, users do not worry about understanding scores; a good validity coefficient satisfies them. The meaning of scores matters when trying to explain or to understand the validity coefficients. What makes biodata predictive? What constructs does it measure? Answers to such questions are especially elusive for biodata, so defining the boundaries of biodata content may be useful.

A guide to those boundaries, provided by Mael (1991), is shown in Table 12.2. It is more than a guide to what may be considered biographical in nature; it is also a guide to kinds of items that can be used sensibly in biodata questionnaires. Briefly, these are the meanings of the headings:

1. Biodata must be *historical,* the items referring to events or experiences that have taken place in the past (in some cases, continuing to occur). Intentions, or presumed behavior given hypothetical circumstances, are not biographical and therefore are outside the boundary.
2. Biodata items are *external* actions. They may involve others. They may be observable by others. They do not involve events solely within one's own head. This restriction does not seem to be widely followed; many forms identified as biodata forms ask questions of the "how did you feel?" variety.
3. The biodata domain is *objective* in the sense that there is a factual, not interpretative, response. It follows that it should

TABLE 12.2

A Taxonomy of Biodata Items

Historical	*Future or hypothetical*
How old were you when you got your first paying job?	What position do you think you will be holding in 10 years? What would you do if another person screamed at you in public?
External	*Internal*
Did you ever get fired from a job?	What is your attitude toward friends who smoke marijuana?
Objective	*Subjective*
How many hours did you study for your real-estate test?	Would you describe yourself as shy? How adventurous are you compared to your coworkers?
Firsthand	*Secondhand*
How punctual are you about coming to work?	How would your teachers describe your punctuality?
Discrete	*Summative*
At what age did you get your driver's license?	How many hours do you study during an average week?
Verifiable	*Nonverifiable*
What was your grade point average in college? Were you ever suspended from your Little League team?	How many servings of fresh vegetables do you eat every day?
Controllable	*Noncontrollable*
How many tries did it take you to pass the CPA exam?	How many brothers and sisters do you have?
Equal access	*Nonequal access*
Were you ever class president?	Were you captain of the football team?
Job relevant	*Not job relevant*
How many units of cereal did you sell during the last calendar year?	Are you proficient at crossword puzzles?
Noninvasive	*Invasive*
Were you on the tennis team in college?	How many young children do you have at home?

Note. From "A Conceptual Rationale for the Domain and Attribute of Biodata Items," by F. A. Mael, 1991, *Personnel Psychology, 44,* 763–792. Copyright 1991 by. Reprinted with permission.

be firsthand information, not attributions to others. An item like "I think my parents were disappointed in me" lies outside the domain on both counts. It attributes to others (the parents) attitudes they may or may not have held, and it probably does so because of subjective interpretations of words, facial expressions, or actions—or of false memories.

4. *Discrete* actions or events have beginnings and endings; a driver's license was in fact obtained (or not) within a time period. By asking for discrete information, the recollection task of the respondent is simplified; there is also the possibility, even if remote, that someone might know or can find out if the answer given is correct. *Verifiable* answers, even if no one is likely to take the trouble to verify them, seem less likely to be faked.

5. There is no point in asking people about things over which they had no *control*. Past experiences that have shaped and influenced present or future behavior are within the boundaries; even if the experiences themselves are beyond the person's control, reactions to them are controllable. Items with specific historical inequalities in accessibility seem inherently discriminatory, such as experience opportunities that have traditionally been closed to females or to certain ethnic minorities.

6. Employment assessment procedures should be seen as *relevant to the job* sought, or the nature of their relevance should be clearly explained; they should have face validity. Items appearing irrelevant to the job are not likely to be very effective even if within biodata boundaries.

7. Items should be *noninvasive*. As a matter of ethics, empathy, or good sense, the boundaries should draw the line excluding background actions or events people are likely to consider none of an employer's business. Some topics are more acceptable than others in a biodata questionnaire, and some topics are more acceptable for some purposes than for others.

Developing Biodata Forms

Biodata items, like others, can be found by plundering forms used by others. Imagination will add a few more, the whole set can be given an empirical trial, and those with "good" item statistics can form the "new" questionnaire. This unpleasant procedure is fairly typical, but the result can be pleasant; Reilly and Chao (1982) found biodata validity coefficients on par with those of standardized tests. Nevertheless, such biodata forms are criticized as excessively empirical, with no clear understanding of what is measured or why it might be working. The alternative is to specify a construct (or several) to be assessed, to develop its theory or rationale, and to generate systematically the kinds of items believed to tap it (e.g., Breaugh & Dossett, 1989).

Efforts to enhance both prediction and understanding begin by clarifying the measurement purpose. For selection, transfer, or promotion, this begins with job analysis. For training and development purposes, it may begin with a diagnostic analysis of problems. Dean, Russell, and Muchinsky (1999) offered further points of departure based on personality and vocational choice theories and suggested procedures for generating items for the constructs identified as likely to be predictive. In theorizing about what trait may account for the predictive validity of biodata measures, the authors dusted off the old term "moxie" to describe a kind of personal resiliency in the face of negative life events. Mael (1993) described a procedure in which biodata items were mapped on to common personality traits. This approach, dubbed "rainforest empiricism," enables the employer to use biographical items instead of personality items to measure personality traits. More recently, P. J. Taylor, Pajo, Cheung, and Stringfield (2004) described the development of reference check items that map on to Big 5 personality traits. This approach avoids self-report distortions by having referees, such as former employers, assess the candidates' personalities. Where biographical data is concerned, a combination of data and thought is surely superior to either thoughtless empiricism or naive theorizing.

INTERVIEWS

Judgments are made during interviews, whether or not formally recorded as ratings, and they include assessments, predictions, and decisions. These judgments are often intuitive and haphazard. Assessment may be no more than "sizing up" an interviewee. Prediction may be no more than a vague hunch that the person sized up will, if hired (retained, promoted, or whatever), be great, not be bad, or just not work out. Assessments are often secondary to decision; some interviewers want only to reach a decision and then get on with other matters. The *Watson v. Ft. Worth* case (chap. 4) affirmed that interviews intended for personnel decisions are psychometric devices, are based on assessments, and should be evaluated by rules applied to other psychometric devices. Moreover, decision making with no concern for quality of assessment and prediction is simply irresponsible.

Researchers often refer to "the" interview as if all interviews were alike. Just as there are many different tests, there are many different interviewers, looking for many different things, and using many different methods. Some are entirely unplanned; others are as tightly structured as any test. Assessment is the avowed purpose of some; it is a hidden purpose in others. Some are short; some are long. Some use one interviewer; others use panels. Some are done by highly skilled interviewers; others are done by people who do not have a clue as to useful procedures. Interview content consists partly of the questions or tasks posed and partly of the medium, the individual interviewer. Interviewers are not as standardized as questions; the same questions can be asked in different ways by different interviewers. Stimulus content consists partly of the attitudes interviewers present or the interviewee perceives.

Interview Research Reviews

Interviews have been considered too unreliable to be valid since Hollingworth (1923) reported rank orders assigned to 57 candidates by each of 12 sales managers—with virtually no agreement.

A 20-year series of narrative reviews consistently identified unreliability as a major problem. It was not until N. Schmitt (1976) that much was said about lumping together data from interviewers varying in skill. Early reviewers also tentatively proposed that *structured interviews,* those with preplanned procedures and sets of questions to be asked, would be better. The idea was later supported in reviews (e.g., Judge, Higgins, & Cable, 2000; Posthuma, Morgeson, & Campion, 2002). Much more is known about assessment by interviewing, and how to make valid, interview-based decisions, than has been communicated to the world at large—where poor interviews remain the rule.

A series of meta-analyses has augmented the narrative reviews and provided explicit generalizations about the validity of (generally) aggregated interviews as predictors of job performance and other criteria. Mean validity coefficients reported in early studies were low but positive; in later analyses, mean coefficients were substantially higher as the literature grew and, perhaps, reported research with better interviews. A reasonable figure is a corrected coefficient (for criterion unreliability and range restriction) of about .36 or .37 (Huffcutt & Arthur, 1994; McDaniel, Whetzel, Schmidt, & Maurer, 1994); Conway, Jako, and Goodman (1996) used upper limits of about .56 for moderately structured interviews and as high as .67 for those that are highly structured (and .34 for poorly structured ones). Interview validity may not be as bad as once believed.

Meta-analytic conclusions evaluate interview validity more favorably than did the narrative reviews. That may be an artifact of the demands of meta-analytic research; a correlation coefficient serving as a data point implies some degree of structure. If validity coefficients for the casual conversations called interviews could be computed, then they would probably be lower on average than those with correlation coefficients computed but still called unstructured (cf. Schmidt & Zimmerman, 2004). Interviews, if well structured, can be quite valid predictors, but too often they are not structured or valid.

Varieties of Structured Interviews

It is not easy to define what is meant by structured. Structured versus unstructured is a rhetorical, not a realistic, dichotomy; there are big differences in the degree and the rigidity of structure. In fact, the descriptive term of choice has changed over the years. Wagner (1949) did not call for *structured* interviews; he called for *standardized* interviews. By the time meta-analyses were examining moderators of interview validity, Wagner's term had almost disappeared, although some authors used both terms interchangeably. They are not synonyms; structure does not necessarily mean standardization. Every time an interviewer decides before an interview what questions will be asked, what judgments will be made, and how they will be recorded, some degree of structure exists; if such structure is developed uniquely for every interview, then it is certainly not standardized. It is structured only to fit an individual candidate. It is preparation for the interview, usually done after examining a candidate's credentials—application form, résumé, any letters of recommendation that might be available, and so forth—and noting some concerns worth exploring.

However, the term structured more typically refers to interviews tailored to fit a job, not an individual candidate. Structuring in this sense begins with the job description, pay classification, promotion patterns, and related data. From such information, traits relevant to performance may be inferred and appropriate questions (to be asked of all candidates) identified. This form of structuring implies at least some standardization.

Different people have different ideas of how interviews should be structured. Four general procedures are described here. The first uses minimal structure, guiding rather than dictating an interviewer's progress through an interview. The second is more tightly structured yet relatively flexible, permitting different candidates to be asked different questions. The other two are more firmly structured, allowing little deviation.

Patterned Interviews. McMurry (1947) developed patterned interviews, a precursor to many lightly structured procedures. It required stating clear, acceptable bases for selection (e.g., desired traits, background experiences, or training). An interviewer's guide provided kinds of questions that might be asked for each of these, and training was supposed to assure understanding of its questions and the selection standards. Appropriate rating scales were provided for recording summary evaluations.

Behavior Description Interviewing. A more complex modification was called the Patterned Behavior Description Interview (see Janz, Hellervik, & Gilmore, 1986). Janz et al. (1986) gave examples of the interview patterns of questions for 16 jobs. The method is based on the aphorism that the best predictor of future behavior is past behavior; all questions in a pattern ask about past behavior, making it an oral personal history inventory. Question development begins from critical incidents classified into dimensions of behavior. Questions (initial and follow-up questions) are written for each dimension unless that dimension can be assessed better by an alternative to an interview (e.g., tests, biodata, credentials). The correspondence of question to dimension need not be one-to-one; the same initial question can, with appropriate follow-up probes, provide information for more than one job dimension. For example, a critical incident for an employment test specialist might have been "Developed a valid hands-on performance test to measure problem-solving skills when informed under court order that written tests would not be permitted." The initial question might be, "Tell me about a time when you solved a measurement problem that precluded conventional testing procedures." Follow-up questions might include, "What was unusual about your solution?" and "How did you get your solution accepted by others?" If the job dimensions included creative problem solving and persuasiveness, then this question and its probes can tap both. After the interview, the candidate is rated on each job dimension on a simple 5-point graphic rating scale. The sum of the dimension ratings provides a total score.

Situational Interviews. Situational interviews are based on goal-setting theory stating that behavior depends in large part on goals or intentions. Theoretically, if people are asked to say how they would respond to critical situations others have faced on a job, their answers reveal their behavioral intentions. Responses can be systematically scored using a scale anchored by behavioral responses.

DEVELOPING A SITUATIONAL INTERVIEW

Latham (1989) outlined the steps in developing a situational interview:

1. Conduct a job analysis using the critical incident technique.
2. Develop an appraisal instrument, such as behavioral observation scales (Latham & Wexley, 1977, 1981), based on the job analysis.
3. Select one or more incidents that formed the basis for the development of performance criteria (e.g., cost consciousness) that constitutes the appraisal instrument.
4. Turn each critical incident into a "what would you do if ..." question.
5. Develop a scoring guide to facilitate agreement among interviewers on what constitutes a good (5), an acceptable (3), or an unacceptable (1) response to each question. If additional anchors (2 and 4) can also be developed, then do so.
6. Review the questions for comprehensiveness in terms of covering the material identified in the job analysis and summarized on the appraisal instrument.
7. Conduct a pilot study to eliminate questions where applicant/interviewees give the same answers, or where interviewers cannot agree on the scoring.

Like behavior description patterns, situational interviews begin with critical incidents but use them differently. Situational interviews emphasize the future, not the past: "what would you do if ...?" rather than "what did you do when ...?" Situational interviews usually use panels of two or more interviewers. According to Latham, the typical panel has two managers from the job area and one human resources staff member. One person reads the questions, but all of them record and evaluate the answers. An example of a question and scoring guide is shown in Figure 12.2.

You are in charge of truck drivers in Philadelphia. Your colleague is in charge of truck drivers 800 miles away in Atlanta. Both of you report to the same person. Your salary and bonus are affected 100% by your costs. Your buddy is in desperate need of one of your trucks. If you say no, your costs will remain low and your group will probably win the Golden Flyer award at the end of the quarter. If you say yes, the Atlanta group will probably win this prestigious award because they will make a significant profit for the company. Your boss is preaching costs, costs, costs, as well as cooperation with one's peers. Your boss has no control over accounting, who are the score keepers. Your boss is highly competitive, he or she rewards winners. You are just as competitive, you are a real winner!

Explain what you would do.

Record answer:

____

____

____

____

Scoring Guide:
(1) I would go for the award. I would explain the circumstances to my buddy and get his or her understanding.
(3) I would get my boss' advice.
(5) I would loan the truck to my buddy. I'd get recognition from my boss and my buddy that I had sacrificed my rear-end for theirs. Then I'd explain the logic to my people.

FIG. 12.2. An example of a question and scoring guide for a situational interview. From Latham, G. P. (1989). The reliability, validity, and practicality of the situational interview. In R. W. Eder & G. R. Ferris (Eds.), *The employment interview: Theory, research, and practice* (pp. 169–182). Newbury Park, CA: Sage Publications. Reprinted with permission.

> Attitude researchers have learned that asking about *intentions* is more effective for predicting behavior, than is asking about attitudes (Ajzen, 1991). The *situational interview* is based on the notion that asking about what you would do (i.e., your intention) is better for predicting what you will do, than is asking about the best thing to do (i.e., your attitude).

Comprehensive Structured Interviews. The term *comprehensive structured interview* is borrowed from Harris (1989) to distinguish the specific procedures described by Campion, Pursell, and Brown (1988) from the generic term *structured interview.* Campion et al. (1988) described their procedure as "more highly structured" than most other approaches. The procedure begins with job analysis to identify KSAs from which interview questions can be developed. Acceptable questions might include those used in behavior description or situational interviews, job knowledge questions, simulations or walk-throughs, and "willingness" questions presenting aspects of realistic job previews. If job requirements differ in importance, then the difference is supposed to be reflected by the relative number of questions related to the different ones. The form of the questions is simpler than the previous two methods, more like those in a printed test; all candidates are asked precisely the same questions, and no prompting or follow-up questions are permitted (although a question may be repeated, if necessary). Moreover, scores of all candidates should be available before the decision is made; this is an explicitly norm-referenced procedure. If feasible, three-member panels are used; the same panel and the same process is to be used for every candidate. The same panel member is to conduct all interviews and ask all questions; all panel members are to take extensive notes. Questions, answers, and candidates are not to be discussed between interviews, but, after all candidates have been interviewed, large discrepancies in ratings may be discussed and appropriate changes may be made. Candidates may not ask questions during the interview, although the procedure calls for a nonevaluative interview with a personnel representative later in which questions are permitted.

Comparison of the Examples. These examples have been presented to show variety, not as prototypes to be matched. All have shown reasonable reliabilities and validity coefficients, statistically significant and competitive with other predictors. All have been defended as practical.

There are, of course, unanswered questions. How much structure is necessary? When comparing the four examples, keep in mind the diminishing returns of structure as identified by meta-analysis (Huffcutt & Arthur, 1994). In doing so, however, other questions surface. The most highly structured interview guides are essentially oral tests with constructed responses. Is testlike standardization an essential feature of interview structure? The same questions could be asked and answered in written form, the responses scored by readers. Would oral and written versions be alike in reliability and validity? Would one form or the other be more susceptible to contaminating sources of variance? Would examinee reaction be the same? Are we ignoring things that should be assessed (e.g., interpersonal communication skills)?

Interview Validity

Interview validity is usually described only with criterion-related validity coefficients; they are apparently higher than formerly supposed. Pooling data across interviewers who differ in individual validity, who make different systematic errors, and whose judgments are not independent may have seriously underestimated validity coefficients. Very little attention has been given to the psychometric validities of interviewers' ratings. What inferences, if any, can be validly drawn about interviewees from interviewers' judgments? General answers are unavailable, so no general principles can be offered for improving the meaningfulness of interviews as assessments. Although interviewer ratings are made in a context different from many other ratings, they are, after all, subject to the problems of other ratings. We will not clearly understand what interviewers can assess until the research enterprise starts to develop theoretical statements of constructs appropriate for interview assessment, train interviewers in their meanings and manifestations, appropriately structure interviews, collect data, and conduct the confirmatory and disconfirmatory research needed to determine whether interviewers' ratings on these constructs lead to valid inferences about them.

Interview guides, rating scales, and general structure of interviews are often content related, relying on job analysis in their development. Lawshe's *content validity ratio* (CVR; Lawshe, 1975) was computed for items in each of three structured interview guides developed by Carrier, Dalessio, and Brown (1990). One of the guides was for use with experienced applicants, the other two for inexperienced ones. For experienced candidates, the approach worked quite well; the highest CVR items combined to form the best criterion-related validity. This is not so for the inexperienced ones. Is content sampling, then, a useful approach to structuring interviews only for experienced people? We can't say. The finding is interesting, but it needs replication.

Interview questions and ratings can be informed by the job analysis or derived from it as content samples. The former is like the choice of predictors in a predictive hypothesis and may lead to more appropriate questions for inexperienced applicants. The latter may distinguish truly experienced candidates from those who merely claim the experience. Inexperienced applicants need to be assessed for aptitudes for the work they have yet to learn; aptitude is surely assessed better by tests than by interviewers' ratings.

Interviewer Characteristics

Research has shown that there are individual differences in the way interviewers use information to reach overall judgments and in the criterion-related validity of those judgments, and the studies have shown that treating different interviewers as mere replications of each other (i.e., pooling data across interviewers) is unwise. In a unique study by Dougherty, Ebert, and Callender (1986), three interviewers audiotaped interviews used in initial screening for entry clerical and technical jobs. Each interviewer saw some applicants and rated them on 8 job-related dimensions and on an overall rating scale. All three interviewers rated all applicants from the tapes. Those hired were subsequently rated by their supervisors on 10 dimensions, including overall performance. Validity coefficients are shown in Table 12.3. ("Live" judgments are those of the actual interviewer at the time of the interview; all other columns refer to judgments based on the tapes.) Again, aggregated interviewer overall judgments were not significantly correlated with supervisory ratings of overall job performance; neither were ratings from two of the interviewers. The third, however, significantly and substantially predicted all supervisory ratings but one. The study went beyond demonstrating individual differences in interviewer validity; it also showed that interviewers can be trained to use more effective policies.

Interviewer Experience and Habit. Most managers prefer people with lots of experience, but sometimes we learn things from experience that are bad habits or misinformation. Gehrlein, Dipboye, and Shahani (1993) demonstrated that experience is not necessarily helpful to interviewers. Admissions officers (experienced interviewers) interviewed college applicants; other applicants were interviewed by alumni, faculty, and others termed "inexperienced." Validity coefficients of interviewer ratings against grade point average (GPA) were nonsignificant for all of the individual experienced interviewers; surprisingly, inexperienced interviewers did much better. The authors suggested that experience tends to breed confidence, even if it is unwarranted. Perhaps the less experienced people compensated for less confidence by planning their interview strategies—in effect, by developing a personal structure for their interviews.

TABLE 12.3

Validity Coefficients for "Live" Overall Judgments, Mean of Overall Judgments, and Individual Interviewer Judgments

			Interviewer		
Criterion Dimension	*Live[a] judgments (n = 57)*	*Mean of[b] judgments (n = 57)*	*1 judgment (n = 56)*	*2 judgments (n = 54)*	*3 judgments (n = 56)*
Learning tasks	.10	.17	.09	.07	.24*
Minimal supervision	.05	.32**	.19	.09	.41**
Organizing	.09	.18	.13	–.05	.26*
Judgment	–.05	.24*	.23*	.07	.26*
Job knowledge	–.09	.12	.07	–.11	.23*
Cooperation	–.04	.09	.13	–.01	.08
Productivity	.03	.19	.12	–.05	.32**
Accuracy	.18	.28*	.25*	.19	.27*
Involvement	.06	.28*	.27*	.04	.34**
Overall performance					
Actual	.06	.21	.15	.02	.26*
Predicted[c]			.23*	.19	.26*

[a]Overall judgments made by interviewers in the actual, live interviews; all other columns are correlations based on judgments from the tape recordings. [b]Mean of the judgments based on tapes by the three interviewers. [c]Using judgments predicted from the interviewer's own policy equation.
*p < .05; **p < .01
Note. Adapted from Dougherty, T. W., Ebert, R. J., & Callender, J. C. (1986). Policy capturing in the employment interview. *Journal of Applied Psychology, 71*, 9–15. Copyright by the American Psychological Association. Reprinted with permission.

Judgment research has generally shown that experience leads to greater confidence, but not to greater ability to predict. Studies using such experts as livestock judges, physicians, psychotherapists, parole officers, and court judges have found experienced judgments to be just as susceptible to error as novice judgments.

Some interviewers habitually talk too much. Daniels and Otis (1950) found that interviewers generally do most of the talking, sometimes two or three times as much as the interviewees. Moreover, it has been shown that interviewers talk more with applicants they accept (C. W. Anderson, 1960). That finding is hard to interpret. Do interviewers talk more to applicants who show signs of success early in the conversation? Or, do they simply feel good about themselves when they talk more, thereby feeling kindly toward the listening applicant?

If the interviewer is seen as an instrument for assessing candidate characteristics through conversation, then it seems logical that the interviewer's contributions to the conversation would be relatively brief, encouraging the candidate to speak freely. When the purpose of the interview is to persuade the candidate to accept an offer, perhaps the interviewer should in fact talk more. But in nearly all other purposes, for example, where public relations is to be enhanced, the interviewer is likely to make a better impression on the interviewee by listening than by talking.

Apparently, the amount and kind of talking done by interviewers depends in large part on prior impressions of the candidates. In a decision-making interview, an interviewer often gets prepared by checking out application materials. The interviewer is likely to talk more and listen less if this preparation produces a favorable impression; there are other first impression effects that bring the validity of interviews into question.

Stereotypes, Prototypes, and Biases. The notion of an ideal applicant need not be stereotypic. Prototypes of ideal candidates can be developed by deliberation, perhaps from job descriptions or with the help of supervisors and senior employees:

> How do different interviewers develop and use prototypes of desired candidates? ... I distinguish between a stereotype (which develops willy-nilly, is widely accepted, and seems implicitly to apply to all members of a group) and a prototype, by which I mean something like a car designer's proto-

> type, a carefully and systematically developed ideal to be achieved; for selection, the prototype should be defined by a set of attributes that not only describe the desired candidates but distinguish them from those less desired.... I suspect that work on the idea of a prototype as a planned ideal will be more fruitful than work on more or less generally accepted stereotypes of what is. (Guion, 1987, p. 202)

Whereas "Similar-to-me" is a bias, "Similar-to-ideal candidate" seems a useful match to an ideal prototype; if the prototype is valid, then matching it should imply valid assessment as well.

Interviewers' biases potentially include demographic variables like gender, race, ethnicity, or age. Research generally reports little or nonsignificant differences in interviewers' ratings of men and women, but differences have been observed for racial and ethnic groups (Huffcut & Roth, 1998). The pessimistic view of these group differences attributes them to interviewer biases against minority group members. The optimistic view is that the group differences in average interview ratings are much smaller than group differences on cognitive ability measures. Research is needed that controls for differences in factors other than race and ethnicity.

A more general "similar-to-me" bias could inflate tendencies toward bias. In one study, racial similarity effects were stronger in conventional than in structured interviews, although mixed-race panels of interviewers avoided the effect (Lin, Dobbins, & Farh, 1992); similarity effects were not found for age. Another study of panels of interviewers showed a similar racial effect, giving higher ratings to candidates of the same racial identity as the majority of the panel (Prewett-Livingston, Feild, Veres, & Lewis, 1996).

Similarity biases are natural, but they are an example of a fundamental flaw in human intuition called judgment by representativeness (Tversky & Kahneman, 1982). *Judgment by representativeness* is the tendency to assume that things that look like each other are like each other. For example, an effective executive who made it to the top without a college education may think that a candidate with only "street smarts" will be similarly effective. That is, if the candidate has the same history as me, then he must be as competent as me. According to Gilovich (1991):

> People assume that "like goes with like": Things that go together should look as though they go together. We expect instances to look like the categories of which they are members; thus, we expect someone who is a librarian to resemble the prototypical librarian. We expect effects to look like their causes; thus, we are more likely to attribute a case of heartburn to spicy rather than bland food, and we are more inclined to see jagged handwriting as a sign of a tense rather than a relaxed personality. (p. 18)

The problem with judgment by representativeness is that it often leads to predictable errors. Consider the aforementioned executive. This successful executive fails to consider the following: (a) How many effective executives have no college education? (b) How many ineffective executives have no college education? (c) How many effective executives have college educations? Odds are that Sets b and c are much larger than Set a. The point is not that the executive should necessarily hire the candidate with a college education, but that the executive should not let similarity on this one attribute interfere with his judgment about the candidates' other strengths and weaknesses.

Interviewee Characteristics

Obviously, characteristics of the person interviewed should influence decisions; they include the characteristics sought. Two special cases, however, merit concern as potential sources of error.

Memory. Interviews generally consist of questions requiring the interviewee to respond with a remembered event, state, or behavior. Personal recall may not be accurate. People may have implicit theories of their own personalities that emphasize stability (e.g., This is how I think now, so I must have thought similarly then). Other people, or the same people for other questions, have implicit theories that lead them to exaggerate changes that have occurred. That is, people make the implicit assumption that behaviors match attitudes. If a person recalls behavior (e.g., leaving a job) associated with an attitude, and if the attitude has changed, then the response may describe behavior more in line with the present attitude than with the earlier reality.

Impression Management. Candidates try to make good impressions, and some are better at it than others. *Impression management* is the attempt to influence the impression made on others. There are surely individual differences in self-presentation skills, but there is little information about kinds of job performance these skills may predict or the kinds of assessments they may contaminate. Interview research needs to study the effect of impression management. Does behavior successfully creating the desired impressions with one interviewer work equally well with another? Can interviewers learn to detect the deceptions implied by the term *impression management?* If so, can they successfully ignore it in making job-relevant assessments or decisions. Kinicki, Lockwood, Hom, and Griffeth (1990) found that two factors described interviewer ratings on six dimensions. One was labeled "interview impression," the other was called "relevant qualifications." The terms are adequately descriptive; only the relevant qualifications factor validly predicted independent job performance ratings.

Ellis, West, Ryan, and DeShon (2002) found that type of interview question influenced the type of impression management engaged in by the interviewee. Specifically, interviewees used more ingratiation tactics when answering situational questions, but they used more self-promotion tactics when they answered experience-based questions. We might expect, therefore, that behavioral description interviews would elicit more self-promotion (i.e., bragging), and that situational interviews would be met with more ingratiation (i.e., kissing up). Impression management tactics also appears to be related to personality (Kristof-Brown, Barrick, & Franke, 2002). Extraverted interviewees engaged in more self-promotion, whereas agreeable interviewees engaged in more ingratiation.

In General

A large body of research on interviewing has given too little practical information about how to structure an interview, how to conduct it, and how to use it as an assessment device. Research suggests that interviews can be valid; for validity, they require structuring and standardization; structure, like many other things, can be carried too far; without carefully planned structure (and maybe even with it) interviewers talk too much; and the interviews made routinely in nearly every organization could be vastly improved if interviewers were aware of and used these conclusions. There is more to be learned and applied.

DISCUSSION TOPICS

1. What kinds of biodata items might be developed to distinguish between high GPA and low GPA students?
2. Can you take these biodata items and turn them into behavioral interview questions? What might you do to reduce faking in the responses?
3. Are there negative consequences associated with using structured interviews?

13

Combining Multiple Assessments

Combining Predictors
Individual Assessment
Assessment Centers

A single predictor of performance is rarely as useful as several. Most personnel decisions are based on multiple assessments. For simple jobs, formal assessment of one truly critical trait may be enough, but even that assessment is likely to be augmented by other information; more complex jobs call for more complex assessment programs. This chapter begins with a brief discussion of the issues involved with combining multiple predictors. This chapter also considers two special cases of multiple assessment, that is, *individual assessment* and group *assessment centers* that usually include assessments of performance on specially developed exercises.

ISSUES IN COMBINING PREDICTORS

Decision Models

The usual prototype of multiple assessment is a battery of tests combined to predict a single criterion. Scores on these tests are added (with or without weights) to form a composite score that, by itself, has no particular meaning beyond a predicted criterion level. Prediction, based on linear multiple regression, is enhanced when scores on each test in the battery predict the criterion and have low correlations with each other, that is, are not redundant.

The use of additive, compensatory models is well established and not to be abandoned capriciously. However, we need a new concept of compensatory batteries. Essentially, the additive model is described with the word *and*: The decision is based on a composite consisting of Test A and Test B and test C, and so on. What is often needed is compensation by alternatives where the operative term is *either or* or *if then*. This seems especially necessary under the accommodation provisions of ADA. Moreover, it seems feasible in algorithms for judgmental policies.

Individual assessments and group assessment centers combine multiple assessments judgmentally, not statistically. One advantage may be that they can facilitate compensation by alternatives—*or* rather than *and*. Of course, what we know of judgmental versus statistical prediction suggests that such a compensatory model can have the serious disadvantage of being less valid.

Tough Choices

For massive, ongoing selection programs, top-down selection makes sense and is probably more efficient. However, it is commonly the case that a bunch of candidates are being considered for a single, often higher level position. The initial stages of selection are usually aimed at narrowing the pool of candidates to arrive at a smaller number of two or three finalists. This small set of finalists is composed of applicants with different strengths and weaknesses—even though they are roughly comparable in overall attractiveness. Although much is known about the relative utility of various predictors for selecting a large number of workers to fill a large number of vacancies, significantly less is known about the factors that influence job-finalist choice (Highhouse, 1997).

Research on choice under conflict has shown that people make inconsistent choices when they are forced to trade-off one quality for another (e.g., How much luxury should be given up to get good gas mileage when buying a car?). In other words, choices are highly dependent on the immediate context—rather than on personal values. One example of this is known as the "decoy effect" in choice. This occurs when an inferior option (a decoy) affects choices between superior options. Highhouse (1996) presented decision makers with two comparable job finalists and one decoy candidate, along with work sample and promotability ratings:

	Work Sample Rating	*Promotability Rating*
Candidate 1	5	80
Candidate 2	7	66
Decoy Candidate A	4	80
Decoy Candidate B	7	54

Participants receiving Decoy Candidate A, along with the choice pair of Candidate 1 versus Candidate 2, preferred Candidate 1 by nearly a 3 to 1 ratio. In contrast, participants receiving Decoy Candidate B with the same choice pair preferred Candidate 2 in nearly the same proportion! Note that the decoy candidates were completely dominated by only one of the two other candidates in both conditions; that is, only one candidate was equal to or better than the decoy on both the work sample and promotability ratings. Thus, the decoys served to increase the relative attractiveness of the dominating candidate. If employers fail to establish beforehand how important the predictors are relative to one another, then they are more likely to be influenced by irrelevant context features like decoys.

Consider a circumstance in which different criteria are predicted, and different predictions suggest different decisions. Such a situation might arise if the predicted criteria are actual job production and a contextual criterion such as dependability or integrity. What should a manager do with a candidate whose predicted level on one of these criteria calls for a favorable decision and calls for rejection on the other?

There seem to be three possible nonevasive solutions to the problem. One is to average predictions, perhaps weighting them by the judged importance of the different criteria. Another is to set minimum acceptable criterion levels on each one (a multiple cut-score approach for predictions). The other is to use managerial judgment, comparing the relative importance of the different criteria to current organizational needs. Long ago, the first author argued that the different predictions should be made and decisions should be based on the criteria most important when the decision must be made (Guion, 1961). We still consider such judgment the best practice.

INDIVIDUAL ASSESSMENT

Individual psychological assessment is commonly used for assessing the suitability of candidates for executive positions or for specialized assignments, such as law enforcement agents (Highhouse, 2002). Characteristic of these positions is a situation where job performance is difficult to define and relatively few people occupy the roles. Individual assessment can be quite expensive, ranging anywhere from $1,500 to $10,000 per candidate. Because of the high prices charged by assessors, along with the fact that assessor performance is difficult to judge, the practice attracts many charlatans.

The high cost of individual assessment also makes it prohibitive for all but the highest level hires. Executive level assessment requires executive sounding dimensions of assessment. Table 13.1 shows dimension labels used for assessment centers, which are usually used for supervisors and middle managers, compared with those used for individual assessment. Although it is quite likely that the assessment center dimensions involve the same behavioral criteria as the individual assessment dimensions, the latter sound much more appropriate for assessing a future Donald Trump.

The distinguishing feature of individual assessment, of course, is that it assesses one person at a time. Ryan and Sackett (1987b) said that an equally important and defining feature is that one psychologist conducts a final, integrating interview and one psychologist (maybe the same one) writes the assessment report. Very little research on individual assessment has been reported, and most published reports are old. Nevertheless, individual assessment is alive and well as an area of professional practice, if not as an area of research.

The Holistic Approach. One very common approach to individual assessment is based on a more clinical tradition in assessment, articulated by psychologists such as Gordon Allport and Henry Murray and referred to as the "whole person," or *holistic,*

TABLE 13.1

Comparison of Assessment Center Dimension Labels With Individual Assessment Dimension Labels

Assessment Center Dimension	*Individual Assessment Dimension*
Judgment	Seasoned Judgment
Persuasiveness	Influencing and Negotiating
Analysis	Visionary Thinking
Work Standards	Shaping Strategy
Behavioral Flexibility	Leadership Versatility
Sensitivity	Inspiring Trust
Oral Communication Skill	Building Organization Relationships
Tenacity	Driving Execution

approach (see Magnusson & Torestad, 1993). Murray was responsible for popularizing the holistic approach to assessment in the United States. He did not believe in the psychometric approach of measuring isolated traits, preferring instead the subjective *diagnosis* of personality. Murray first applied this practice to the assessment of future spies for the Office of Strategic Services, an earlier version of the CIA (Highhouse, 2002). The holistic approach remains controversial, with little empirical research to support its use over the more traditional psychometric approach.

A Psychometric Emphasis. In the 1950s, a research and consulting group at Western Reserve University[1] developed an assessment program for "higher level" sales and managerial personnel. The program description is still the most complete in easily accessible literature (e.g., J. T. Campbell, 1962; J. T. Campbell, Otis, Liske, & Prien, 1962; Huse, 1962; Otis, J. T. Campbell, & Prien, 1962). The seven-article series is a prototype for assessment and assessment research, and highly recommended for careful study. The basic program included:

1. A staff member visited clients to learn about the job to be filled, the organization, and the social environment; information gained was used to tailor the assessment program.
2. Two psychologists together interviewed candidates, independently rating them on several scales. They did not have access to test data.
3. Projective test responses were analyzed by a clinical psychologist who rated the candidate on the same scales without seeing the candidate personally and without knowledge of other test results.
4. A test battery was developed specifically for the job in question; the battery minimally included two personality inventories, an interest inventory, and tests of abilities considered important to the job.

[1]After a merger, the university became Case–Western Reserve.

5. One psychologist–interviewer wrote a report describing social skills, intellectual functioning, drive and ambition, personal adjustment, and a judgment of probable effectiveness.

The program emphasized the battery of psychometric tests, which were generally the most valid components of the program.

Two other model programs, developed after World War II, were implemented for the identification of management talent at Standard Oil of New Jersey (now Exxon) and Sears, Roebuck and Company. The test batteries included measures of things such as verbal ability, inductive reasoning, situational judgment, and personality. The researchers reported multiple correlations in the area of .70–.75 in the prediction of a managerial success index (e.g., a combination of position level, salary, and ranking by executives). Based on this research, Bentz (1967) speculated that there is a cluster of psychological characteristics associated with executive success, including forcefulness, dominance, assertiveness, and confidence. This has been supported in subsequent research.

Programs described and evaluated in the literature are old ones, generally dating to the 1950s and 1960s. Legal uncertainties of the EEO era may have inhibited publication of such programs. Legal uncertainty remains; Ryan and Sackett (1987b) reported that nearly 30% of their respondents were not sure that their practices were consistent with the Uniform Guidelines. Their survey also supported the notion that newer programs have introduced few innovations.

INDIVIDUAL ASSESSMENT IN PRACTICE

Ryan and Sackett (1987) surveyed members of the Society for Industrial and Organizational Psychology (SIOP) and found that those doing individual assessments are likely to be full-time, licensed consultants, and to be one of several in the organization who do such assessments. Many who conduct individual assessment, however, are not SIOP members, and were trained in subdisciplines such as clinical, counseling, or educational psychology.

The SIOP respondents reported many purposes of individual assessment; selection and promotion (including planning for succession) and outplacement were the major ones. They also reported that assessment typically required at least a half day; some were shorter, and some required two full days. Assessment tools for individual assessors usually include personal history data, ability tests, personality and interest inventories, interviews, and often projective devices. The general pattern for arriving at conclusions about assessees is strictly judgmental; mechanistic techniques for setting specific composite scores as cutoffs for recommendations tend to be unpopular.

Information about organizations and positions was typically gathered through conversations and interviews, not from more systematic organizational and job analyses. Information sought included the usual emphasis on tasks and responsibilities, KSAs, and critical incidents involving prior successes and failures. Individual assessments were thought to need a wider variety of information than is common in job analysis: interpersonal relationships, supervisory expectations, and broad statements of functions were common, and some respondents mentioned such considerations as organizational climate, opportunities for advancement, subordinate characteristics, and the criteria used in evaluating performance in the position.

Written reports were usually followed by telephone or face-to-face discussions with the client. Reports rarely included actual test scores, but strengths and weaknesses and suggestions for personal development were usually included. Reports did not necessarily include recommendations; about one third of the respondents reported making ratings on specific traits or expected performance dimensions.

Criticisms of Individual Assessment

People who conduct individual assessments are often extremely confident in their ability to make clinical judgments, despite the fact that evidence for expertise in predicting human behavior is decidedly bleak (see Camerer & Johnson, 1991; Highhouse, 2002). When asked to provide validity evidence, the common response is that psychometrics does not apply to this kind of selection situation, or that assessors would not be in business long if they were not valid (Hansen & Conrad, 1991). Both statements are false; individual assessment is subject to the same standards as any other method of assessment for selection, and many people pay for selection techniques that are void. Individual assessment programs are open to some other criticisms:

1. Individual assessment is rarely subjected to serious validation efforts. Traditional validation is often not possible, but job-related constructs could be identified and evidence could be acquired to evaluate the validity of inferences drawn. Program evaluation methods could also be used, at least in firms doing a lot of assessment.
2. Assessment conclusions are often unreliable. Different assessors evaluate candidates differently, perhaps because they rely on different information and perhaps because they have no standard basis for consistency. An intractable reliability problem exists insofar as different readers of a report draw different inferences from it. Three assessors described by Ryan and Sackett (1989) did not agree on ratings of suitability for the position.
3. Assessment summaries are too often influenced by one or two parts of the assessment program that could have been used alone. This is not surprising; assessment summaries are judgments of the report writer, and judgment research shows that judgments are typically based on only a few of the available (usually negative or early) cues.

4. Great emphasis is placed on personality assessment without matching evidence of the relevance of the traits assessed. Where assessments are statistically validated against job performance criteria, scores on one or two traditional cognitive tests are usually more valid than scores or clinical judgments based on personality tests.
5. Individual assessments, limited to one person, cannot assess interpersonal skills from actual interpersonal behavior. Most individual assessment is done with candidates for managerial or sales work, work that requires interaction with others; assessment without such interaction may be deficient; this may be one reason why group assessment center approaches have dominated the assessment literature in recent years.
6. It may be ethically and legally questionable to seek information not explicitly relevant to the work to be done, yet individual assessments typically include intellectual and personality exploration, gathering general and diverse data about a person. Many people think collecting information without direct job relevance is an unwarranted invasion of privacy. On the other hand, some consider it unfair or unethical to base decisions on one or two traits without a complete picture of the individual.

All of these points can be answered by appropriate design. Validation efforts combining evidence of relevance of traits assessed with evidence of the construct validities of the assessments provide better validity evidence than a single validity coefficient; that is, well-developed predictive hypotheses should dictate and justify assessment content. Greater use of work samples (or of exercises based on them) could provide easy justifications of content. The absence of interpersonal behavior in the assessment process itself is not so serious if personal records of interpersonal achievements can be assessed by achievement records and other biodata, or where interview structure focuses on such history.

ASSESSMENT CENTERS

Instead of measuring characteristics of one person at a time, *assessment centers* evaluate small groups of people at more or less the same time. Instead of one person being responsible for the final assessments, a group of observers may work together to form a consensus about assessees. Like individual assessments, assessment center programs use multiple methods of assessment to make multiple assessments. The methods may not include literal work samples or simulations, but they nearly always include exercises chosen to reflect a major aspect of job performance.

> Whereas *individual assessment* deemphasizes structure and emphasizes the expertise of the assessor, the modern *assessment center* emphasizes structure, and deemphasizes the role of assessor expertise.

Assessment Center Purposes

Most assessment centers are organization specific. Consulting firms may provide generic assessment center services, primarily for smaller organizations, but they are more likely to assist organizations in developing their own programs. Most assessment centers, especially for managerial purpose, are built around organizationally specific values and practices. This may be because many are used for employee development and feedback, rather than for employee selection. They are not always designed for managers; many are for salespeople or public safety jobs.

Purposes differ within occupational categories. Thornton and Byham (1982) divided managerial assessments into those for early identification of potential managers, for promotions, or for management development. The different purposes call for differences in program design. Different purposes may call for assessments of different constructs. Some diagnostic purposes may require psychologists or educators as assessors, but other developmental purposes may be better accomplished with managers as assessors—managers similar to those to whom assessees will later report. An overall assessment rating (OAR) may have no importance for diagnostic purposes but may be crucial for personnel decisions like hiring or promotion. The discussion here focuses on selection or promotion.

Assessment Center Components

An organizing principle of assessment center development is that the program should be a *multiattribute* assessment, covering several dimensions relevant to the decision to be made. A further principle is that the assessments should not depend on specific methods of assessment—they should be *multimethod* assessments. Any attribute is to be assessed by more than one method. The multimethod aspect of assessment center programs is not merely a matter of numbers for increasing reliability, although it may serve that purpose. The reason is "rather that the process of seeking confirmation from several exercises leads to more validity of measurement of complex dimensions" (Thornton & Byham, 1982, p. 227). It leads to greater validity through more comprehensive domain sampling and through the convergent evidence of validity of dimensional assessments.

Assessment centers have many components. Job or task analysis provides background; special exercises are based on task analyses. Standardized tests are often chosen for important KSAs. Any component should be clearly relevant to the job, provide reliable and valid assessments, and contribute meaningfully to an OAR, if one is used. Some varieties of assessment procedures are briefly discussed here, but the list is not at all exhaustive.

Tests and Inventories. Traditional tests and inventories are included in most assessment centers. Their role in an OAR raises some questions. How should they be combined with various ratings? Statistically? In an additive model with nominal weights? If given to the assessors as information to consider with exercise ratings in arriving at the OAR, should they be given as raw scores, or as z scores, percentiles, or other interpretive scores?

Tests and inventories, by themselves, often have validities as high as any overall composite of assessment center components. This may be due to superior reliabilities but, whatever the reason, should they be given credence beyond that of the exercises? This is, in part, a reprise of the performance test versus traditional test issues of chapter 10, but it is more than that. When considering the importance of interpersonal skills in many kinds of jobs, do the group exercises provide more important assessments than those obtained with traditional tests and inventories?

Exercises. Most assessment center exercises are performance tests; they are samples or abstractions of aspects of the jobs for which people are assessed. Many are low in fidelity to the job, but high fidelity simulations would be inappropriate for assessees who do not yet know the job. It is content sampling of sorts, but it is content suggested by (highly abstracted from) the job, not literal job content.

The most frequently used assessment center simulation is an *In-Basket* exercise. In-Basket tests simulate administrative work, usually with a set of reasonably typical memos, clippings, letters, reports, messages, and even junk mail that can accumulate on a person's desk. Instructions generally tell the assessee to play the role of a person new to the job, working when no one else is around, trying to clear the desk; In-Baskets are not group exercises. Materials range from simple to complex, from trivial to urgent, and are often interrelated. Additional documents may or may not be provided as reference material (e.g., a file cabinet containing both relevant and unrelated items of information). The assessee may be interviewed after the exercise to explain reasons for actions taken, with ratings based on the interview. Some In-Basket tests, however, have scoring protocols and require no further information from the assessee.

An equally common exercise, not clearly a simulation, is the *Leaderless Group Discussion*. The group is given a problem to solve, a time limit in which to do so, and perhaps a requirement for a written solution. No one is assigned the role of chair; leadership functions must emerge during the discussion. Specific roles might be assigned to the various group members, often with the competitive requirement of trying to convince others to adopt a particular position. Many variants on the theme have been used.

Interviews. Assessment centers usually use interviews, but they are not like employment interviews. Various examples include stress interviews, interviews as role-playing simulations, and panel interviews. Ordinary problems of interviews occur in these, but assessment center interviews can be more standardized, without being testlike, than other interviews.

> An example of a *role play* simulation might include having the job candidate play the part of a candy bar sales representative who is charged with making a phone call to a buyer for a chain of gas stations. The job candidate would have to convince the buyer (played by the assessor) to stock the new candy bar in the gas station convenience stores. The buyer would make the sales representative's job more difficult by feigning indifference and asking difficult questions about the product's characteristics.

Assessors

Functions of Assessors. Zedeck (1986) identified three assessor functions. A major function is as an *observer and recorder* of behavior in the exercises. Behavior is commonly recorded in descriptive (and perhaps evaluative) reports written about the observations. Fulfillment of this function requires careful, standard training. Ratings for a given dimension may be made by different assessors in different exercises. Differences in the behavior observed and the dimensional inferences drawn from it are necessarily attributable in part to the differences in exercises, but they should not be attributable to different assessors having different understandings of the nature of the dimension. A related problem is that the observers may also be part of the stimulus, and different observers may stimulate different reactions. Videotaped exercise performance may help with this; the assessors can observe tapes using "instant replay," if needed (Ryan et al., 1995).

A second function is as a *role player,* an active participant in an assessment exercise. In many exercises, assessors are interviewers, usually with another assessor in a purely observer role. In such exercises, an assessor serves as a stimulus to which the assessee responds. One problem for this function is lack of standardization. Role players may change their own behavior during the sequence of interviews. In a stress interview, for example, some may get harsher over a sequence of interviews whereas others may say, in effect, to heck with it—and cause less stress. If different assessors play the same role, then standardization is still more unlikely. Trying to be an actor and an observer simultaneously is cognitively difficult, and assessors are unlikely to be good actors. It is probably best if assessors are as unobtrusive as possible.

Zedeck's third function is as a *predictor*. Assessors may make explicit predictions, or prediction may be based on the ratings, whether dimensional ratings or OARs.

Assessor Qualifications. Assessors may be psychologists, HR staff, or job experts (e.g., managers in managerial assessment centers). Staff psychologists may be assessors with managers, they may chair assessor panel discussions, or they may simply be resource people. Assessors from whatever source should receive intensive training with frequent refreshers; they should be fully familiar with the exercises and the kinds of behavior they may observe, and they should fully understand the language and concepts related to the ratings they are asked to make.

Numbers of Assessors Needed. Typically, the ratio of assessees to assessors is 2:1. Thornton and Byham (1982) considered this a desirable ratio. Cognitive demands on observers are heavy and can be reduced by adding more assessors, but that can be daunting for the assessees. It may be better to use fewer assessors over a longer time period viewing videotapes.

Other questions emerge. Should assessors become specialists? Should one assessor be a specialist in the leaderless group discussion and another a specialist in personal history interviews? Perhaps a specialist for certain dimensions? In group exercises, should each assessor try to observe and rate all candidates in the group or be assigned to observe and rate no more than two at a time? These are questions about ways to use assessors as observers and raters to maximize reliability and validity of the assessments provided. They must be answered locally; no general answers have been empirically found.

Dimensions to Be Assessed

There is disagreement about the dimensions to be rated. The dimensions (constructs) might be personal traits, job-defined competencies, or performance levels on aspects of jobs reflected in simulations. Assessors might be asked to rate only overall performance in an exercise, or perhaps component aspects of exercise performance. Traits rated might be generalized, habitual behaviors. Task performance may be rated in terms of outcomes or processes. A dimension can be defined by behavior exhibited only in particular kinds of situations. All of these constructs, except the last one, should generalize across situations, therefore across exercises. The last one is an idea of a dimension that has not been traditionally espoused in the assessment center literature. An example of typical assessment center dimensions for a supervisory position is shown in Table 13.2.

In early assessment centers, personal traits (largely personality traits that were thoroughly defined and discussed by psychologists like Henry Murray) were rated; more recent centers favor behavioral categories that, unfortunately, are often poorly defined. The

TABLE 13.2

Typical Assessment Center Dimensions and Their Definitions

Dimension	*Definition*
Tolerance for Stress	Stability of candidate's performance under pressure and/or opposition.
Oral Communication Skill	Effective expression in individual or group situations (including gestures and nonverbal communication).
Work Standards	Setting high goals or standards of performance for self, subordinates, others, and the organization.
Persuasiveness/ Sales Ability	Utilizing appropriate interpersonal styles and methods of communication to obtain agreement or acceptance of an idea, plan, activity, or product from clients.
Sensitivity	Actions that indicate appropriate consideration for the feelings and needs of others.
Behavioral Flexibility	Modifying behavior to reach a goal when obstructed by the attitudes, beliefs, opinions, or behavior of another person or persons.
Analysis	Relating and comparing data from different sources, identifying issues, securing relevant information, and identifying relations.
Judgment	Developing alternative courses of action and making decisions that are based on logical assumptions and reflect factual information.
Organization Sensitivity	Perceiving the impact and implications of decisions on other components of the organization.
Tenacity	Staying with a plan of action until the desired objective is achieved or is no longer reasonably attainable.

literature on assessment center dimensions is not exemplary. More bluntly, much of it is silly. Dimensions are given names, but the names are not defined. Trait constructs are often rejected by some who mistakenly define traits simply as personality variables that "cause" behavior, apparently irrespective of circumstances. Task competencies are often rejected because they are seen as being concerned only with outcomes, another unwarranted restriction in definition. Thornton and Byham (1982, p. 118) preferred to refer to "behavioral dimensions," which are inferred from job analysis, defined behaviorally in terms of directly observable behaviors, and free of any inferences about underlying personality traits.

It seems the real issue is not about whether the dimensions should be called traits, competencies, or behavioral dimensions; after all, they can all be defined in behavioral terms. The real problem is in the operations defining the dimensions. For most assessment center exercises, ratings are the assessments, so the issue is the typical problem with ratings.

Ratings. Exercises stimulate behavior, the behavior is observed by assessors, and the observations are the foundation for the ratings—which, like scores on tests, must have a meaning to be validated. If ratings of an attribute are valid, and if the same attribute is rated in two or more different exercises, then permissible inferences from ratings of the attribute should be at least somewhat consistent across those exercises; if not, they are not assessing a common construct.

The logic of multiple assessment is that prediction is better, because assessment is more reliable when assessments are replicated. In assessment centers, replication implies measuring a predictor in more than one way. If the predictors are the rated dimensions, then assessments (ratings) of an attribute in one exercise should generalize to (be correlated with) assessments in another. This is not a psychometric statement of parallel or equivalent forms; it is a statement that, if two exercises are designed so that they reveal (for example) skill in oral communication, then the communication effectiveness in one should be similar to the communication effectiveness in the other. As we see later, it rarely works out that way.

Overall Assessments. Most assessment centers call for an overall assessment rating (OAR). Different programs use different procedures for developing the OAR. Is the OAR an operational definition of a definable attribute? It might be, but often it is not; it is likely to be analogous to the composite score computed implicitly in multiple regression, when the composite is simply a complex predictor variable composed of a set of essentially unrelated but valid predictors. Other procedures might call for a mechanical averaging of overall ratings given to individual candidates by the various assessors. More commonly, however, there is a consensus meeting at which candidates are discussed, ratings on attributes are agreed on, independent OARs are made and shared, differences are discussed and resolved, and a consensus achieved. Many people consider the consensus meeting a key feature of the assessment center concept.

ASSESSMENT CENTER PROBLEMS AND ISSUES

There is no one orthodox "best" way in assessment center design; each program is different, in part to fit its different set of circumstances. The differences also highlight some problems of program design and some issues on which experts may disagree.

Construct Validities of Dimension Assessments

The biggest issue focuses on the dimensions, or constructs, rated by observers. Can internally consistent constructs be validly assessed by substantially different assessment exercises? Converging validity evidence is consistency in assessments of the same construct across exercises in which it is rated. Lack of convergence may not indicate invalid ratings; it may indicate only confusion about what is being assessed.

Dimensional Consistency. If the attribute (construct or dimension) is defined and the exercises developed so that the attribute rated reflects the same construct in two different exercises, then the correlation between the two ratings on the dimension should not be high, but substantial. Exercises are not designed as parallel forms, so correlations need not approximate reliability coefficients. The multitrait–multimethod logic should apply, however, where different exercises are intended to tap the same constructs. Correlations between ratings of the same dimensions on different exercises should be larger than the correlations between ratings on different dimensions within the same exercise; factor analysis of such a matrix should yield factors consistent with the dimensional constructs.

Results of Factor Analyses. Factor analysis results for a police assessment center are summarized in Table 13.3.[2] Clearly, the factors are defined, not by the dimensions, but by the exercises. The factor analysis provides no support for the construct validity of the dimension ratings and, in fact, supports the alternative position that dimension ratings are exercise specific rather than generalizable over exercises (and, by extension, to comparable aspects of performance on the job). This is not an isolated example. Sackett and Dreher (1982) analyzed data from three independent assessment centers and, in all three cases, found factors that were defined by exercises, not attributes. Many others have reported similar results.

Silverman, Dalessio, Woods, and Johnson (1986) looked for convergence experimentally in an assessment center with three exercises, each rated on the same six dimensions. In a within-exercise method, candidates were rated on each relevant dimension immediately at the conclusion of the exercise. A within-dimension method, a modification of the AT&T procedure, made dimension ratings after a staff conference. In the within-exercise method, all factors were exercise factors. Results were less clear for the within-dimension method, however. It also gave three factors, somewhat like the three within-exercise factors, but there were strong secondary loadings. Ratings of leadership, for example, had factor

[2]This was done in an unpublished study by Dennis Sweeney, then at Bowling Green State University.

TABLE 13.3

Rotated Factor Pattern of Police Assessment Center Ratings

Exercise and Dimension	Factor[a] *I*	*II*	*III*	*IV*	*V*	*VI*	h^2	*rxx*[b]
Leaderless Group Discussion (NR)								
Assertiveness—1[c]	30			88			88	70
Persuasiveness—1				88			87	66
Oral communication skill—1			81			75	58	
Assertiveness—2	32			82			80	75
Persuasiveness—2				60			40	64
Oral communication skill—2			82			78	40	
Leaderless Group Discussion (AR)								
Assertiveness—1	87						86	79
Persuasiveness—1	88						86	73
Oral communication skill—1	79						70	65
Assertiveness—2	82						78	76
Persuasiveness—2	57						38	68
Oral communication skill—2	75						63	52
Competitive Exercise								
Assertiveness—1			83				77	76
Team spirit—1			83				72	72
Assertiveness—2			83				76	70
Team spirit—2			86				78	67
Analysis Interview								
Reasoning—1						88	83	89
Reasoning—2						89	84	85
Stress Interview								
Stress tolerance—1					87		78	83
Stress tolerance—2					87		77	71
Situations Test								
Reasoning—1		88				79	42	
Written communication skill—1		83				69	32	
Reasoning—2		63					37	50

[a]Only factor loadings of .30 or higher are listed; decimal points omitted. [b]Interrater reliability coefficients. These are spuriously low; acceptable reliability estimates are necessarily higher than communalities. [c]1 indicates graphic ratings, 2 indicated checklist summated ratings.

loadings of at least .35 on all three exercises. In short, these were not dimension factors supporting the validity of construct inferences from dimensional ratings, but neither did they form the clear alternative factor pattern. Their results suggest that procedural adjustments can improve the construct validity of the ratings.

Reasons for Inconsistency in Dimension Ratings. Dimensions can be viewed from two extreme points of view. Neither makes much sense but, together, they help focus on the problem posed by the factor analysis results. At one extreme, the dimensions are viewed as unalterable traits (not necessarily genetic, but well-established by adulthood) exhibited consistently in behavior in virtually all circumstances. From this extreme view, multiple assessments of a dimension would serve no purpose other than increasing reliability, but they would converge. At the other extreme, the dimensions are simply aspects of behavior in a given situation, without generalizability to any other situation. Carrying this position to its logical extreme, prediction of future performance is impossible; even generalization from one exercise to another—even where both call for somewhat similar behaviors—is unlikely.

The extremes are obviously false; behavior can have both typical and situationally determined components. Low consistency across exercises may reflect inconsistent behavior; typical behavior may not be elicited in atypical situations or in situations having their own intrinsic behavioral imperatives. A person who is typically judgmental and vocal may be judgmental and vocal in a leaderless group discussion but inhibit that typical behavior in a simulation where one is to help two conflicting parties negotiate or reconcile their differences. Ratings on forcefulness of oral communication in these two exercises cannot reasonably be expected to correlate highly.

Many reasons might be offered to explain the tendency to get only exercise factors. The specificity of situational demands, described earlier, is one. Another is that rating dimensions with the same names does not necessarily mean the same constructs were rated. Constructs to be rated are rarely defined thoroughly; the usual case settles at best for a brief definitional phrase. Developers of assessment centers, perhaps even more than developers of other assessment methods, need to be extraordinarily precise in presenting their dimension definitions to the raters who must use them.

Solutions? The most common suggestion for solving the problem is the use of behaviorally based ratings or checklists. Reilly, Henry, and Smither (1990) asked assessors to write examples of behavior corresponding to dimensions they had rated previously on 5-point scales. A large pool of items remained after editing, and the Smith–Kendall retranslation procedure was used (P. C. Smith & Kendall, 1963). Items that were almost always assigned to the intended dimensions were placed in checklists for the dimensions, and assessors were instructed to use the checklists immediately after an exercise, indicating 0 (*behavior did not occur*), 1 (*behavior occurred once*), or 2 (*behavior occurred more than once*). Ratings on the dimension, for that exercise, were then made on the same 5-point scale previously used. Much better convergent validity was found when the checklist was used.

The use of a different sort of construct might help. Joyce, Thayer, and Pond (1994) classified possible dimensions as either person-oriented ("traditional" dimensions) or task oriented (their alternative to traditional dimensions). Examples of task-oriented dimensions included "Structuring and staffing tasks: Allocating manpower and resources to tasks, delegating assignments, and organizing the work of subordinates," and "Establishing effective work group relationships: Recognizing, praising, and encouraging employees and co-workers; maintaining a high level of morale" (Joyce et al., 1994, p. 113). A natural experiment was possible because two essentially parallel assessment centers were run by the same organization. One of these assessed managers as they entered a management training program, the other assessed them again 2 years later at the completion of the program. The first used traditional dimensions; the second used task-oriented dimensions. Results were familiar. Factor analysis of the dimensions, whether personal attributes or job functions, resulted in factors defined by exercises, not by either of the alternatives.

Recent meta-analytic research has suggested that the OAR may just be a combination of a small number of cognitive and personality factors (Arthur, Day, McNelly, & Edens, 2003; Collins et al., 2003). For example, Arthur and his colleagues (2003) found that the dimensions problem solving and influencing others had correlations with performance that, by themselves, exceeded the OAR-performance correlation. Collins and her associates (2003) similarly purported that cognitive ability and extraversion accounted for most of what was being measured by the OAR. It may be that a small number of dimensions would be sufficient for prediction purposes, and may result in the expected dimension factors.

Using meta-analysis to examine if assessment center methodology had an impact on the construct validity of dimension ratings, Woehr and Arthur (2003) indicated that better convergent validity across exercises was present when fewer dimensions were rated by the assessors. The researchers also noted that dimension ratings showed better convergent and discriminant validity when ratings were made by dimension across exercises, rather than within exercises.

Criterion-Related Validities

Despite many problems, assessment centers have amassed a good record of criterion-related validities. We do not know the underlying constructs, and we have little evidence to say that ratings of these (usually) poorly defined constructs are valid assessments. Nevertheless, dimension ratings and OARs have been valid predictors of future performance. Meta-analyses have found a mean corrected validity coefficient in the area of .36 to .37, with a lower bound of the 95% confidence interval well above 0, indicating generalized validity (Arthur et al., 2003; Gaugler, Rosenthal, Thornton, & Bentson, 1987).

There are, however, differences in validities across studies. This is not surprising; different assessment centers have different exercises, performance is rated on different (and different kinds of) dimensions, rater training varies widely, purposes differ, and different kinds of criteria are predicted. A review of meta analytic results suggests the following conclusions:

1. Predictive validity is higher when more kinds of assessment exercises are included. The multiple exercises should be multiple samples of job-related behavior, and multiple assessments of the same constructs.
2. Validities are higher in those assessment centers where peer evaluations are included. This point, and the preceding one, may merely indicate that more thoroughly developed programs are more valid.
3. Assessors' backgrounds and training moderate validity. OARs in assessment centers using psychologists as assessors are more valid than those where managers were the assessors.
4. Although the typical assessment center involves ratings on 10 or more dimensions, approximately 4 dimensions account for the assessment center's ability to predict performance. Demanding fewer dimension ratings from assessors is also related to better convergent validity across exercises.
5. Validities are much higher for ratings of potential for management progress than for predictions of future performance.

> Assessor judgments appear to be highly influenced by the candidate's ability to *solve problems* and *influence others*. Exercises used in traditional assessment centers may be best suited to the assessment of these two abilities.

Some skepticism is warranted. Apparent validity may be attributed to common stereotypes. A "good leader" stereotype can influence both assessments and criteria, providing no more than an illusion of validity. A contaminating source of variance destroys validity—unless it contaminates both assessment and criterion, in which case it gives an illusion of increasing validity by increasing the coefficient.

A Point of View

Both educational and managerial assessment people have been uncomfortable with traditional testing, questioning its appropriateness for their purposes. The discomfort has not been a traditional concern over reliability and validity so much as a concern about whether the right things have been measured. In-Basket tests, for example, became widely used assessment center exercises not because of superior reliability or predictive power but because they tap the everyday decision-making skills of managerial work.

Some validity coefficients for assessment centers, especially when ratings of potential are correlated with advancement over time, are very good. Others, however, seem ordinary, even low. The corrected validity coefficient for predicting performance was .36–.37 in the meta-analyses. Corrected validity coefficients for some paper-and-pencil methods are as high as .50. Why would one go to the trouble and expense of developing an assessment center that, on the average, might yield a lower validity than achieved by less expensive, more traditional methods? And how much confidence can one have that even the best validities cannot be explained away as the result of common stereotypes?

Skepticism implies questioning, not rejection. The questions should lead to research, not to abandonment or undue abbreviation of assessment centers. Some explanatory research has been done, and suggestions for redesign of assessment procedures have been offered. Many researchers explain the problem of construct validity as due to excessive cognitive demands on assessors. Perhaps assessors should be specialists for a few dimensions or a few exercises.

Two questions seem to require data. How many dimensions are needed to arrive at a stable OAR? How many are needed to predict the criterion? For either question, assessment center development requires an analog of the item analysis procedures of traditional test development. That is, the developer should determine, for each dimension and for each exercise, what it does in fact contribute both to the judgment and to the prediction. This requires pilot studies and a willingness to discard and perhaps replace dimensions or exercises that do not contribute.

DISCUSSION TOPICS

1. What are some ways to improve the reliability and validity of employment decisions based on individual assessments?
2. How can clinical judgment best be used in the process of assessing the suitability of a candidate for a position?
3. Viewing assessment center exercises as test items, how might we make the assessment center a more reliable and valid test?

References

Age Discrimination in Employment Act of 1967, 29 U.S.C. Sec 621 et seq. (1967).

Ajzen, I. (1991). The theory of planned behavior. *Organizational Behavior & Human Decision Processes, 50,* 179–211.

Albemarle Paper Company v. Moody, 422 U.S. 405 (1975).

Allen v. Alabama State Board of Education, No. 81-697-N (consent decree filed with U.S. District Court for the Middle District of Alabama Northern Division, 1985).

American Educational Research Association, American Psychological Association, & National Council on Measurement in Education. (1985). *Standards for educational and psychological testing*. Washington, DC: American Psychological Association.

American Psychological Association, American Educational Research Association, & National Council on Measurements Used in Education. (1954). Technical recommendations for psychological tests and diagnostic techniques. *Psychological Bulletin, 51,* 201–238.

American Psychological Association, American Educational Research Association, & National Council on Measurement in Education. (1966). *Standards for educational and psychological tests and manuals*. Washington, DC: American Psychological Association.

Anderson, C. W. (1960). The relation between speaking times and decision in the employment interview. *Journal of Applied Psychology, 44,* 267–268.

Anderson, N., & Burch, G. S. (2004). Measuring person–team fit: Development and validation of the team selection inventory. *Journal of Managerial Psychology, 19*(4), 406–426.

Arthur, W., Day, E. A., McNelly, T. L., & Edens, P. S. (2003). A meta-analysis of the criterion-related validity of assessment center dimensions. *Personnel Psychology, 56,* 125–154.

Ash, R. A., Johnson, J. C., Levine, E. L., & McDaniel, M. A. (1989). Job applicant training and work experience evaluation in personnel selection. *Research in Personnel and Human Resource Management, 7,* 183–226.

Ashton, M. C., Lee, K., & Goldberg, L. R. (2004). A hierarchical analysis of 1,710 English personality-descriptive adjectives. *Journal of Personality and Social Psychology, 87,* 707–721.

Balzer, W. K. (1986). Biases in the recording of performance-related information: The effects of initial impression and centrality of the appraisal task. *Organizational Behavior and Human Decision Processes, 37,* 329–347.

Balzer, W. K., & Sulsky, L. M. (1992). Halo and performance appraisal research: A critical examination. *Journal of Applied Psychology, 77,* 975–985.

Barrett, G. V., Phillips, J. S., & Alexander, R. A. (1981). Concurrent and predictive validity designs: A critical reanalysis. *Journal of Applied Psychology, 66,* 1–6.

Barrick, M. R., & Mount, M. K. (1993). Autonomy as a moderator of the relationships between the big five personality dimensions and job performance. *Journal of Applied Psychology, 78,* 111–118.

Barrick, M. R., Mount, M. K., & Judge, T. A. (2001). Personality and performance at the beginning of the new millennium: What do we know and where do we go next? *International Journal of Selection and Assessment, 9,* 9–31.

Bennett, R. E. (1993). On the meanings of constructed response. In R. E. Bennett & W. C. Ward (Eds.), *Construction versus choice in cognitive measurement: Issues in constructed response, performance testing, and portfolio assessment* (pp. 1–27). Hillsdale, NJ: Lawrence Erlbaum Associates.

Bennett, R. E., Rock, D. A., & Wang, M. (1991). Equivalence of free-response and multiple-choice items. *Journal of Educational Measurement, 28,* 77–92.

Bennett, R. E., & Ward, W. C. (Eds.). (1993). *Construction versus choice in cognitive measurement: Issues in constructed response, performance testing, and portfolio assessment.* Hillsdale, NJ: Lawrence Erlbaum Associates.

Bentz, V. J. (1967). The Sears experience in the investigation, description, and prediction of executive behavior. In F. R. Wickert & D. E. McFarland (Eds.), *Measuring executive effectiveness* (pp. 147–205). New York: Appleton-Century-Crofts.

Bernardin, H. J. (1987). Development and validation of a forced choice scale to measure job-related discomfort among customer service representatives. *Academy of Management Journal, 30,* 162–173.

Bernardin, H. J., & Beatty, R. W. (1984). *Performance appraisals: Assessing human behavior at work.* Boston: Kent.

Bernardin, H. J., & Buckley, M. R. (1981). Strategies in rater training. *Academy of Management Review, 6,* 205–212.

Bernardin, H. J., & Smith, P. C. (1981). A clarification of some issues regarding the development and use of behaviorally anchored rating scales (BARS). *Journal of Applied Psychology, 66,* 458–463.

Binning, J. F., & Barrett, G. V. (1989). Validity of personnel decisions: A conceptual analysis of the inferential and evidential bases. *Journal of Applied Psychology, 74,* 478–494.

Bobko, P., Karren, R., & Parkington, J. J. (1983). Estimation of standard deviations in utility analysis: An empirical test. *Journal of Applied Psychology, 68,* 170–176.

Boring, E. G. (1961). The beginning and growth of measurement in psychology. In H. Woolf (Ed.), *Quantification: A history of the meaning of measurement in the natural and social sciences* (pp. 108–127). Indianapolis: Bobbs-Merrill.

Borman, W. C. (1979). Format and training effects on rating accuracy and rater errors. *Journal of Applied Psychology, 64,* 410–421.

Borman, W. C. (1986). Behavior-based rating scales. In R. A. Berk (Ed.), *Performance assessment: Methods and applications* (pp. 100–120). Baltimore: Johns Hopkins University Press.

Borman, W. C. (1987). Personal constructs, performance schemata, and "folk theories" of subordinate effectiveness: Explorations in an army officer sample. *Organizational Behavior and Human Decision Processes, 40,* 307–322.

Borman, W. C., & Motowidlo, S. J. (1993). Expanding the criterion domain to include elements of contextual performance. In N. Schmitt & W. C. Borman (Eds.), *Personnel selection* (pp. 71–98). San Francisco: Jossey-Bass.

Bourassa, G. L., & Guion, R. M. (1959). A factorial study of dexterity tests. *Journal of Applied Psychology, 43,* 199–204.

Bowman, M. L. (1989). Testing individual differences in ancient China. *American Psychologist, 44,* 576–578.

Bray, D. W., Campbell, R. J., & Grant, D. L. (1974). *Formative years in business: A long-term AT&T study of managerial lives.* New York: Wiley.

Breaugh, J. A., & Dossett, D. L. (1989). Rethinking the use of personal history information: The value of theory-based biodata for predicting turnover. *Journal of Business & Psychology, 3,* 371–385.

Bridgeman, B. (1992). A comparison of quantitative questions in open-ended and multiple-choice formats. *Journal of Educational Measurement, 29,* 253–271.

Brogden, H. E. (1946). On the interpretation of the correlation coefficient as a measure of predictive efficiency. *Journal of Educational Psychology, 37,* 65–76.

Brogden, H. E. (1949). When testing pays off. *Personnel Psychology, 37,* 65–76.

Brogden, H. E., & Taylor, E. K. (1950). The dollar criterion—applying the cost accounting concept to criterion construction. *Personnel Psychology, 3,* 133–154.

Brooks, M. E., & Highhouse, S. (2006). Can good judgment be measured? In J. A. Weekley & R. E. Ployhart (Eds.), *Situational judgment tests.* Lawrence Erlbaum Associates.

Burch, G. S. J., & Anderson, N. (2004). Measuring person–team fit: Development and validation of the team selection inventory. *Journal of Managerial Psychology, 21,* 406–426.

Bureau of National Affairs. (1990). ADA: Americans With Disabilities Act of 1990: Text and analysis. *Labor Relations Reporter, 134*(11), S-3-S-47. (Supplement)

Camerer, C. F., & Johnson, E. J. (1991). The process-performance paradox in expert judgment: How can experts know so much and predict so badly? In K. A. Ericsson & J. Smith (Eds.), *Toward a general theory of expertise: Prospects and limits* (pp. 195–217). Cambridge, England: Cambridge University Press.

Campbell, D. T., & Fiske, D. W. (1959). Convergent and discriminant validation by the multitrait-multimethod matrix. *Psychological Bulletin, 56,* 81–105.

Campbell, J. P., McCloy, R. A., Oppler, S. H., & Sager, C. E. (1992). A theory of performance. In N. Schmitt & W. C. Borman (Eds.), *Personnel selection in organizations* (pp. 35–70). San Francisco: Jossey-Bass.

Campbell, J. P., McCloy, R. A., Oppler, S. H., & Sager, C. E. (1993). A theory of performance. In N. Schmitt & W. C. Borman (Eds.), *Personnel selection* (pp. 35–70). San Francisco: Jossey-Bass.

Campbell, J. T. (1962). Assessments of higher level personnel: I. Background and scope of the research. *Personnel Psychology, 15,* 57–62.

Campbell, J. T., Otis, J. L., Liske, R. E., & Prien, E. P. (1962). Assessments of higher level personnel: II. Validity of the overall assessment process. *Personnel Psychology, 15,* 63–74.

Campion, M. A., Pursell, E. D., & Brown, B. K. (1988). Structured interviewing: Raising the psychometric properties of the employment interview. *Personnel Psychology, 41,* 25–42.

Carrier, M. R., Dalessio, A. T., & Brown, S. H. (1990). Correspondence between estimates of content and criterion-related validity values. *Personnel Psychology, 43,* 85–100.

Carroll, J. B. (1993). *Human cognitive abilities: A survey of factor-analytic studies.* Cambridge, England: Cambridge University Press.

Cattell, J. M. (1890). Mental tests and measurements. *Mind, 15,* 373–380.

Cattell, R. B. (1963). Theory of fluid and crystallized intelligence: A critical experiment. *Journal of Educational Psychology, 54,* 1–22.

Chan, D., & Schmitt, N. (1997). Video-based versus paper-and-pencil method of assessment in situational judgment tests: Subgroup differences in test performance and face validity perceptions. *Journal of Applied Psychology, 82,* 143–159.

Chan, D., & Schmitt, N. (2002). Situational judgment and job performance. *Human Performance, 15,* 233–254.

Chow, S. L. (1991). Some reservations about power analysis. *American Psychologist, 46,* 1088.

Civil Rights Act of 1964, 42 U.S.C. § 253 (1964).

Claudy, J. G. (1978). Multiple regression and validity estimation in one sample. *Applied Psychological Measurement, 2,* 595–607.

Cleary, T. A. (1968). Test bias: Prediction of grades of Negro and White students in integrated colleges. *Journal of Educational Measurement, 5,* 115–124.

Cohen, J. (1960). A coefficient of agreement for nominal scales. *Educational and Psychological Measurement, 20,* 37–46.

Cohen, J. (1977). *Statistical power analysis for the behavioral sciences*. New York: Academic Press.

Cohen, J. (1983). The cost of dichotomization. *Applied Psychological Measurement, 7,* 249–253.

Cohen, J. (1990). Things I have learned (so far). *American Psychologist, 45,* 1304–1312.

Cole, M. (1953). *Robert Owen of New Lanark*. New York: Oxford University Press.

Cole, N. S. (1973). Bias in selection. *Journal of Educational Measurement, 10,* 237–255.

Cole, N. S., & Moss, P. A. (1989). Bias in test use. In R. L. Linn (Ed.), *Educational measurement* (pp. 201–219). New York: American Council on Education/Macmillan.

Collins, J. M., Schmidt, F. L., Sanchez-Ku, M., Thomas, L., McDaniel, M. A., & Le, H. (2003). Can basic individual differences shed light on the construct meaning of assessment center evaluations? *International Journal of Selection and Assessment, 11,* 17–29.

Connecticut v. Teal, 457 U. S. 440 (1982).

Conway, J. M., Jako, R. A., & Goodman, D. F. (1996). A meta-analysis of interrater and internal consistency reliability of selection interviews. *Journal of Applied Psychology, 80,* 565–579.

Cooper, W. H. (1981). Ubiquitous halo. *Psychological Bulletin, 90,* 218–244.

Costa, P. T., McCrae, R. R., & Kay, G. G. (1995). Persons, places and personality: Career assessment using the revised NEO Personality Inventory. *Journal of Career Assessment, 3,* 123–139.

Coward, W. M., & Sackett, P. R. (1990). Linearity of ability-performance relationships: A reconfirmation. *Journal of Applied Psychology, 75,* 297–300.

Cranny, C. J., & Doherty, M. E. (1988). Importance ratings in job analysis: Note on the misinterpretation of factor analysis in industry and the public sector. In S. Gael (Ed.), *The job analysis handbook for business, industry and government* (Vol. 2, pp. 1051–1071). New York: Wiley.

Crocker, J. (1981). Judgment of variation by social perceivers. *Psychological Bulletin, 87,* 272–292.

Cronbach, L. J. (1951). Coefficient alpha and the internal structure of tests. *Psychometrika, 16,* 297–334.

Cronbach, L. J. (1971). Test validation. In R. L. Thorndike (Ed.), *Educational measurement* (2nd ed., pp. 443–507). Washington, DC: American Council on Education.

Cronbach, L. J. (1975). Beyond the two disciplines of scientific psychology. *American Psychologist, 30,* 116–127.

Cronbach, L. J. (1988). Five perspectives on validity argument. In H. Wainer & H. I. Braun (Eds.), *Test validity* (pp. 3–17). Hillsdale, NJ: Lawrence Erlbaum Associates.

Cronbach, L. J., & Gleser, G. C. (1957). *Psychological tests and personnel decisions*. Urbana, IL: University of Illinois Press.

Cronbach, L. J., Gleser, G. C., Nanda, H., & Rajaratnam, N. (1972). *The dependability of behavioral measurements: Theory of generalizability for scores and profiles.* New York: Wiley.

Cuesta v. State of New York Office of Court Administration, 42 EPD Section 36,949 (SD, NY, 1987).

Cullen, M. J., Hardison, C. H., & Sackett, P. R. (2004). Using SAT-grade and ability-job performance relationships to test predictions derived from stereotype threat theory. *Journal of Applied Psychology, 89,* 220–230.

Cureton, E. E. (1950). Validity. In E. F. Lindquist (Ed.), *Educational measurement* (pp. 621–694).

Dachler, H. P. (1989). Selection and the organizational context. In P. Herriot (Ed.), *Assessment and selection in organizations: Methods and practice for recruitment and appraisal* (pp. 45–69). Chichester, England: Wiley.

Dalessio, A., & Imada, A. S. (1984). Relationships between interview selection decisions and perceptions of applicant similarity to an ideal employee and self: A field study. *Human Relations, 37,* 67–80.

Dalessio, A. T. (1994). Predicting insurance agent turnover using a video-based situational judgment test. *Journal of Business and Psychology, 9,* 23–32.

Daniels, H. W., & Otis, J. L (1950). A method for analyzing employment interviews. *Personnel Psychology, 3,* 425–444.

Dawes, R. M., & Corrigan, B. (1974). Linear models in decision making. *Psychological Bulletin, 81,* 95–106.

Day, D. V., & Sulsky, L. M. (1995). Effects of frame-of-reference training and information configuration on memory organization and rating accuracy. *Journal of Applied Psychology, 80,* 158–167.

Dean, M. A., Russell, C. J., & Muchinsky, P. M. (1999). Life experiences and performance prediction: Toward a theory of biodata. *Research in Human Resources Management, 17,* 245–281.

Deaux, K. (1993). Commentary: Sorry, wrong number—A reply to Gentile's call. *Psychological Science, 4,* 125–126.

Dothard v. Rawlinson, 15 FEP Cases 11 (1977).

Dougherty, T. W., Ebert, R. J., & Callender, J. C. (1986). Policy capturing in the employment interview. *Journal of Applied Psychology, 71,* 9–15.

Drasgow, F. (1987). Study of the measurement bias of two standardized psychological test. *Journal of Applied Psychology, 72,* 19–29.

Drever, J. (1952). *A dictionary of psychology.* Baltimore: Penguin.

DuBois, P. H. (1970). *The history of psychological testing.* Boston: Allyn & Bacon.

Dunnette, M. D. (1963). A modified model for test validation and selection research. *Journal of Applied Psychology, 47,* 317–323.

Dunnette, M. D., & Borman, W. C. (1979). Personnel selection and classification. *Annual Review of Psychology, 30,* 477–525.

Dwight, S. A., & Donovan, J. J. (2003). Do warning not to fake reduce faking? *Human Performance, 16,* 1–23.

Eels, R., & Walton, C. (1961). *Conceptual foundations of business.* Homewood, IL: Irwin.

Einhorn, H. J., & Bass, A. R. (1971). Methodological considerations relevant to discrimination in employment testing. *Psychological Bulletin, 75,* 261–269.

Ellis, A. P. J., West, B. J., Ryan, A. M., & DeShon, R. P. (2002). The use of impression management tactics in structured interviews: A function of question type? *Journal of Applied Psychology, 87,* 1200–1208.

England, G. W. (1971). *Development and use of weighted application blanks.* Dubuque, IA: Brown.

English, H. B., & English, A. C. (1958). *A comprehensive dictionary of psychological and psychoanalytic terms.* New York: Longmans, Green and Co.

Equal Employment Opportunity Commission. (1970). Guidelines on employee selection procedures. *Federal Register, 35*(149), 12333–12336.

Equal Employment Opportunity Commission, Civil Service Commission, Department of Labor, & Department of Justice. (1978). Uniform guidelines on employee selection procedures. *Federal Register, 43*(166), 38290–38315.

Faley, R. H., Kleiman, L. S., & Lengnick-Hall, M. L. (1984). Age discrimination and personnel psychology: A review and synthesis of the legal literature with implications for future research. *Personnel Psychology, 37,* 327–350.

Farrell, J. N., & McDaniel, M. A. (2001). The stability of validity coefficients over time: Ackerman's (1988) model and the General Aptitude Test Battery. *Journal of Applied Psychology, 86,* 60–79.

Fine, S. A., & Cronshaw, S. F. (1999). *Functional job analysis: A foundation for human resource management.* Mahwah, NJ: Lawrence Erlbaum Associates.

Flanagan, J. C. (1954). The critical incident technique. *Psychological Bulletin, 51,* 327–358.

Fleishman, E. A., & Reilly, M. E. (1992a). *Administrator's guide: F-JAS, Fleishman Job Analysis Survey.* Palo Alto, CA: Consulting Psychologists Press.

Fleishman, E. A., & Reilly, M. E. (1992b). *Handbook of human abilities: Definitions, measurements and job task requirements.* Palo Alto, CA: Consulting Psychologists Press.

Flexner, S. B. (Ed.). (1987). *Random House dictionary of the English language* (2nd ed., unabridged). New York: Random House.

Frederiksen, N., & Melville, S. D. (1954). Differential predictability in the use of test scores. *Educational and Psychological Measurement, 14,* 647–656.

French, J. W. (Ed.). (1951). The description of aptitude and achievement tests in terms of rotated factors. *Psychometric Monographs,* (5).

Freyd, M. (1923). Measurement in vocational selection: An outline of research procedure. *Journal of Personnel Research, 2,* 215–249, 268–284, 377–385.

Funder, D. C. (1991). Global traits: A neo-Allportian approach to personality. *Psychological Science, 2,* 31–39.

Gael, S. (1988). Subject matter expert conferences. In S. Gael (Ed.), *The job analysis handbook for business, industry, and government* (Vol. 1, pp. 432–445). New York: Wiley.

Ganzach, Y., Kluger, A. N., & Klayman, N. (2000) Making decisions from an interview: Expert measurement and mechanical combination. *Personnel Psychology, 53,* 1–20.

Gaugler, B. B., Rosenthal, D. B., Thornton, G. C., III, & Bentson, C. (1987). Meta-analysis of assessment center validity. *Journal of Applied Psychology, 72,* 493–511.

Gehrlein, T. M., Dipboye, R. L., & Shahani, C. (1993). Nontraditional validity calculations and differential interviewer experience: Implications for selection interviewers. *Educational and Psychological Measurement, 52,* 457–469.

Ghiselli, E. E. (1956). Dimensional problems of criteria. *Journal of Applied Psychology, 40,* 1–4.

Ghiselli, E. E. (1964). Dr. Ghiselli comments on Dr. Tupes' note. *Personnel Psychology, 17,* 61–63.

Ghiselli, E. E. (1966). *The validity of occupational aptitude tests.* New York: Wiley.

Gilovich, T. (1991). *How we know what isn't so: The fallibility of human reason in everyday life.* New York: The Free Press.

Gladwell, M. (2005). *Blink: The power of thinking without thinking.* Boston: Little Brown.

Glaser, R. (1963). Instructional technology and the measurement of learning outcomes. *American Psychologist, 18,* 519–521.

Glaser, R. (1994). Criterion-referenced tests: Part I. Origins. *Educational Measurement: Issues and Practice, 13*(4), 9–11.

Glaser, R., & Klaus, D. J. (1962). Proficiency measurement: Assessing human performance. In R. Gagné (Ed.), *Psychological principles in system development* (pp. 421–427). New York: Holt, Rinehart & Winston.

Goals 2000: Educate America Act, Pub. L. No. 103-227, 108 Stat. 125 (1994, March 31).

Goffin, R. D., & Christiansen, N. D. (2003). Correcting personality tests for faking: A review of popular personality tests and an initial survey of researchers. *International Journal of Selection and Assessment, 11,* 340–344.

Goldberg, L. R. (1993). The structure of phenotypic personality traits. *American Psychologist, 48,* 26–34.

Goldberg, L. R. (1999). The Development of Five-Factor Domain Scales from the IPIP Item Pool. [On-line]. Available URL: http://ipip.ori.org/ipip/memo.ht

Goldberg, L. R., Grenier, J. R., Guion, R. M., Sechrest, L. B., & Wing, H. (1991). *Questionnaires used in the prediction of trustworthiness in pre-employment selection decisions: An APA task force report.* Washington, DC: American Psychological Association.

Golden Rule Insurance Company et al. v. Washburn et al., No. 419-76 (stipulation for dismissal and order dismissing cause, Circuit Court of Seventh Judicial Circuit, Sangamon County, IL, 1984).

Goleman, D. (1995). *Emotional intelligence.* New York: Bantam.

Gottfredson, G. D., & Holland, J. L. (1994). *Position Classification Inventory.* Odessa, FL: Psychological Assessment Resources.

Gough, H. G. (1985). A work orientation scale for the California Psychological Inventory. *Journal of Applied Psychology, 70,* 505–513.

Gratz v. Bollinger, 539 U.S. (2003).

Griggs v. Duke Power Co., 401 U.S. 424 (1971).

Guilford, J. P. (1954). *Psychometric methods* (2nd ed.). New York: McGraw-Hill.

Guilford, J. P. (1959). *Personality*. New York: McGraw-Hill.

Guion, R. M. (1961). Criterion measurement and personnel judgments. *Personnel Psychology, 14,* 141–149.

Guion, R. M. (1965). *Personnel testing*. New York: McGraw-Hill.

Guion, R. M. (1966). Employment tests and discriminatory hiring. *Industrial Relations, 5,* 20–37.

Guion, R. M. (1980). On trinitarian doctrines of validity. *Professional Psychology, 11,* 385–398.

Guion, R. M. (1987). Changing views for personnel selection. *Personnel Psychology, 40,* 199–213.

Guion, R. M. (1991). Personnel assessment, selection, and placement. In M. D. Dunnette & L. M. Hough (Eds.), *Handbook of industrial and organizational psychology* (2nd ed., Vol. 2, pp. 327–397). Palo Alto, CA: Consulting Psychologists Press.

Guion, R. M. (1996). Evaluation of performance tests for work readiness. In L. R. Resnick & J. G. Wirt (Eds.), *Linking school and work: Roles for standards and assessment* (pp. 267–303). San Francisco: Jossey-Bass.

Guion, R. M. (1998). *Assessment, measurement, and prediction for. personnel decisions*. Mahwah, NJ: Lawrence Erlbaum Associates.

Guion, R. M., & Gottier, R. F. (1965). Validity of personality measures in personnel selection. *Personnel Psychology, 18,* 135–164.

Guion, R. M., Highhouse, S., Reeve, C., & Zickar, M. J. (2005). *The Self-Descriptive Index.* Sequential Employment Testing. Bowling Green, OH.

Guion, R. M., & Ironson, G. H. (1983). Latent trait theory for organizational research. *Organizational Behavior and Human Performance, 31,* 54–87.

Gulliksen, H. (1950). *Theory of mental tests*. New York: Wiley.

Gutman, A. (2000). *EEO law and personnel practices*. Newbury Park, CA: Sage.

Guttman, L. (1945). A basis for analyzing test–retest reliability. *Psychometrika, 10,* 255–282.

Hakel, M. D. (1989). The state of employment interview theory and research. In R. W. Eder & G. R. Ferris (Eds.), *The employment interview: Theory, research, and practice* (pp. 285–293). Newbury Park, CA: Sage.

Hanson, C. P., & Conrad, K. A. (1991). *A handbook of psychological assessment in business*. New York: Quorum Books.

Harris, M. M. (1989). Reconsidering the employment interview: A review of recent literature and suggestions for future research. *Personnel Psychology, 42,* 691–726.

Hartigan, J. A., & Wigdor, A. K. (Eds.). (1989). *Fairness in employment testing: Validity generalization, minority issues, and the General Aptitude Test Battery*. Washington, DC: National Academy Press.

Hattrup, K., Schmitt, N., & Landis, R. S. (1992). Equivalence of constructs measured by job-specific and commercially available aptitude tests. *Journal of Applied Psychology, 77,* 298–308.

Hausknecht, J. P., Day, D. V., & Thomas, S. C. (2004). Applicant reactions to selection procedures: An updated model and meta-analysis. *Personnel Psychology, 57,* 639–683.

Hawk, J. A. (1970). Linearity of criterion-GATB aptitude relationships. *Measurement and Evaluation in Guidance, 2,* 249–251.

Hazer, J. T., & Highhouse, S. (1997). Factors influencing managers' reactions to utility analysis: Effects of SD_y method, information frame, and focal intervention. *Journal of Applied Psychology, 82,* 104–112.

Hedge, J. W., Teachout, M. S., & Laue, F. J. (1990). *Interview testing as a work sample measure of job proficiency.* AFHRL-TP-89-60. Brooks Air Force Base, TX: Air Force Systems Command.

Helmreich, R. L., Sawin, L. L., & Carsrud, A. L. (1986). The honeymoon effect in job performance: Temporal increases in the predictive power of achievement motivation. *Journal of Applied Psychology, 71,* 185–188.

Henle, C. A. (2004). Case review of the legal status of banding. *Human Performance, 17*(4), 415–432.

Highhouse, S. (1996a). Context-dependent selection: The effects of decoy and phantom job candidates. *Organizational Behavior and Human Decision Processes, 65,* 68–76.

Highhouse, S. (1996b). The utility estimate as a communication device: Practical questions and research directions. *Journal of Business and Psychology, 11,* 85–100.

Highhouse, S. (1997). Understanding and improving job-finalist choice: The relevance of behavioral decision research. *Human Resource Management Review, 7,* 449–470.

Highhouse, S. (2002). Assessing the candidate as a whole: A historical and critical analysis of individual psychological assessment for personnel decision making. *Personnel Psychology, 55,* 363–396.

Hofstee, W. K. B., de Raad, B., & Goldberg, L. R. (1992). Integration of the big five and circumflex approaches to trait structure. *Journal of Personality and Social Psychology, 63,* 146–163.

Hogan, J. (1991a). Physical abilities. In M. D. Dunnette & L. M. Hough (Eds.), *Handbook of industrial and organizational psychology* (2nd ed., Vol. 2, pp. 753–831). Palo Alto, CA: Consulting Psychologists Press.

Hogan, J. (1991b). Structure of physical performance in occupational tasks. *Journal of Applied Psychology, 76,* 495–507.

Hogan, J., Hogan, R., & Busch, C. M. (1984). How to measure service orientation. *Journal of Applied Psychology, 69,* 167–173.

Hogan, J., & Quigley, A. M. (1986). Physical standards for employment and the courts. *American Psychologist, 41,* 1193–1217.

Hogan, R., & Hogan, J. (1992). *Hogan Personality Inventory: Manual.* Tulsa, OK: Hogan Assessment Systems.

Hogarth, R. (2001). *Educating intuition.* University of Chicago Press.

Holland, P. W., & Wainer, H. (Eds.). (1993). *Differential item functioning.* Hillsdale, NJ: Lawrence Erlbaum Associates.

Hollingworth, H. L. (1923). *Judging human character.* New York: Appleton.

Hough, L. M. (1992). The "Big Five" personality variables—construct confusion: Description versus prediction. *Human Performance, 5,* 139–155.

Hough, L., & Tippins, N. (1994, April). New designs for selection and placement systems: The Universal Test Battery. In N. Schmitt (Chair), *Cutting edge developments in selection.* Symposium at meeting of the Society for Industrial and Organizational Psychology, Nashville, TN.

Howard, A. (1986). College experiences and managerial performance. *Journal of Applied Psychology, 71,* 530–555.

Huffcutt, A. I., & Arthur, W., Jr. (1994). Hunter and Hunter (1984) revisited: Interview validity for entry-level jobs. *Journal of Applied Psychology, 79,* 184–190.

Huffcutt, A. I., & Roth, P. L. (1998). Racial group differences in employment interview evaluations. *Journal of Applied Psychology, 83,* 179–189.

Hull, C. L. (1928). *Aptitude testing.* Yonkers-on-Hudson: World Book.

Humphreys, L. G. (1952). Individual differences. *Annual Review of Psychology, 3,* 131–150.

Humphreys, L. G. (1979). The construct of general intelligence. *Intelligence, 3,* 105–120.

Hunter, J. E. (1983). *Test validation for 12,000 jobs: An application of job classification and validity generalization analysis to the General Aptitude Test Battery (GATB)* (Test Research Rpt. No. 45). Washington, DC: U.S. Employment Service, U.S. Department of Labor.

Hunter, J. E., & Schmidt, F. L. (1990). *Methods of meta-analysis: Correcting error and bias in research findings.* Newbury Park, CA: Sage.

Hurtz, G. M., & Donovan, J. J. (2000). Personality and job performance: The Big Five revisited. *Journal of Applied Psychology, 85,* 869–879.

Huse, E. F. (1962). Assessments of higher level personnel. IV. The validity of assessment techniques based on systematically varied information. *Personnel Psychology, 15,* 195–205.

International Brotherhood of Teamsters v. United States, 431 U. S. 324 (1977).

Inwald, R. (1992). *Hilson Job Analysis Questionnaire.* Kew Gardens, NY: Hilson Research.

Ironson, G. H., Guion, R. M., & Ostrander, M. (1982). Adverse impact from a psychometric perspective. *Journal of Applied Psychology, 67,* 419–432.

Jackson, D. N., & Messick, S. (1958). Content and style in personality assessment. *Psychological Bulletin, 55,* 243–252.

Jaeger, R. M. (Ed.). (1976). On bias in selection [Special issue]. *Journal of Educational Measurement, 13,* 3–99.

James, L. R. (1998). Measurement of personality via conditional reasoning. *Organizational Research Methods, 1,* 131–163.

James, L. R., McIntyre, M. D., Glisson, C. A., Bowler, J. L., & Mitchell, T. R. (2004). The Conditional Reasoning Measurement System for aggression: An overview. *Human Performance, 17,* 271–295.

Janz, T., Hellervik, L., & Gilmore, D. C. (1986). *Behavior description interviewing.* Boston: Allyn & Bacon.

Jeanneret, P. R. (1994, July). *Accommodation: State of the research and practice when complying with the Americans With Disabilities Act.* Address to the American Psychological Society, Washington, DC.

Jeanneret, P. R., & Strong, M. H. (2003). Linking O*Net job analysis information to job requirement predictors: An O*Net application. *Personnel Psychology, 56*, 465–492.

Johnson, H. W. (1975). The Hawthorne studies: The legend and the legacy. In E. L. Cass & F. G. Zimmer (Eds.), *Man and work in society* (pp. 273–277). New York: Van Nostrand Reinhold.

Joyce, L. W., Thayer, P. W., & Pond, S. B., III. (1994). Managerial functions: An alternative to traditional assessment center dimensions? *Personnel Psychology, 47,* 109–121.

Judge, T. A., & Cable, D. M. (2004). The effect of physical height on workplace success and income: Preliminary test of a theoretical model. *Journal of Applied Psychology, 89,* 428–441.

Judge, T. A., Erez, A., Bono, J. E., & Thoresen, C. J. (2003). The Core Self-Evaluations Scale: Development of a measure. *Personnel Psychology, 56,* 303–331.

Judge, T. A., Higgins, C. A., & Cable, D. M. (2000). The employment interview: A review of recent research and recommendations for future research. *Human Resource Management Review, 10,* 383–406.

Kane, J. S. (1987, April 22). *Wish I may, wish I might, wish I could do performance appraisal right.* Unpublished manuscript, School of Management, University of Massachusetts, Amherst, MA.

Kanfer, R., & Ackerman, P. L. (1989). Motivation and cognitive abilities: An integrative/aptitude treatment interaction approach to skill acquisition. *Journal of Applied Psychology, 74,* 657–690.

Kehoe, J. F., & Tenopyr, M. L. (1994). Adjustment in assessment scores and their usage: A taxonomy and evaluation of methods. *Psychological Assessment, 6,* 291–303.

Kichuk, S. L., & Wiesner, W. H. (1998). Work teams: Selecting members for optimal performance. *Canadian Psychology, 39,* 23–32.

Kinicki, A. J., Lockwood, C. A., Hom, P. W., & Griffeth, R. W. (1990). Interviewer predictions of applicant qualifications and interviewer validity: Aggregate and individual analyses. *Journal of Applied Psychology, 75,* 477–486.

Kinslinger, H. J. (1966). Application of projective techniques in personnel psychology since 1940. *Psychological Bulletin, 66,* 134–149.

Kuder, G. F., & Richardson, M. W. (1937). The theory of estimation of test reliability. *Psychometrika, 2,* 151–160.

Kuncel, N. R., Hezlett, S. A., & Ones, D. S. (2004). Academic performance, career potential, creativity, and job performance: Can one construct predict them all? *Journal of Personality and Social Psychology, 86,* 148–161.

Kraiger, K. (1990, April). *Generalizability of performance measures across four Air Force specialities* (Technical Paper AFHRL-TP-89-60). Brooks AFB, TX: Air Force Systems Command.

Kraiger, K., & Ford, J. K. (1985). A meta-analysis of ratee race effects in performance ratings. *Journal of Applied Psychology, 70,* 56–65.

Kriedt, P. H., & Dawson, R. I. (1961). Response set and the prediction of clerical job performance. *Journal of Applied Psychology, 45,* 175–178.

Kristof-Brown, A., Barrick, M. R., & Franke, M. (2002). Applicant impression management: Dispositional influences and consequences for recruiter perceptions of fit and similarity. *Journal of Management, 28,* 27–46.

Landy, F. J. (1989). *Psychology of work behavior.* Pacific Grove, CA: Brooks/Cole.

Latham, G. P. (1989). The reliability, validity, and practicality of the situational interview. In R. W. Eder & G. R. Ferris (Eds.), *The employment interview: Theory, research, and practice* (pp. 169–182). Newbury Park, CA: Sage.

Latham, G. P., & Wexley, K. N. (1977). Behavioral observation scales for performance appraisal. *Personnel Psychology, 30,* 255–268.

Latham, G. P., & Wexley, K. N. (1981). *Increasing productivity through performance appraisal.* Reading, MA: Addison-Wesley.

Lawshe, C. H. (1952). What can industrial psychology do for small business? (A symposium). 2. Employee selection. *Personnel Psychology, 5,* 31–34.

Lawshe, C. H. (1975). A quantitative approach to content validity. *Personnel Psychology, 28,* 563–575.

Lawshe, C. H. (1979). Shrinking the cosmos: A practitioner's thoughts on alternative selection procedures. In P. Griffin (Ed.), *The search for alternative selection procedures: Developing a professional stand* (pp. 1–26). Los Angeles: Personnel Testing Council of Southern California.

Lawshe, C. H. (1987a). Adverse impact: Is it a viable concept? *Professional Psychology: Research and Practice, 18,* 492–497.

Lawshe, C. H. (1987, November). *A practitioner's thoughts on job analysis.* Paper presented at Content Validity III, Bowling Green State University, Bowling Green, OH. (Updated July 1987)

Lawshe, C. H., & Balma, M. J. (1966). *Principles of personnel testing* (2nd ed.). New York: McGraw-Hill.

Lawshe, C. H., Kephart, N. C., & McCormick, E. J. (1949). The paired comparison technique for rating performance of industrial employees. *Journal of Applied Psychology, 33,* 69–77.

Lawshe, C. H., & Schucker, R. E. (1959). The relative efficiency of four test weighting methods in multiple prediction. *Educational and Psychological Measurement, 19,* 103–114.

Levy, P. E., & Williams, J. R. (2004). The social context of performance appraisal: A review and framework for the future. *Journal of Management, 30,* 881–905.

Li, H., Rosenthal, R., & Rubin, D. B. (1996). Reliability of measurement in psychology: From Spearman-Brown to maximal reliability. *Psychological Methods, 1,* 98–107.

Lievens, F., Highhouse, S., & De Corte, W. (2005). The importance of traits and abilities in supervisors' hirability decisions as a function of method of assessment. *Journal of Occupational and Organizational Psychology.*

Lievens, F., Sanchez, J. I., & De Corte, W. (2004). Easing the inferential leap in competency modeling: The effects of task-related information and subject matter expertise. *Personnel Psychology, 57,* 881.

Likert, R. (1932). A technique for the measurement of attitudes. *Archives of Psychology, 140,* 44–53.

Lilienfeld, S. O., Wood, J. M., & Garb, H. N. (2000). The scientific status of projective techniques. *Psychological Science in the Public Interest, 1,* 27–66.

Lindemann, B., & Grossman, P. (1996). *Employment discrimination law* (3rd ed.). Washington, DC: Bureau of National Affairs.

Linn, R. L. (1994). Criterion-referenced measurement: A valuable perspective clouded by surplus meaning. *Educational Measurement: Issues and Practice, 13*(4), 12–14.

Linn, R. L., & Werts, C. E. (1971). Considerations for studies of test bias. *Journal of Educational Measurement, 8,* 1–4.

Lin, T. R., Dobbins, G. H., & Farh, J. (1992). A field study of race and age similarity effects on interview ratings in conventional and situational interviews. *Journal of Applied Psychology, 77,* 367–371.

Lord, F. M., & Novick, M. R. (1968). *Statistical theories of mental test scores.* Reading, MA: Addison-Wesley.

Macan, T. H., & Highhouse, S. (1994). Communicating the utility of human resource activities: A survey of I/O and HR professionals. *Journal of Business and Psychology, 8,* 425–436.

Mael, F. A. (1991). A conceptual rationale for the domain and attribute of biodata items. *Personnel Psychology, 44,* 763–792.

Mael, F. A. (1993). Rainforest empiricism and quasi-rationality: Two approaches to objective biodata. *Personnel Psychology, 46,* 719–738.

Magnusson, D., & Torestad, B. (1993). A holistic view of personality: A model revisited. *Annual Review of Psychology, 44,* 427–452.

Management Scientists, Inc. (1982). *Development/validation of written examination for uniformed court officer/senior court officer, Office of Court Administration, State of New York* (Vol. 3). Philadelphia: MSI.

Martin, L. (1991). *A report on the glass-ceiling initiative.* U.S. Department of Labor.

Martinez, M. E. (1991). A comparison of multiple-choice and constructed figural response items. *Journal of Educational Measurement, 28,* 131–145.

Matthews, G., Roberts, R. D., & Zeidner, M. (2004). Seven myths about emotional intelligence. *Psychological Inquiry, 15*(3), 179–196.

Matthews, G., Zeidner, M., & Roberts, R. D. (2002). *Emotional intelligence: Science and myth.* Cambridge, MA: MIT Press.

Mayer, J. D., & Salovey, P. (1997). *What is emotional intelligence?* New York: Basic Books.

McAdams, D. P. (1992). The five factor model *in* personality: A clinical appraisal. *Journal of Personality, 60,* 329–361.

McClough, A. C., & Rogelberg, S. G. (2003). Selection in teams: An exploration of the Teamwork Knowledge, Skills, and Ability test. *International Journal of Selection & Assessment, 11,* 56–66.

McCormick, E. J. (1959). Applications of job analysis to indirect validity. *Personnel Psychology, 12,* 402–413.

McCormick, E. J. (1979). *Job analysis.* New York: AMACOM.

McCormick, E. J., & Ilgen, D. R. (1980). *Industrial psychology* (7th ed.). Englewood Cliffs, NJ: Prentice-Hall.

McCrae, R. R. (Ed.). (1992). The five-factor model: Issues and applications [Special issue]. *Journal of Personality, 60*(2), 175–532.

McDaniel, M. A., & Nguyen, N. T. (2001). Situational judgment tests: A review of practice and constructs assessed. *International Journal of Selection and Assessment, 9,* 103–113.

McDaniel, M. A., Schmidt, F. L., & Hunter, J. E. (1988b). A meta-analysis of the validity of methods for rating training and experience in personnel selection. *Personnel Psychology, 41,* 283–314.

McDaniel, M. A., Whetzel, D. L., Schmidt, F. L., & Maurer, S. D. (1994). The validity of employment interviews: A comprehensive review and meta-analysis. *Journal of Applied Psychology, 79,* 599–616.

McMurry, R. N. (1947). Validating the patterned interview. *Personnel, 23,* 263–272.

Meehl, P. E. (1954). *Clinical versus statistical prediction.* Minneapolis: University of Minnesota Press.

Meehl, P. E. (1967). What can the clinician do well? In D. N. Jackson & S. Messick (Eds.), *Problems in human assessment* (pp. 594–599). New York: McGraw-Hill.

Mehrens, W. A. (1992). Using performance assessment for accountability purposes. *Educational Measurement: Issues and Practice, 11*(1), 3–9, 20.

Messick, S. (1989). Validity. In R. L. Linn (Ed.), *Educational measurement* (3rd ed., pp. 13–103). New York: American Council on Education & Macmillan.

Messick, S. (1995). Standards of validity and the validity of standards in performance assessment. *Educational Measurement: Issues and Practice, 14*(4), 5–8.

Miner, M. G., & Miner, J. B. (1978). *Employee selection within the law.* Washington, DC: Bureau of National Affairs.

Micceri, T. (1989). The unicorn, the normal curve, and other improbable creatures. *Psychological Bulletin, 105,* 156–166.

Miller, C. S., Kaspin, J. A., & Schuster, M. H. (1990). The impact of performance appraisal methods on age discrimination in Employment Act cases. *Personnel Psychology, 43.*

Mischel, W. (1968). *Personality and assessment.* New York: Wiley.

Morgeson, F. P., Delaney-Klinger, K., Mayfield, M. S., Ferrara, P., & Campion, M. A. (2004). Self-presentation processes in job analysis: A field experiment investigating inflation in abilities, tasks, and competencies. *Journal of Applied Psychology, 89*(4), 674–686

Murphy, K. R. (1989). Is the relationship between cognitive ability and job performance stable over time? *Human Performance, 2,* 183–200.

Murphy, K. R., Balzer, W. K., Lockhart, M. C., & Eisenman, E. J. (1985). Effects of previous performance on evaluations of present performance. *Journal of Applied Psychology, 70,* 72–84.

Murray, H. A. (1938). *Explorations in personality.* New York: Oxford University Press.

National Commission on Testing and Public Policy. (1990). *From gatekeeper to gateway: Transforming testing in America.* Chestnut Hill, MA: National Commission on Testing and Public Policy, Boston College.

Offermann, L. R., & Gowing, M. K. (1993). Personnel selection in the future: The impact of changing demographics and the nature of work. In N. Schmitt & W. C. Borman (Eds.), *Personnel selection in organizations* (pp. 385–417). San Francisco: Jossey-Bass.

Officers for Justice v. Civil Service Commission of the City and County of San Francisco. (1991). U.S. District, LEXIS 8259.

Oppler, S. H., Peterson, N. G., & McCloy, R. A. (1994, April). *A comparison of peer and supervisory ratings as criteria for the validation of predictors.* Paper presented to the Society for Industrial and Organizational Psychology, Nashville, TN.

Otis, J. L., Campbell, J. T., & Prien, E. P. (1962). Assessment of higher level personnel: VII. The nature of assessments. *Personnel Psychology, 15,* 441–446.

Parkinson, C. N. (1962). Genius by the yard. *Saturday Review, 45*(41), 32–33.

Pearlman, K., Schmidt, F. L., & Hunter, J. E. (1980). Validity generalization results for tests used to predict job proficiency and training success in clerical occupations. *Journal of Applied Psychology, 65,* 373–406.

Pedhazur, E. J., & Schmelkin, L. P. (1991). *Measurement, design, and analysis: An integrated approach.* Hillsdale, NJ: Lawrence Erlbaum Associates.

Petersen, N. S., & Novick, M. R. (1976). An evaluation of some models for culture-fair selection. *Journal of Educational Measurement, 13,* 3–29.

Peterson, N. G., Borman, W. C., Hanson, M. A., & Kubisiak, U. C. (1999). Summary of results, implications for O*NET applications, and future directions. *An occupational information system for the 21st century: The development of O*NET* (pp. 289–295). American Psychological Association, Washington, DC, US xii, 336pp.

Ployhart, R. E., & Ehrhart, M. G. (2003). Be careful what you ask for: Effects of response instructions on the construct validity and reliability of situational judgment tests. *International Journal of Selection and Assessment, 11,* 1–16.

Posthuma, R. A., Morgeson, F. P., & Campion, M. A. (2002). Beyond employment interview validity: A comprehensive narrative review of recent research and trends over time. *Personnel Psychology, 55,* 1–81.

Prewett-Livingston, A. J., Feild, H. S., Veres, J. G., III, & Lewis, P. M. (1996). Effects of race on interview ratings in a situational panel interview. *Journal of Applied Psychology, 81,* 178–186.

Raju, N. S., Edwards, J. E., & LoVerde, M. A. (1985). Corrected formulas for computing sample sizes under indirect range restriction. *Journal of Applied Psychology, 70,* 565–566.

Raju, N. S., Steinhaus, S. D., Edwards, J. E., & DeLessio, J. (1991). A logistic regression model for personnel selection. *Applied Psychological Measurement, 15,* 139–152.

Rasch, G. (1980). *Probabilistic models for some intelligence and attainment tests*. Chicago: University of Chicago Press. (Originally work published 1960)

Raymark, P. H., Schmit, M. J., & Guion, R. M. (1997). Identifying potentially useful personality constructs for employee selection. *Personnel Psychology, 50*(3), 723–736.

Regents, University of California v. Bakke, 438 U. S. 265 (1978).

Reilly, R. R., & Chao, G. T. (1982). Validity and fairness of some alternative employee selection procedures. *Personnel Psychology, 35,* 1–62.

Reilly, R. R., Henry, S., & Smither, J. W. (1990). An examination of the effects of using behavior checklists on the construct validity of assessment center dimensions. *Personnel Psychology, 43,* 71–84.

Richardson, M. W. (1941). The combination of measures. In P. Horst (Ed.), *The prediction of personal adjustment* (pp. 379–401). New York: Social Science Research Council.

Richardson, M. W., & Kuder, F. (1939). The calculation of test reliability coefficients based upon the method of rational equivalence. *Journal of Educational Psychology, 30,* 681–687.

Robie, C., & Ryan, A. M. (1999). Effects of nonlinearity and heteroscedasticity on the validity of conscientiousness in predicting overall job performance. *International Journal of Selection and Assessment, 7*, 157–169.

Rounds, J. (1995). Vocational interests: Evaluating structural hypotheses. In D. Lubinski & R. V. Dawis (Eds.), *Assessing individual differences in human behavior* (pp. 177–232). Palo Alto, CA: Davies-Black.

Ruch, F. L., & Ruch, W. W. (1967). The *K* factor as a (validity) suppressor variable in predicting success in selling. *Journal of Applied Psychology, 51,* 201–204.

Ryan, A. M., Daum, D., Bauman, T., Grisez, M., Mattimore, K., Nalodka, T., & McCormick, S. (1995). Direct, indirect, and controlled observation and rating accuracy. *Journal of Applied Psychology, 80,* 664–670.

Ryan, A. M., & Lasek, M. (1991). Negligent hiring and defamation: Areas of liability related to pre-employment inquiries. *Personnel Psychology, 44,* 293–319.

Ryan, A. M., & Sackett, P. R. (1987a). Pre-employment honesty testing: Fakability, reactions of test takers, and company image. *Journal of Business and Psychology, 1,* 248–256.

Ryan, A. M., & Sackett, P. R. (1987b). A survey of individual assessment practices by I/O psychologists. *Personnel Psychology, 40,* 457–487.

Ryan, A. M., & Sackett, P. R. (1989). Exploratory study of individual assessment practices: Interrater reliability and judgments of assessor effectiveness. *Journal of Applied Psychology, 74,* 568–579.

Sackett, P. R., & Dreher, G. F. (1982). Constructs and assessment center dimensions: Some troubling empirical findings. *Journal of Applied Psychology, 67,* 401–410.

Sackett, P. R., & DuBois, C. L. Z. (1991). Rater–ratee race effects on performance evaluation: Challenging meta-analytic conclusions. *Journal of Applied Psychology, 76,* 873–877.

Sackett, P. R., & Laczo, R. M. (2003). Job and work analysis. *Handbook of Psychology: Industrial and Organizational, 12,* 21–37.
Sackett, P. R., & Ostgaard, D. J. (1994). Job-specific applicant pools and national norms for cognitive ability tests: Implications for range restriction corrections in validation research. *Journal of Applied Psychology, 79,* 680–684.
Sackett, P. R., & Wade, B. E. (1983). On the feasibility of criterion-related validity: The effects of range restriction assumptions on needed sample size. *Journal of Applied Psychology, 68,* 374–381.
Sanchez, J. I., & Levine, E. L. (2001). The analysis of work in the 20th and 21st centuries. In N. Anderson & D. S. Ones, *Handbook of industrial, work and organizational psychology: Vol. 1. Personnel psychology* (pp. 71–89). London: Sage.
Saunders, D. R. (1956). Moderator variables in prediction. *Educational and Psychological Measurement, 16,* 209–222.
Schippmann, J. S., Ash, R. A., Battista, M., Carr, L., Eye, L. D., Hesketh, B., Kehoe, J., Pearlman, K., Prien, E. P., & Sanchez, J. I. (2000). The practice of competency modeling. *Personnel Psychology, 53,* 703–740.
Schmidt, F. L., & Hunter, J. E. (1977). Development of a general solution to the problem of validity generalization. *Journal of Applied Psychology, 62,* 529–540.
Schmidt, F. L., & Hunter, J. E. (1981). Employment testing: Old theories and new research findings. *American Psychologist, 36,* 1128–1137.
Schmidt, F. L., & Hunter, J. E. (1998). The validity and utility of selection methods in personnel psychology: Practical and theoretical implications of 85 years of research findings. *Psychological Bulletin, 124,* 262–274.
Schmidt, F. L., Hunter, J. E., Croll, P. R., & McKenzie, R. C. (1983). Estimation of employment test validities by expert judgment. *Journal of Applied Psychology, 68,* 590–601.
Schmidt, F. L., Hunter, J. E., & Urry, V. W. (1976). Statistical power in criterion-related validation studies. *Journal of Applied Psychology, 61,* 473–485.
Schmidt, F. L., Law, K., Hunter, J. E., Rothstein, H. R., Pearlman, K., & McDaniel, M. (1993). Refinements in validity generalization methods: Implications for the situational specificity hypothesis. *Journal of Applied Psychology, 78,* 3–12.
Schmidt, F. L., & Zimmerman, R. D. (2004). A counterintuitive hypothesis about employment interview validity and some supporting evidence. *Journal of Applied Psychology, 89,* 553–561.
Schmit, M. J., Kihm, J., & Robie, C. (2000). Development of a global measure of personality. *Personnel Psychology, 53*(1), 153–193.
Schmitt, A. P., & Crocker, L. (1981, April). *Improving examinee performance on multiple-choice tests.* Paper presented at the convention of the American Educational Research Association, Los Angeles.
Schmitt, N. (1976). Social and situational determinants of interview decisions: Implications for the employment interview. *Personnel Psychology, 29,* 79–101.

Schoorman, F. D. (1988). Escalation bias in performance evaluations: An unintended consequence of supervisor participation in hiring decisions. *Journal of Applied Psychology, 73,* 58–62.

Silverman, W. H., Dalessio, A., Woods, S. B., & Johnson, R. L., Jr. (1986). Influence of assessment center methods on assessors' ratings. *Personnel Psychology, 39,* 565–578.

Smith v. City of Jackson, Mississippi, No. 03-1160 (U. S. March 30, 2005).

Smith, F. J. (1977). Work attitudes as predictors of attendance on a specific day. *Journal of Applied Psychology, 62,* 16–19.

Smith, P. C., & Kendall, L. M. (1963). Retranslation of expectations: An approach to the construction of unambiguous anchors for rating scales. *Journal of Applied Psychology, 47,* 149–155.

Snow, R. E. (1993). Construct validity and constructed-response tests. In R. E. Bennett & W. C. Ward (Eds.), *Construction versus choice in cognitive testing: Issues in constructed response, performance testing, and portfolio assessment* (pp. 45–60). Hillsdale, NJ: Lawrence Erlbaum Associates.

Society for Industrial and Organizational Psychology. (1987). *Principles for the validation and use of personnel selection procedures* (3rd ed.). College Park, MD: SIOP.

Spearman, C. (1927). *The abilities of man.* New York: Macmillan.

Spence, J. T., Helmreich, R. L., & Pred, R. S. (1987). Impatience versus achievement strivings in the Type A pattern: Differential effects on students' health and academic achievement. *Journal of Applied Psychology, 72,* 522–528.

Stanley, J. C. (1971). Reliability. In R. L. Thorndike (Ed.), *Educational measurement* (2nd ed., pp. 356–442). Washington, DC: American Council on Education.

Steele, C. M., & Aronson, J. (1995). Stereotype threat and the intellectual performance of African Americans. *Journal of Personality and Social Psychology, 69,* 797–811.

Sternberg, R. J., & Detterman, D. K. (Eds.). (1986). *What is intelligence?* Norwood, NJ: Ablex.

Stevens, M. J., & Campion, M. A. (1994). The knowledge, skill, and ability requirements for teamwork: Implications for human resource management. *Journal of Management, 20,* 503–530.

Stevens, M. J., & Campion, M. A. (1999). Staffing work teams: Development and validation of a selection test for teamwork settings. *Journal of Management, 25,* 207–228.

Stricker, L. J., & Ward, W. C. (2004). Stereotype threat, inquiring about test takers' ethnicity and gender, and standardized test performance. *Journal of Applied Social Psychology, 34*(4), 665–693.

Super, D. E. (1960). The biographical inventory as a method for describing adjustment and predicting success. *Bulletin of the International Association of Applied Psychology, 9,* 18–39.

Taylor, H. C., & Russell, J. T. (1939). The relationship of validity coefficients to the practical effectiveness of tests in selection. *Journal of Applied Psychology, 23,* 565–578.

Taylor, P. J., Pajo, K., Cheung, G. W., & Stringfield, P. (2004). Dimensionality and validity of a structured telephone reference check procedure. *Personnel Psychology, 57,* 745–772.

Tenopyr, M. L. (2004, April). *The University of Michigan cases: Promises and problems*. Paper presented at the 19th annual conference of the Society for Industrial and Organizational Psychology, Chicago, IL.

Tett, R. P., Jackson, D. N., & Rothstein, M. (1991). Personality measures as predictors of job performance: A meta-analytic review. *Personnel Psychology, 44,* 703–742.

Thoresen, C. J., Bradley, J. C., Bliese, P. D., & Thoresen, J. D. (2004). The big five personality traits and individual job performance grow trajectories in maintenance and transitional job stages. *Journal of Applied Psychology, 89,* 835–853.

Thorndike, E. L. (1920). A constant error in psychological ratings. *Journal of Applied Psychology, 4,* 25–29.

Thorndike, R. L. (1949). *Personnel selection: Test and measurement techniques.* New York: Wiley.

Thorndike, R. L. (1971). Concepts of culture-fairness. *Journal of Educational Measurement, 8,* 63–70.

Thornton, G. C., III, & Byham, W. C. (1982). *Assessment centers and managerial performance*. New York: Academic Press.

Thurstone, L. L. (1928). Attitudes can be measured. *American Journal of Sociology, 33,* 529–554.

Thurstone, L. L. (1931). *The reliability and validity of tests.* Ann Arbor: Edwards.

Thurstone, L. L. (1938). Primary mental abilities. *Psychometric Monographs,* (1).

Thurstone, L. L. (1947). *Multiple factor analysis*. Chicago: University of Chicago Press.

Tinsley, H. E. A., & Weiss, D. J. (1975). Interrater reliability and agreement of subjective judgements. *Journal of Counseling Psychology, 22*, 358–376.

Tryon, R. C. (1957). Reliability and behavior domain validity: Reformulation and historical critique. *Psychological Bulletin, 54,* 229–249.

Tversky, A., & Kahneman, D. (1982). Judgment of and by representativeness. In D. Kahneman, P. Slovic, & A. Tversky (Eds.), *Judgment under uncertainty: Heuristics and biases* (pp. __–__). Cambridge, England: Cambridge University Press.

Tzelgov, J., & Henik, A. (1991). Suppression situations in psychological research: Definitions, implications, and applications. *Psychological Bulletin, 109,* 524–536.

U.S. Commission on Civil Rights. (1993). *The validity of testing in education and employment.* Washington, DC: U.S. Commission on Civil Rights.

U.S. Department of Labor. (1972). *Handbook for analyzing jobs.* Washington, DC: U.S. Government Printing Office.

U.S. Department of Labor. (1972). *Dictionary of occupational titles: Definitions of titles* (4th ed.). Washington, DC: U.S. Government Printing Office.

U.S. Department of Labor. (1977). *Dictionary of occupational titles. Definitions of titles*. 4th ed. Washington, DC: U.S. Government Printing Office.

van der Zee, K. I., Bakker, A. B., & Bakker, P. (2002). Why are structured interviews so rarely used in personnel selection? *Journal of Applied Psychology, 87,* 176–184.

Van de Ven, A. H., & Ferry, D. L. (1980). *Measuring and assessing organizations*. New York: Wiley.

Van Vianen, A. E., & Willemsen, T. M. (1992). The employment interview: The role of sex stereotypes in the evaluation of male and female job applicants in the Netherlands. *Journal of Applied Social Psychology, 22,* 471–491.

Viglione, D. J., & Hilsenroth, M. J. (2001). The Rorschach: Facts, fictions, and future. *Psychological Assessment, 13,* 452–471.

Villanova, P., Bernardin, H. J., Johnson, D. L., & Dahmus, S. A. (1994). The validity of a measure of job compatibility in the prediction of job performance and turnover of motion picture theater personnel. *Personnel Psychology, 47,* 73–90.

Villanova, P., & Bernardin, J. (1994). The validity of a measure of job compatibility in the prediction of job performance and turnover of motion picture theater personnel. *Personnel Psychology, 47,* 73–90.

Wainer, H., & Thissen, D. (1992). *Combining multiple-choice and constructed response test scores: Toward a Marxist theory of test construction* (Program Statistics Research, Tech. Rep. No. 92–23). Princeton, NJ: Educational Testing Service.

Wainer, H., & Thissen, D. (1996). How is reliability related to the quality of test scores? What is the effect of local dependence on reliability? *Educational Measurement: Issues and Practice, 15*(1), 22–29.

Wagner, R. (1949). The employment interview: A critical summary. *Personnel Psychology, 2,* 17–46.

Wallace, S. R. (1965). Criteria for what? *American Psychologist, 20,* 411–417.

Wanous, J. P. (1980). *Organizational entry: Recruitment, selection, and socialization of newcomers*. Reading, MA: Addison-Wesley.

Ward, W. C. (1982). A comparison of free-response and multiple-choice forms of verbal aptitude tests. *Applied Psychological Measurement, 6,* 1–11.

Wards Cove Packing Co. v. Atonio, 109 S. Ct. 2115 (1989).

Washington v. Davis, 426 U. S. 229 (1976).

Watson v. Fort Worth Bank & Trust, 108 S. Ct. 2777 (1988).

Watson, G., & Glaser, E. M. (1980). *Watson–Glaser Critical Thinking Appraisal*. San Antonio, TX: Psychological Corporation.

Waung, M., & Highhouse, S. (1997). Fear of conflict and empathic buffering: Two explanations for the inflation of performance feedback. *Organizational Behavior and Human Decision Processes, 71,* 37–54.

Weber v. Kaiser Aluminum & Chemical Corporation, 563 F. 2d 2126 (CA 5 1977).

Webster, E. C. (1964). *Decision making in the employment interview*. Montreal: Industrial Relations Centre, McGill University.

Westen, D., & Weinberger, J. (2004). When clinical description becomes statistical prediction. *American Psychologist, 59,* 595–613.

Wherry, R. J. (1931). A new formula for predicting the shrinkage of the coefficient of multiple correlation. *Annals of Mathematical Statistics, 2,* 446–457.

Wherry, R. J., Sr., & Bartlett, C. J. (1982). The control of bias in ratings: A theory of rating. *Personnel Psychology, 35,* 521–551.

Whyte, W. H., Jr. (1957). *The organization man.* New York: Doubleday.

Wigdor, A. K., & Sackett, P. R. (1993). Employment testing and public policy: The case of the General Aptitude Test Battery. In H. Schuler, J. L. Farr, & M. Smith (Eds.), *Personnel selection and assessment* (pp. 183–204). Hillsdale, NJ: Lawrence Erlbaum Associates.

Witt, L. A., & Ferris, G. R. (2003). Social skill as moderator of the conscientiousness–performance relationship: Convergent results across four studies. *Journal of Applied Psychology, 88,* 809–821.

Woehr, D. J., & Arthur, W. (2003). The construct related validity of assessment center ratings: A review and meta-analysis of the role of methodological factors. *Journal of Management, 29,* 231–258.

Zammuto, R. F., London, M., & Rowland, K. M. (1982). Organization and rater differences in performance appraisals. *Personnel Psychology, 35,* 643–658.

Zedeck, S. (1986). A Process analysis of the assessment center method. In B. M. Staw & L. L. Cummings (Eds.), *Research in organizational behavior* (Vol. 8, pp. 259–296). Greenwich, CT: JAI Press.

Zeidner, M. (1987). Test of the cultural bias hypothesis: Some Israeli findings. *Journal of Applied Psychology, 72,* 38–48.

Author Index

A

Ackerman, P. L., 59
Ajzen, I., 245, 303
Alexander, R. A., 13
Anderson, C. W., 308
Anderson, G. S., 79
Anderson, N., 79
Aronson, J., 213
Arthur, W., 336, 337
Arthur, W., Jr., 298, 304
Ash, R. A., 49, 78
Ashton, M. C., 72

B

Bakker, A. B., 291
Bakker, P., 291
Balma, M. J., 264
Balzer, W. K., 277, 278, 282
Barrett, G. V., 13, 52, 53, 54, 54fn
Barrick, M. R., 71, 186, 311
Bass, A. R., 207fn
Battista, M., 49
Bauman, T., 327
Beatty, R. W., 282
Bentson, C., 337
Bentz, V. J., 319
Bernardin, H. J., 264, 279, 282, 288
Binning, J. F., 52, 53, 54, 54fn
Bliese, P. D., 55
Bono, J. E., 72
Boring, E. G., 116fn
Borman, W. C., 41, 60, 64, 135, 269, 270, 279
Bowler, J. L., 288
Bowman, M. L., 7
Bradley, J. C., 55
Breaugh, J. A., 296
Brogden, H. E., 202
Brooks, M. E., 246
Brown, B. K., 303
Brown, S. H., 305
Buckley, M. R., 279, 282
Burch, G. S., 79
Busch, C. M., 72
Byham, W. C., 323, 324, 327, 330

C

Cable, D. M., 277, 298
Callender, J. C., 306, 307
Camerer, C. F., 321
Campbell, D. T., 142

Campbell, J. P., 59, 62, 259
Campbell, J. T., 318
Campion, M. A., 35, 79, 298, 303
Carr, L., 49
Carrier, M. R., 305
Carroll, J. B., 67
Carsrud, A L., 55
Cattell, J. M., 116
Cattell, R. B., 67
Chan, D., 243, 245, 249
Chao, G. T., 296
Cheung, G. W., 296
Christiansen, N. D., 288
Claudy, J. G., 184
Cohen, J., 169, 170
Cole, M., 259
Cole, N. S., 213, 214
Collins, J. M., 336
Conrad, K. A., 321
Conway, J. M., 298
Cooper, W. H., 277
Corrigan, B., 179
Costa, P. T., 41
Coward, W. M., 157
Cranny, C. J., 36
Cronbach, L. J., 130, 135, 147, 202, 276
Cronshaw, S. F., 28
Cullen, M. J., 213
Cureton, E. E., 129

D

Dachler, H. P., 15
Dahmus, S. A., 288
Dalessio, A., 332
Dalessio, A. T., 249, 305
Daniels, H. W., 308
Daum, D., 327
Dawes, R. M., 179
Day, D. V., 197, 280, 290
Day, E. A., 336, 337
De Corte, W., 49, 291
de Raad, B., 70
Dean, M. A., 296
Delaney-Klinger, K., 35
DeShon, R. P., 311
Digman, J. M., 71
Dipboye, R. L., 306
Dobbins, G. H., 309
Doherty, M. E., 36
Donovan, J. J., 72, 289
Dossett, D. L., 296
Dougherty, T. W., 306, 307
Drasgow, F., 217
Dreher, G. F., 332
Drever, J., 12, 134
DuBois, C. L. Z., 276
DuBois, P. H., 7
Dunnette, M. D., 135
Dwight, S. A., 289

E

Ebert, R. J., 306, 307
Edens, P. S., 336, 337
Eels, R., 6
Ehrhart, M. G., 245
Einhorn, H. J., 207fn
Eisenman, E. J., 278
Ellis, A. P. J., 311
England, G. W., 292
English, A. C., 57
English, H. B., 57
Erez, A., 72
Eye, L. D., 49

F

Faley, R. H., 105
Farh, J., 309
Farrell, J. N., 55
Feild, H. S., 309
Ferrara, P., 35
Ferris, G. R., 179
Ferry, D. L., 23
Fine, S. A., 28
Fiske, D. W., 142
Flanagan, J. C., 28
Fleishman, E. A., 45, 48, 49, 75, 76, 77, 246, 248
Ford, J. K., 276
Franke, M., 311
Frederiksen, N., 178
French, J. W., 52
Freyd, M., 7, 11

Funder, D. C., 72

G

Ganzach, Y., 204
Garb, H. N., 287
Gaugler, B. B., 337
Gehrlein, T. M., 306
Ghiselli, E. E., 55, 158
Gilmore, D. C., 300
Gilovich, T., 310
Gladwell, M., 291
Glaser, R., 238fn
Gleser, G. C., 147, 202
Glisson, C. A., 288
Goffin, R. D., 288
Goldberg, L. R., 41, 69, 70, 71, 72
Goleman, D., 78
Goodman, D. F., 298
Gottfredson, G. D., 41
Gottier, R. F., 68, 73
Gough, H. G., 72
Grenier, J. R., 71
Griffeth, R. W., 311
Grisez, M., 327
Grossman, P., 94
Guilford, J. P., 72, 141, 264
Guion, R. M., 41, 68, 71, 73, 75, 87, 133, 135, 166, 181, 207, 216, 248, 254, 261, 263, 292, 309, 316
Gulliksen, H., 161
Gutman, A., 94
Guttmann, L., 130

H

Hanson, C. P., 321
Hanson, M. A., 41
Hardison, C. H., 213
Harris, M. M., 303
Hartigan, J. A., 100, 221
Hattrup, K., 240, 241
Hausknecht, J. P., 197, 290
Hawk, J. A., 157
Hedge, J. W., 243
Hellervik, L., 300
Helmreich, R. L., 55, 72
Henle, C. A., 224
Henry, S., 335
Hesketh, B., 49
Hezlett, S. A., 64
Higgins, C. A., 298
Highhouse, S., 41, 203, 246, 279, 286, 287, 291, 315, 316, 318, 321
Hilsenroth, M. J., 287
Hofstee, W. K. B., 70
Hogan, J., 72, 74, 75, 76, 77, 198
Hogan, R., 72, 198
Hogarth, R., 204
Holland, J. L., 41
Holland, P. W., 217
Hollingworth, H. L., 297
Hom, P. W., 311
Hough, L., 287
Hough, L. M., 72
Howard, A., 78
Huffcutt, A. I., 298, 304, 309
Hull, C. L., 116
Humphreys, L. G., 67
Hunter, J. E., 78, 185, 186, 221, 242
Hurtz, G. M., 72
Huse, E. F., 318

I

Ilgen, D. R., 248
Inwald, R., 41
Ironson, G. H., 216

J

Jackson, D. N., 72, 74, 289
Jako, R. A., 298
James, L. R., 288
Janz, T., 300
Jeanneret, P. R., 41, 46, 106
Johnson, D. L., 288
Johnson, E. J., 321
Johnson, H. W., 201
Johnson, J. C., 78
Johnson, R. L., Jr., 332
Joyce, L. W., 335
Judge, T. A., 71, 72, 277, 298

K

Kahneman, D., 309
Kane, J. S., 259
Kanfer, R., 59
Kay, G. G., 41
Kehoe, J., 49
Kendall, L. M., 264, 335
Kephart, N. C., 264
Kichuk, S. L., 79
Kihm, J., 255
Kinicki, A. J., 311
Kinslinger, H. J., 286
Klaus, D. J., 238fn
Klayman, N., 204
Kleiman, L. S., 105
Kluger, A. N., 204
Kraiger, K., 275, 276
Kristof-Brown, A., 311
Kubisiak, U. C., 41
Kuder, F., 130
Kuder, G. F., 129
Kuncel, N. R., 64

L

Laczo, R. M., 49
Landis, R. S., 240, 241
Landy, F. J., 28
Lasek, M., 108fn
Latham, G. P., 267, 268, 301, 302
Laue, F. J., 243
Lawshe, C. H., 32, 45, 179, 215, 264, 305
Le, H., 336
Lee, K., 72
Lengnick-Hall, M. L., 105
Levine, E. L., 37, 78
Levy, P. E., 281
Lewis, P. M., 309
Li, H., 133
Lievens, F., 49, 291
Lilienfeld, S. O., 287
Lin, T. R., 309
Lindemann, B., 94
Linn, R. L., 238fn
Liske, R. E., 318
Lockhart, M. C., 278
Lockwood, C. A., 311

M

Macan, T. H., 203
Mael, F. A., 293, 294fn, 296
Magnusson, D., 318
Martin, L., 4
Matthews, G., 78
Mattimore, K., 327
Maurer, S. D., 298
Mayer, J. D., 78
Mayfield, M. S., 35
McAdams, D. P., 73
McClough, A. C., 79
McCloy, R. A., 59, 62, 259, 280
McCormick, E. J., 25, 30, 31, 46, 248, 264
McCormick, S., 327
McCrae, R. R., 41, 69
McDaniel, M. A., 55, 78, 245, 298, 336
McIntyre, M. D., 288
McMurry, R. N., 300
McNelly, T. L., 336, 337
Meehl, P. E., 194
Melville, S. D., 178
Merron, J., 240
Messick, S., 135, 289
Micceri, T., 171
Miner, 286
Mischel, W., 68
Mitchell, T. R., 288
Morgeson, F. P., 35, 298
Moss, P. A., 213, 214
Motowidlo, S. J., 60
Mount, M. K., 71, 186
Muchinsky, P. M., 296
Murphy, K. R., 54, 278

N

Nalodka, T., 327
Nanda, H., 147
Nguyen, N. T., 245

O

Ones, D. S., 64

Oppler, S. H., 59, 62, 259, 280
Ostgaard, D. J., 166
Ostrander, M., 216
Otis, J. L., 308, 318

P

Pajo, K., 296
Pearlman, K., 49
Pedhazur, E. J., 164, 167
Peterson, N. G., 41, 280
Phillips, J. S., 13
Ployhart, R. E., 245
Pond, S. B., III, 335
Posthuma, R. A., 298
Pred, R. S., 72
Prewett-Livingston, A. J., 309
Prien, E. P., 49, 318
Pursell, E. D., 303

Q

Quigley, A. M., 74

R

Rajaratnam, N., 147
Raymark, P. H., 41
Reeve, C., 41
Reilly, M. E., 45, 48, 49, 75, 76, 77, 246, 248
Reilly, R. R., 296, 335
Richardson, M. W., 129
Roberts, R. D., 78
Robie, C., 157, 255
Rogelberg, S. G., 79
Rosenthal, D. B., 337
Rosenthal, R., 133
Roth, 202
Roth, P. L., 309
Rothstein, M., 72, 74
Rounds, J., 41
Rubin, D. B., 133
Russell, C. J., 296
Ryan, A. M., 108fn, 157, 290, 311, 317, 319, 321, 327

S

Sackett, P. R., 49, 157, 166, 213, 276, 290, 317, 319, 321, 332
Sager, C. E., 59, 62, 259
Salovey, P., 78
Sanchez, J. I., 37, 49
Sanchez-Ku, M., 336
Sawin, L. L., 55
Schippmann, 202
Schippmann, J. S., 49
Schmelkin, L. P., 164, 167
Schmidt, F. L., 78, 185, 186, 242, 298, 336
Schmit, M. J., 41, 255
Schmitt, N., 240, 241, 243, 245, 249, 298
Schoorman, F. D., 278
Schucker, R. E., 179
Sechrest, L. B., 71
Shahani, C., 306
Silverman, W. H., 332
Sisson, 271
Smith, F. J., 58
Smith, P. C., 264, 335
Smither, J. W., 335
Spearman, C., 67
Spence, J. T., 72
Steele, C. M., 213
Stevens, M. J., 79
Stricker, L. J., 213
Stringfield, P., 296
Strong, M. H., 41
Sulsky, L. M., 277, 280
Switzer, 202

T

Taylor, P. J., 296
Teachout, M. S., 243
Tenopyr, M. L., 103
Tett, R. P., 72, 74
Thayer, P. W., 335
Thissen, D., 132, 133
Thomas, L., 336
Thomas, S. C., 197, 290
Thoresen, C. J., 55, 72
Thoresen, J. D., 55

Thorndike, E. L., 277
Thorndike, R. L., 252
Thornton, G. C., III, 323, 324, 327, 330, 337
Thurstone, L. L., 121
Tinsley, H. E. A., 273
Tippins, N., 287
Tomkins, 286
Torestad, B., 318
Tryon, R. C., 123
Tversky, A., 309

V

Van de Ven, A. H., 23
van der Zee, K. I., 291
Veres, J. G., III, 309
Viglione, D. F., 287
Villanova, P., 288
Vinchur, 202

W

Wagner, R., 299
Wainer, H., 132, 133, 217
Walton, C., 6
Ward, W. C., 213
Waung, M., 279
Weinberger, J., 204
Weiss, D. J., 273
West, B. J., 311
Westen, D., 204
Wexley, K. N., 267, 268, 301
Wherry, R. J., 184
Whetzel, D. L., 298
Whyte, W. H., Jr., 63
Wiesner, W. H., 79
Wigdor, A. K., 100, 221
Williams, J. R., 281
Wing, H., 71
Witt, L. A., 179
Woehr, D. J., 336
Wood, J. M., 287
Woods, S. B., 332

Z

Zedeck, S., 326
Zeidner, M., 78
Zickar, M. J., 41, 150
Zimmerman, R. D., 298

Subject Index

A

Absenteeism, 58
Accuracy (vs. reliability and validity), 124–126
Achievement orientation, 55
Acquiescent response set, 289
Activity level (personality construct), 72
Adjustments to scores, 220–222
Adverse impact
  analysis of, 98–99
  and item response theory, 151
  and Uniform Guidelines on Employee Selection Procedures, 84–87
  vs. test bias, 212–215
Advertisements, 83
Aerobic capacity, 75, 76, 77
Affirmative action, 101–104, *see also* quotas
  and social policy, 219–220
Age Discrimination in Employment Act, 104–105
Agreeableness, 55, 70
Aliens, 83
Alpha coefficient, 130
Alternative selection procedures, 86–87
Americans With Disabilities Act, 105–107
  and physical and sensory competencies, 74
  and use of small data sets, 132
Applicant populations, defining, 54
Applicant reactions to tests, 289–291
Application forms, questions on, 106–107
Assessment
  scales for, 196–197
  vs. measurement, 115
Assessment centers, 16
  dimensions assessed, 328–331
    construct validities, 331–336
    criterion-related validities, 336–338
  methods used by, 324–326
  purposes of, 323–324
  staff of, 326–328
Assessors, 326–328
Associative memory, 66
Assumptions
  of personnel selection, 8
  statistical, 171–172

Attenuation, 123–124
Attributes, theories of, 144

B

Background checks
  and Americans With Disabilities Act, 107
  and negligent hiring, 110
Balance, sense of, 76, 77
Bands, 91, 222
  decisions within, 223–224
  fixed, 224–226
  sliding, 226–230
  and validation of selection procedures, 86
  width of, 222–223
BARS (behaviorally anchored rating scales), 264–267
Basic skills (O*NET system), 67
Behavioral descriptions
  behaviorally anchored rating scales (BARS), 264–267
  behavioral observation scales (BOS), 267–269
  behavior summary scales (BSS), 269–271
Behavior description interviewing, 300–301
BFOQs (bona fide occupational qualifications), 103–104
Bias, statistical
  defined, 206–207
  vs. adverse impact, 212–215
Biases of interviewers, 309
Bible, 7
Biodata, 16, 293–296
Bivariate regression, 155–158
Bona fide occupational qualifications (BFOQs), 103–104
BOS (behavioral observation scales), 267–269
BSS (behavior summary scales), 269–271
Burden of persuasion, 96, 99
Business necessity, 86
  and 1991 amendment to Civil Rights Act, 100
  defined, 84–85
  diversity as, 103–104
  and *Griggs vs. Duke Power Co.*, 95
  and test bias, 218

C

Cardiovascular endurance, 75, 76
Career stages, 54–55
Case law
  defined, 93–94
  and EEO regulations, 94–99
CAT (computerized adaptive tests), 150–151, 250
Categories (of inventory items), 32
Central tendency errors, 276
Change in organizations, 63
Checklists, 285
China, ancient, 7
Civil Rights Act, 81–83
  1991 Amendment, 100, 220
  and personality testing, 68
  and physical and sensory competencies, 74
  and Type II error, 170
Clinical prediction, 193–194, 204
Cluster analysis for task statements, 36
Cognitive abilities
  defined, 64–65
  examples of, 65, 66
  as performance predictors, 54–55
  tests of, 239–241
Combining predictors, *see* multivariate statistics
Commercial tests, use of, 240–241
Communication style (of interviewers), 308
Comparisons (rating method), 262–264
Compensatory prediction models, 173–180
  in multiple assessments, 314
  multiple correlation analysis, 176–177
  regression equations, 174–176, 179
  suppressor and moderator variables, 177–179
  unit weighting, 179–180

Competency modeling, 49
Comprehensive structured interviews, 303–304
Computerized testing, 150–151, 249–250
Conceptual definitions (of criterion variables), 58
Concurrent vs. predictive research designs, 73
Conditional reasoning tests, 288
Conference methods of need analysis, 22–23
Confirmatory evidence, 141–142
Connecticut vs. Teal, 97–98
Conscientiousness, 70–72
Constructs
  defined, 235
  in performance ratings, 272
  predictor and criterion, 51–52
  validity of, 53–54, 89–90, 135
Consultants, 24–25
Content validity, 88–89, 135
Content validity ratio (CVR), 305
Contextual performance, 63
  defined, 60
Coordination, 75, 76, 77
Correlated error, 163
Correlates, patterns of, 141–144
Correlation
  basic concepts, 158–162
  of dimensions vs. patterns, 15–16
  Pearson's coefficient of, 116
  product-moment coefficients, 162–167
  statistical significance, 167–170
Cost-benefit analysis, *see* utility analysis
Credential requirements, 78
Criterion bias, 216
Criterion choice, 9, 63
Criterion constructs
  defined, 51–52, 57
  and hypothesis development, 52–54
  inferring from measures, 58–59
Criterion measures, 51, 53, 58–59
Criterion-referenced testing, 238–239
Criterion-related validation, 135
  defined, 153–154
  and Uniform Guidelines on Employee Selection Procedures, 87–88
Critical incident interviews, 28–29
Cross-cultural testing, 255–256
Cross-functional skills, 67
Cross-validation, 182–184
Crystallized intelligence, 67
Cultural bias, 206–207
Cut scores, 91–92, 251–254
  as alternative selection procedure, 86
  and content validation, 89
  multiple, 180–181
  sequential, 182
  and validation of selection procedures, 86
CVR (content validity ratio), 305

D

Data collection, 11
Declarative knowledge, 59
Decoy effect, 315
Demanded vs. preferred qualifications, 79
Demographics, 10
Descriptive inferences, 135–136
Determination, coefficients of, 160–161
Diary keeping (in performance rating), 279, 281–282
Dictionary of Occupational Titles, 40
Differential Aptitude Test Battery, 240–241
Differential item functioning (DIF), 216–217
Dimensional consistency (in multiple assessments), 331–336
Disabilities, 105–107
Disconformatory evidence, 142
Discrimination
  fair vs. unfair, 207
  against groups, 208–209
Disparate treatment, 84–87
Distributions, 166–167

differences in, 209–212
Diversity, 10
and assessment, 17
as business necessity, 103–104
Domain-referenced testing, 238–239
Dothard vs. Rawlinson, 96
Drug testing, 247
Duties (job analysis), 26

E

Education requirements, 78–79
Elements (job analysis), 26
Eligibility lists, 92
Elimination of selection procedures, 86
Emotional intelligence, 78
Emotional stability, 70
Employee comparisons (rating method), 262–264
Equal Employment Opportunity Commission (EEOC), 83–84, 102
Equal employment opportunity law, 20, 81
Equivalence, coefficients of, 128–129
Error
correlated, 163
systematic, 212
Escalation bias, 278
Estimate, errors of, 159
Evidence, types of, 141–142
Expectancy data
charts, 197–199
graphs, 199–201
Experience samples, 27–28

F

Factor analysis, 144–147
defined, 65
of personality traits, 69
for task statements, 36
Fairness, 207
Faking responses, 287–289
Fidelity, (of simulations and exercises), 243, 325
Fitness testing, 246–247
Five-factor personality model, 69–73
FJA (Functional Job Analysis), 28
Fleishman Job Analysis Survey, 45, 48–49
Flexibility, 76, 77
Fluency, 65, 66
Fluid intelligence, 67
Folk theories, 64
Follow-up research design, 12
Forced choice inventories, 271, 285, 288–289
Forced distributions, 263
Foreign countries, 81
80% (four fifths) rule, 85, 215
Four fifths (80%) rule, 85, 215
Frame of reference (FOR) training, 279–280
Functional Job Analysis (FJA), 28
Functional relationships (between variables), 55–57

G

Gender discrimination, 82, 83
General Aptitude Test Battery (GATB), 221
Generalizability, 10
of performance ratings, 275
from research sample to population, 154–155
theory of, 147–148
of validity research, 14, 90–91, 216
G (general intelligence), 67
Gideon (biblical character), 7
Glass-Ceiling initiative, 4
Global vs. specific assessments, 15–16
Graphic rating scales, 260–262
Gratz vs. Bollinger, 103
Griggs vs. Duke Power Co., 94–96
Group differences, reasons for, 209–210
Group heterogeneity, 167
Guidelines, *see* Uniform Guidelines on Employee Selection Procedures

H

Halo errors, 277
Handbook for Analyzing Jobs, 40
Hearing ability, 75
Height and weight requirements, 96
Heterogeneity, group, 167
Heteroscedasticity, 163
Higher level jobs, testing for, 91
Hogan Personality Inventory, 72
Holistic assessment, 15–16
Homoscedasticity, 163
Honeymoon stage, 54–55
Human resources management positions, 4
Humility (personality construct), 72
Hypothesis, null, 161–162, 168
Hypothesis development
  defined, 51–52
  local nature of, 80
  theory and practice, 52–54
Hypothesis formation, 9–10

I

Immigrants, 110
Impression management, 311–312
In-Basket tests, 325, 338
Incident files, 281–282
Incumbents (and task sampling), 35–36
Indifference, ranges of, 222
Individual psychological assessment, 316
  criticisms of, 321–322
  holistic, 317–318
  psychometric, 318–319
  SIOP survey on, 319–320
Inductive reasoning, *see* reasoning ability
Inferences
  and concept of validity, 134
  descriptive and relational, 135–136
  and hypothesis development, 53–54
Injuries, 107–110
Integrity, 70–72
Intellectance, 55, 70
Intelligence, 65, 67
Intent (in discrimination cases), 95, 100, 105
Internal consistency, coefficients of, 129–130
International Brotherhood of Teamsters vs. United States, 85
International Personality Item Pool (IPIP), 41
Interpersonal skills, 79
Interrater agreement, 131, 272–274
Interviewees, characteristics of, 310–312
Interviewers, characteristics of, 305–310
Interviewing (job analysis), 28
Interviews, employment
  at assessment centers, 326
  questions about disabling conditions, 106–107
  reviews of, 297–298
  validity of, 304–305
  varieties of, 299–304
Inventories, 284–285
  applicant reactions, 289–291
  distorting responses, 287–289
  items on, 31–32
  task, *see* task inventories
  varieties of, 285–287
IPIP (International Personality Item Pool), 41
IRT, *see* item response theory
Item bias, *see* differential item functioning
Item matching, 255
Item response theory (IRT), 148–151
  and computerized testing, 249

J

Job analysis, 9, 74
  construct and content validation, 88–89
  observational methods, 25–30
  personality-based, 41–44
  potential problems, 39–40
  ready-to-use methods, 40–49
  subjective nature of, 49–50
  survey methods, 30

and work samples, 243
Job descriptions (job analysis), 26
Job families (job analysis), 26
Job knowledge
components of, 59–60
vs. job skill, 60
Job-oriented inventories, 30
Job Performance Measurement Project, 275
Job-relatedness vs. validity, 95
Job requirements inventories, *see* task inventories
Job Requirements Inventory, 32, 45
Job requirements (job analysis), 37–39
Job specific knowledge, 67–68
Judgment aids, 195–197
assessment scales, 196–197
expectancy charts, 197–199
expectancy graphs, 199–201
utility analysis, 201–203
Judgments
and prediction, 193–194, 204
in traditional research, 14–15
of validity, 190–192

K

Know-how, *see* job specific knowledge
Knowledge (procedural vs. declarative), 59
KSAs (Knowledges, Skills, and Abilities), 37–39
and content validation, 88
and team selection, 79
Kuder-Richardson estimates, 129–130

L

Labor unions, 83
Leaderless Group Discussions, 326
Learning period, length of, 55
Leniency errors, 276–277
Linearity, assumption of, 157–158
Linear testing, 250
Locus of control (personality construct), 72

M

Maintenance stage (of career development), 54–55
Managers, use of psychometric tests by, 192
Mean scores (vs. other distributional characteristics), 209–210
Measurement, 115–117
errors in
and error variance, 117–122
and reliability, 122–125
methods of, 10, *see also* tests
Measures, evaluation of, 190–192
Medical examinations, 107
Memory, 65, 66
in interviewees, 310–311
Mental abilities, *see* cognitive abilities
Mental tests, early, 116
Merit (as basis for personnel decisions), 6
Meta-analysis and validity generalization, 184–187
Minnesota Multiphasic Personality Inventory (MMPI), 285, 287
Minority groups, *see* protected groups
MMPI (Minnesota Multiphasic Personality Inventory), 285, 287
Moderator variables, 178–179
Modifications
to selection procedures, 15, 85–86
to tests, 218
Monotonic relations, 155–156
Motivation
defined, 59
of raters, 280–281
Motivational variables, 55
Multiple assessments
of groups, *see* assessment centers
of individuals, *see* individual psychological assessment
Multiple-choice tests, 285
alternatives to, 16
Multiple component promotion systems, 97–98
Multiple correlation analysis, 176–177

Multiple hurdles, 180–181
Multiple predictors, *see* predictors, combining
Multiple regression analysis, 174–176, 179
Multivariate statistics
  compensatory prediction models, 173–180
  noncompensatory prediction models, 180–182
  replication and cross-validation, 182–184
  validity generalization, 184–187
Muscular strength, 75, 76, 77

N

National Commission on Testing and Public Policy, 16–17
National Commission on Testing and Public Policy recommendations, 16–17
National origin, 82
Need analysis, *see* job analysis; organizational need analysis
Negligent hiring, 107–110, 246–247
NEO Job Profiler, 41
Noncognitive performance tests, 246–248
Noncompensatory prediction models, 180–182
Nonlinearity, 162–163
Normal distribution, assumption of, 171–172
Normal law of error, 116
Norm-referenced testing, 236–238
Null hypothesis, 161–162, 168
Number facility, 65, 66

O

OAI (Organizational Assessment Instruments), 23
Observation (job analysis method), 27–28
Observe-and-question method (of job analysis), 45
Occupational Information Network, *see* O*NET
Occupations, defined (for job analysis), 26
Occupation-specific skills, 67
O*NET (Occupational Information Network), 40–41
  categorization of occupational skills, 67
  and personality traits, 69
Openness, 55
Operational definitions (of criterion variables), 58
Organizational Assessment Instruments (OAI), 23
Organizational assessment surveys, 23
Organizational need analysis, 9, 20–25
  approaches, 22–25
  and organizational outcomes, 21–22
  uses of, 20–21
Outliers, 167
Overall assessment ratings (OARs), 324, 330–331, 336

P

Paired comparisons, 263–264
PAQ (Position Analysis Questionnaire), 41, 45, 46–47
Part-time employees, 110
Pass-fail scoring, *see* cut scores
Patterned interviews, 300–301
PAT (Tomkins–Horn Picture Arrangement Test), 285
Pearsonian coefficients, 162–167
Pearson's coefficient of correlation, 116
Peer ratings, 280
Perceptual speed, 65, 66
Performance, components of, 59–60, 61–62
Performance ratings
  by assessment centers, 330
  limitations, 258–259
  methods of, *see* rating methods
  observational aids, 281–282
  research on, 271–276

role of rater, 276–282
Performance tests, 241–248
at assessment centers, 325–326
noncognitive performance, 246–248
situational judgments, 244–246
work samples and simulations, 242–244
Personal history assessment
biodata, 293–296
weighted application blanks, 291–292
Personality-based job analysis, 41–44
Personality inventories, 68–70
predictive value of, 73–74
Personnel assessment, perceived importance of, 3–4
Philadelphia Plan, 101–102
Physical competencies, 74–77
Pilot studies (for task inventories), 34–35
Plato, 7
Polygraph protection act, 110
Population, specification of, 54
Position Analysis Inventory, 32
Position Analysis Questionnaire (PAQ), 41, 45, 46–47
Position Classification Inventory, 41
Positions (in job analysis), 26
Power, statistical, 170
Predicted yield policy, 252–253
Prediction
and combining imperfect measures, 16–17
and hypotheses, 51–54
statistical vs. judgmental, 193–194
Predictors
combining, 11, 313–316, *see also* multivariate statistics
for team selection, 79
theoretical vs. practical sources of, 64
validation of, 11–12
Preferred vs. demanded qualifications, 79
Present-employee research design, 12
Prior impressions (among raters), 277–278
Problem recognition, 66
Procedural knowledge, 59
Procedural planning, 196
Product–moment coefficients, 162–167
Project A, 276
Projective personality assessments, 285–287
Protected groups, 208–209
and test bias, 216–217
test scores of, 209–212
Prototypes (vs. stereotypes), 308–309
Proximate causes, 108fn
Psychometrics (defined), 6
Psychometric theory, extensions of, 144–147
Psychometric validity, 11–12, 136–137
types of evidence for, 137–144
Psychomotor tests, 248

Q

Quetelet, 115–116
Quotas, 100
and adverse impact, 221–222
and *Regents, University of California vs. Bakke*, 96–97
and university admissions, 103–104

R

Race-norming, 100, 221
Racial discrimination, 94–96
Rainforest empiricism, 296
Range restriction, 164–166
Ranking, 86, 91
Rank order comparisons, 262
Raters
characteristics of, 278–281
errors made by, 276–278
Rating methods
behavioral descriptions, 264–271
employee comparisons, 262–264

graphic rating scales, 260–262
Ratings, *see* performance ratings
Reasonable accomodation, 106
Reasoning ability, 65, 66, 67
Record keeping
in performance rating, 281
and Uniform Guidelines on Employee Selection Procedures, 93
Reduced variance, 164–166
Reference checks, 109
Regents, University of California vs. Bakke, 96–97
Regression, bivariate, 155–158
Regression equations
coefficients, 175–176
and cut scores, 253–254
Rehnquist, William, 104
Relational inferences, 135–136
Reliability
coefficients of, 133–134
interrater, 131
and validity, 122–126, 140–141
Reliability estimates, 125–127
comparisons between, 131–132
equivalence, 128–129
internal consistency, 129–130
interpretation of reliability coefficients, 133–134
stability, 127–128
standard error of measurement, 132–133
Religious organizations, 83
Replication (and combined predictors), 182
Representativeness, judgment by, 309–310
Research design, 10–11
and personality test validation, 73–74
theory and practice, 52–54
Research subjects, employment status of, 13
Residuals, 159
Response scales, 32–34
Response sets, 287–289
Retranslation, 266
Reverse discrimination, 102
Revised NEO Personality Inventory, 41

S

Sampling
and small applicant pools, 14
for task inventories, 35
Scaled response inventories, 285
Scatterplots, 155
Score adjustments, 220–222
Scores, permitted use of, 91–93
Self-Descriptive Index, 41
Self-evaluation (personality construct), 72
Self-management skills, 79
Sensory competencies, 75–77
Sensory tests, 248
Sequential hurdles, 182
Service orientation, 72
Severity errors, 276–277
Significance, statistical, 167–170
Similar-to-me bias, 309
Simulations, 242–243
Single positions, selection for, 132
SIOP, *see* Society for Industrial and Organizational Psychology
Situational interviews, 301–303
Situational judgment tests, 244–246
Situation specificity hypothesis, 185
Sixteen Personality Factor Questionnaire, 285
Social desirability response set, 287
Social policy and affirmative action, 219–220
Society for Industrial and Organizational Psychology (SIOP)
definition of performance, 59
individual assessment survey, 319–320
Souter, David, 104
Span memory, 66
Spatial ability, 65, 66
Stability, coefficients of, 127–128
Stamina, 75, 76, 77
Standard deviation, 116
Standardization, 11, 235–236

Statistical analysis, role in personnel research, 187
Statistical power, 170
Statistical significance, 167–170
Status quo (and criterion choice), 63
Stereotypes
  and criterion validity, 338
  by interviewers, 308–310
Stereotype threat, 213
Strength, 75, 76, 77
Structured interviews, 299–304
Subjective assessments, 98–99
Supervisors, task sampling by, 35–36
Suppressor variables, 177
Surgency, 70
Surveys
  for job analysis, 30
  for organizational assessment, 23
Systematic error, 121, 212

T

Talk-through interviews, 243
Task inventories
  administering, 35–36
  analyzing, 36–39
  developing, 30–35
Tasks (in job analysis), 26
Task statements, 29, 31
Team selection, 79
Team Selection Inventory, 79
Teamwork Test, 79
Test-retest correlation, 128
Tests, 10
  bias in, 213–215
  controversial aspects, 256–257
  defined, 235–236
  development of, 137–140
  norm-referenced vs. domain-referenced, 236–239
  and public policy, 16–17
Theory, importance of, 17–18
Third variables, 161
Time intervals, specification of, 54–55
Tomkins-Horn Picture Arrangement Test (PAT), 286
Tort law, 107–110
Trade-offs between traits, 57
Trade unions, 101–102
Trainability tests, 16
Transitional stage (of career development), 54–55
Translations of tests, 255–256
Transportability of validity research, 14, 90–91
Type A personality construct, 72
Type I and Type II errors, 169–170

U

Unfitness, 107–110
Uniform Guidelines on Employee Selection Procedures, 15
  and adverse impact, 84–87
  case law concerning, 93–99
  and individual psychological assessment, 319
  requirements for validation, 87–90
  and test bias, 217–218
  and validity of selection procedures, 90–93
United States Employment Service (USES), 221, 276
Unit weighting, 179–180
Unreliability, 163–164
Utility analysis, 201–203

V

Validation
  and adverse impact, 86–87
  on "common sense" grounds, 86
  as hypothesis testing, 154–155
  procedures for, 8–12
Validity
  coefficients of, 142–143
  concepts of, 11–12, 124–126, 134–137
  differential, 213–214
  of interviews, 304–305
  judgments of, 190–192
  psychometric, 136–144
Validity generalization, 184–187
Variables, third, 161

Variance
  and measurement error, 117–122
  reduced, 164–166
Verbal comprehension, 65, 66
Vision, 75
Vocabulary tests, 67
Voluntary affirmative action, 102

W

Wards Cove Packing Co. vs. Atonio, 99
Wasting human resources, 7
Watson vs. Fort Worth Bank & Trust, 98–99, 297
Weight and height requirements, 96
Weighted application blanks, 291–292
Wisdom, 4–5
Women, 4
Wonderlic Personnel Test, 240
Worker characteristics
  assessment of, 45–49
  and job analysis, 37–39
Worker functions (in Functional Job Analysis), 28
Worker-oriented inventories, 31
Work orientation, 72
Work samples, 16, 242–244